THE HASKELL LECTURES IN
COMPARATIVE RELIGION

EPOCHS IN BUDDHIST HISTORY

THE UNIVERSITY OF CHICAGO PRESS
CHICAGO, ILLINOIS

THE BAKER & TAYLOR COMPANY
NEW YORK

THE CAMBRIDGE UNIVERSITY PRESS
LONDON

THE MARUZEN-KABUSHIKI-KAISHA
TOKYO, OSAKA, KYOTO, FUKUOKA, SENDAI

THE MISSION BOOK COMPANY
SHANGHAI

SĀKYAMUNI

(Japanese painting of the Kano School, sixteenth century.)

EPOCHS IN BUDDHIST HISTORY

THE HASKELL LECTURES, 1921

By

KENNETH J. SAUNDERS

Author of "The Story of Buddhism," "Gotama Buddha"
Editor of "The Heart of Buddhism," "The Buddha's Way of Virtue"
Professor of the History of Religion, Pacific School of
Religion, Berkeley, and Lecturer in the
University of California

THE UNIVERSITY OF CHICAGO PRESS
CHICAGO ILLINOIS

COPYRIGHT 1924 BY
THE UNIVERSITY OF CHICAGO

All Rights Reserved

Published January 1924

Composed and Printed By
The University of Chicago Press
Chicago, Illinois, U.S.A.

INTRODUCTION

That Buddhism is a stream which has its source in the complex and elusive system of Brahmanism known today as Hinduism; that it is rightly called by the name of Gotama Buddha, the great moral reformer of the sixth century B.C. because he shaped its course and purified its waters; that as the stream flowed in an ever widening bed out over the Eastern World, tributaries poured into it from every side, swelling, coloring, and sometimes defiling it—all this is generally accepted. This book is an attempt to describe that remarkable process; and as in the case of the great sister-religion, Christianity, it is difficult to say anything which does not need qualification. The tributaries of both religions are many and diverse, and the streams are very complex. In Buddhism, in the first place, there are several philosophical systems, ranging from a naïve realism to a subtle mystical pantheism, and all claiming to be derived from the words of Sākyamuni. The person of the Founder has, in the second place, played a widely different rôle in different schools, from that of an ethical teacher, "supernormal perhaps but not supernatural," to that of supreme god among the gods. In the third place, the moral reform for which he is so justly famous has been variously interpreted, as different emphasis has been placed now upon one and now upon another part of his teachings, until the Buddhist world finds itself divided between the ideals of a self-centered, individualistic mind-culture, on the one hand, and a passionate, altruistic self-sacrifice, on the other.

Such is the destiny of great and complex teachers; and it is my purpose in this book to show how the noble qualities which he embodied have led almost inevitably to a polytheistic cult, as the stream has found its way into other lands, and first one then another was emphasized and embodied in a new "god," and to trace its course and the tributaries which have entered it. To put all this into more Buddhistic imagery—the lotus of Buddhism has grown apace; its seeds have germinated and borne rich fruitage. But some have been pollinated from plants of another species, producing hybrids, and some have germinated in desert swamps, becoming weeds. In describing this process it is not my object to criticize or to discriminate between the true and false growths. That must be left to the Buddhist world. My task is merely that of a sympathetic chronicler; yet it is my sincere desire to help Christian and Buddhist scholars toward a friendly and frank discussion. I belonged for some time to a group representing many religions in India; and many were the delightful evenings we spent without heat or conscious propaganda, learning one another's point of view and growing, as we all believed, in the process. I remember the great Buddhist scholar, Oldenberg, coming into our midst and saying: "I did not know such a thing was possible." It *is* possible, and it ought to be done in every intellectual center in the world;[1] indeed, the mutual respect and understanding of the nations cannot be based upon rock until numerous groups of this kind are meeting in an honest attempt to study the great streams which have made our civilizations what they are.

To scholars of the West and of the East I am deeply indebted, but it is to the East that I have naturally turned

[1] A very interesting group of this kind, numbering over a hundred, meets in Tokyo.

for my information, and today there are Eastern scholars trained in the scientific methods of the West who yet see Buddhism from within as adherents. Among these I would mention with special gratitude my teacher in Ceylon the Pundit Wagiswara and my friend, Dr. M. Anesaki, whose name is justly revered wherever Buddhism is studied. And with them I would thank the courteous and genial monks of many a monastery from Ceylon to Japan, whose guest I have been. In these quiet haunts I have caught something of the spirit of the great and noble Order of the Yellow Robe, which, in spite of perversions, has shown an amazing power of recovery.

And of the thoughts which have come to me during twelve years' study of the religion of Gotama Buddha, I will here set down by way of introduction these: (1) that the great keynotes of our modern scientific thinking, causality and the unity of the universe, even if Gotama did not first formulate them, were popularized by him; and that this is one of the most remarkable achievements in the history of human thought; (2) that the conviction which rings through his words of a moral purpose governing the universe, of the sure reward of good and evil, is even more sublime; (3) that his anticipation of modern psychological theories deserves close and respectful study; (4) that his "religion," the influence of his words and deeds, is still very much alive, and still supplies a felt want in Asia; (5) that with all its accretions and corruptions it still has much to teach the Western World; (6) and that what men have made of it is eloquent of what they are made of: for its rationalism has needed to be reinforced by mysticism; its moral code has been driven to seek other sanctions than the enlightened common sense he appealed to; and the devotion he strove to disentangle from his own person has clung tenaciously to it.

What Buddhism has become is to Christians a vindication also of many of the teachings of Jesus—the Fatherhood of God, the brotherhood of man, the harmonizing of the individual and corporate life in a divine Kingdom on earth: and, even more remarkable, it is a vindication also of some of the less simple and more controversial of the dogmas of Christianity, such as the *Logos* doctrine, the triune nature of the Godhead, and the Atonement.

The Buddhist, on the other hand, may see in some of the more philosophical and mystical expressions of Christianity a Buddhist element;[1] and this is true—that there are in Christianity elements which are not much understood or used by the Christian church, but which are the very breath of life to the devout Buddhist; such, for instance, as the doctrine of the unity of all life and the practice of communion with it.   The followers of the two Ways have every reason to associate in friendship and to unite in social service.   They are both faced with immensely difficult problems of social and international relations.   I hope this book[2] may in some measure be a bridge between them.   "They who have lived with the eternal Word are Christians—even though we call them atheists."[3]   And the spirit of Christ can only pass between us who call ourselves by his august Name and our Buddhist friends, if we are trying to understand and to respect one another.

K. J. S.

BERKELEY, CALIFORNIA
    Easter, 1922

[1] Cf. Dr. Anesaki in *Hibbert Journal*, IV, 9.

[2] Much of the contents of this book was given as Haskell Lectures in the University of Chicago in 1921.   Chapter vi has appeared in the *Journal of Religion* and Appendix I in the *International Review of Missions*.

[3] Justin Martyr.

CONTENTS

xi

PREFATORY NOTES

I. THE TERMS HĪNAYĀNA AND MAHĀYĀNA

Much confusion exists as to the great divisions of Buddhism, and the terms, "Southern and Northern," "Hīnayāna and Mahāyāna," are all used generally, but quite inaccurately, to describe the primitive and the developed forms of this very complex religion. Many writers who condemn the Mahāyāna as heretical naïvely use its contemptuous name Hīnayāna for the orthodox! The following scheme may prove helpful as an indication of the theory worked out in this book.

1. The teachings and example of Sākyamuni are the original Buddhism (560–480 B.C.). All schools claim to be true to the Founder and his Precepts, and we are dependent upon their interpretations and records. It is the task of critical scholarship to edit these, and to separate the various strata within the books. It is impossible, except in rare cases, to be sure which are *ipsissima verba* of the Founder, but of his main tenets there is little question.

2. They were not written down for some centuries, but preserved in the memory of the monks, who very soon began to differ in the emphasis placed on certain great doctrines, yet continued to live side by side in the same monasteries, and to comment upon the traditions, agreeing to differ as to the letter and the spirit.

3. A great popularization of the Buddhist ethic took place in the Asokan era (250 B.C.), and the layman gained a new significance as the note of service was struck, and a Buddhist world-order envisaged.

4. A less austere Buddhism began to make itself felt, and to call itself Mahāyāna (Great Way), labeling the more stoical way Hīnayāna (the Narrow Sect or Way) and accusing it of losing the spirit of the Founder. The followers of this way are represented best by the Theravāda (School of the Elders) of Ceylon, and in my opinion the early criticism of the Mahāyāna that they were too aloof is justified; they neither attained Arhatship about which they centered their lives, nor appreciated the nobler ideal of the Bodhisattva.

5. In the Mahāyāna there are differences not only of ethical and philosophical interpretation but of Buddhology; its stages may be connoted by the following terms: (*a*) the Halfway Mahāyāna (*ca.* 50 B.C.–50 A.D.); (*b*) the Paradise Mahāyāna (*ca.* 100 A.D.); (*c*) the Full Mahāyāna (*ca.* 100–400 A.D.).

6. The philosophical schools of the last-named which flourished from about 100 A.D. to about 400 A.D., or from the *Avatamsaka Sūtra* to the *Yogācāra*, are concerned with the nature of Reality, and tend for the most part toward monism, though with many differences of emphasis.

7. The various schools are harmonized by Chi-i and others in China (sixth century A.D.) in a pantheistic realism.

8. In the later Mantrayāna (*ca.* 700 A.D.) this philosophy is further developed and made the basis for a sensuous polytheism and a magic cultus, degenerating at last into Tantric or Sakta Buddhism.

II. THE NATURE OF MAN AND THE PHENOMENAL WORLD

1. For primitive Buddhism the doctrine of transiency is cardinal; this is expressed by two words: anattā, aniccā. Anattā means that man is an ever changing stream of

consciousness without substantial entity; yet it is taken
for granted that he is free to choose the direction in which
this stream shall flow. The term aniccā as applied to the
phenomenal world indicates that this also is a continual
process of change without abiding entity. The doctrine
of Karma is taken over from Hinduism, and the causality
of the universe is recognized, but a *Causa causans* is ignored.

2. The Hīnayāna schools have their own interpretations of these doctrines; some are realist, some idealist
(see Appendix IV). A *Causa causans* is denied.

3. The Mādhyamaka school of Mahāyāna carries on
the process of analysis, and teaches that all phenomena are
unreal, or have only a relative reality; the life of man is
either a dream or a total illusion.

4. The Yogācāra school finds a *Causa causans* in the
evolution of the Ālayavijñāna or receptacle of consciousness, which contains all human minds and all phenomena,
and is responsible for the illusion of separate existence.

5. The comprehensive schools of T'ien-t'ai and others
find an indwelling Absolute, the Tathatā, which gives
reality alike to the noumenal and phenomenal. This
culminates in:

6. The Mantrayāna doctrine of Ādi-Buddha or First
Cause.

III. NIBBĀNA AND NIRVĀNA

Nibbāna is the Pāli word used by early Buddhists, and
should be kept to distinguish their view of the ultimate
goal alike from that of contemporary Hindu teachers,
and that of the Mahāyāna: for these views the Sanskrit
Nirvāna may be used.

Of Nibbāna two interpretations are to be recognized:
(1) that of primitive Buddhism, which places the emphasis
upon the dying-out of the flame of Tanhā, or craving, and

indicates that with this the transient world of Samsāra comes to an end in an ineffable state of calm, cool joy beyond human categories; (2) that of the Hīnayāna school-men of a later, more negative, age who tend to place less emphasis upon the ethical content, and at times teach that it is the cessation not merely of becoming but of being. They differ little in fact from the annihilationists whom their master condemned.

Of Nirvāna similarly there are various interpretations: (1) that of some parts of the Upanishads, which think of it as a waking-up to the fact of the substantial unity of the soul, or ātman, with the supreme Ātman, or Brahman; (2) that of the Mahāyāna, which rejects the negative interpretation of the Hīnayāna, and regards Nirvāna as a permanent supreme Reality, blissful and serene, though ineffable. Some schools interpret it as a life of conscious union with the universal Buddha, and some as the awakening of the true Buddha-self in the human heart. (For synonyms see Appendix III.)

IV. THE WAYS TO NIBBĀNA AND NIRVĀNA

Inasmuch as the Buddhist schools differ mainly as to the way to Nibbāna, or Nirvāna, as it is called in Sanskrit Buddhism, the outline given above may be amplified as follows:

a) The Founder, conceiving himself as the Seer of Reality, teaches both the Arhat ideal of strenuous self-realization by way of detachment, and the Bodhisattva ideal by way of service. The goal in either case is Nibbāna —the end of Tanhā and of Samsāra—the only Absolute recognized in early Buddhism. The Founder may also have made a distinction between Pacceka Buddha (solitary, reticent Buddha) and Sammā-sam-buddha (per-

fect Buddha who teaches). These distinctions are all
based upon phases of his own experience; he had been
Arhat but "out of pity for the world" remained to teach
it; i.e., he refused to be Pacceka Buddha, but became
Buddha, fulfilling his true Bodhisattva nature. He seems
himself to have made little distinction between Buddha,
Bodhisattva, and Arhat. They are all "in Nibbāna";
i.e., in them Tanhā and Samsāra are at an end; but the
Bodhisattva remains on earth or in a heaven to help
mankind and all living things.

b) As the teachings of the Founder were systematized
by the monastic Hīnayāna commentators four stages
are to be distinguished:

1. The stage of the Sāvaka who is either (*a*) Sotāpanno,
i.e., one who has set his feet upon the upward path, or
"entered the stream"; (*b*) Sakadāgamino, i.e., one who
has made such progress that he will only be once more a
man and will then attain Nibbāna; (*c*) Anāgāmino, i.e.,
one who attains Nibbāna "without returning"; (*d*)
Arhat, he who is already free, having broken the bonds,
and is already in Nibbāna.

2. The stage of the Pacceka Buddha, i.e., a fully
enlightened Buddha who keeps his knowledge to himself.

3. The stage of Bodhisattva, who is potentially both
Arhat and Buddha, but who prefers to help all sentient
things.

4. The stage of the Buddha, who, having reached full
and complete Nibbāna, is the source of truth and the guide
to all.

c) Though he does not use the words, Asoka in all his
services to his people and in his interpretation of the
Dhamma emphasizes the Bodhisattva rather than the
Arhat ideal. He is regarded by the Theravāda as an

upāsika or lay-adherent, and his works of civilization as by-products.

d) Halfway or incipient Mahāyāna carried on this Bodhisattva tendency, but recognized in deference to the more austere members of the Sangha that Arhatship is one way to Nibbāna—even if no one now achieves the goal. Faith in the Buddha begins to supplement and to supplant works.

e) The Full Mahāyāna of the "Lotus" (*ca.* 100 A.D.) roundly declares that there is only one way, that the Buddha has destined all to Buddhahood, and only by his "skilful strategy" accommodates truth and speaks of the ways of Sāvaka, Pacceka-Buddha, and Bodhisattva. In this Mahāyāna is probably nearer than Hīnayāna to original Buddhism.

f) The Paradise Mahāyāna, agreeing in theory that Buddhahood or Nirvāna is the goal, offers to ordinary folk the alluring vision of the Paradise of Amitābha as more easily reached and more satisfying, and develops a progressive emphasis upon faith rather than works as the way of salvation.

V. BUDDHOLOGY

Side by side with this shifting of emphases went on a growing Buddhology which may for schematic purposes be expressed as follows:

1. The Teacher proclaims himself the "Elder Brother of Mankind," supernormal but not supernatural; he ignores any supreme God, and teaches that the gods of his people are unable to help, being themselves in bondage to Karma and Samsāra.

2. He is variously regarded by the monks of the Hīnayāna as (*a*) an omniscient Teacher, source of all truth (Theravāda); (*b*) a supernatural Being, not subject

to human passion (Mahāsanghika); this is the germ of later Mahāyāna teachings.

3. The Asokan laity regard him as one of several Buddhas and pay worship to his symbols; this they call "worshiping the Lord" (cf. Asokan sculpture).

4. The early Halfway Mahāyāna represents him as a God surrounded by adoring Bodhisattvas and other beings (cf. Gandhāran sculpture).

5. For the Full Mahāyāna of the "Lotus" he is the almost Eternal Lord and Father, one of many Buddhas whom he now supersedes.

6. For the Paradise Mahāyāna of the *Sukhāvatī Vyūha* he disappears behind the eternal or semi-eternal Amitābha, and in the *Amitāyur-dhyāna Sūtra* points to him.

7. For the Mādhyamaka and Yogācāra schools he is an embodiment more or less real of the Dharmakāya.

8. For the *Avatamsaka* he is one of innumerable forms in which the primeval Buddha Vairochana is manifest.

9. For the Mantrayāna he is an emanation of the self-existent Adi-Buddha.

The abbreviation *B.N.* refers to Dr. Bunyiu Nanjio's *Catalogue of the Chinese Tripitaka*, Oxford, 1883; *S.B.E.* to the *Sacred Books of the East*; *B.T.* to Warren's *Buddhism in Translations*; *E.R.E.* to the *Encyclopaedia of Religion and Ethics*; *P.T.S.* to the Pāli Text Society; *J.R.A.S.* to the *Journal of the Royal Asiatic Society*.

CHAPTER I

RĀJAGAHA; THE MIDDLE PATH

The Differentia of the Buddhist Reform (ca. 525 B.C.)

*"He that seeth the Dhamma seeth me." "That there is effective action, resultant action, and power within to do this or that, I, even I, proclaim." "As the ocean has but one flavour so my teaching has but one essence— deliverance." "Engineers control the stream: the wise controlleth himself." "Of all that springs from causes the Tathāgata has explained the cause."—*SĀKYAMUNI.

The country of Magadha is famous in Indian literature for its beauty and fertility. On the east side of its ancient capital, Rājagaha, the King's House, is a natural rampart of five wooded hills, to which from time immemorial have gathered the religious teachers of India; and thither they still come, followed by eager pilgrim crowds, wistfully seeking peace and comfort. To these hills with their wooded slopes and bare cliffs, honeycombed with hermitages, came the young Siddhartha about the middle of the sixth century B.C., seeking guidance, and here some nine years later he began his work as a reformer of the religion of India, and as her greatest moral teacher.

It is not difficult to picture the young reformer whose story has been so often told:[1] lonely at first, subject to periods of depression at the stupidity and inertia of those about him, repelled as he ate the first meal of scraps thrown into his begging-bowl, but gathering courage and inspiration as disciples began to attach themselves to him, and to help him formulate the rules of a new religious order. We may think of them during the rains in peace-

[1] I have tried to retell it in a biographical sketch, *Gotama Buddha*. New York: Association Press, 1921; London: Oxford Press, 1923.

ful retreat upon these hills, gazing down upon the fertile
plains of the Ganges Valley, or gathered about him on
the bare Peak of the Vulture that rose clear above the
wooded slopes, and pouring out in that serene air a paean
of thanksgiving and joy in their new-found liberty of mind
and peace of soul.

> As swans who soar in tracks of sunlit air,
> As sorcerers in realms of space are free;
> So does the sage win through to mastery
> Of Māra, and the transient world's despair.

In order to give them this liberty, however, the new
teacher first convinced them of the universality of law.
Before they could be free in the universe they must realize
that it is lawful to the core.   This was a truth already
accepted in theory,[1] but men were ignoring it in practice.
Among the first of the converts were two Brahmins,
Moggallāna and Sāriputta, and from the story of their
conversion we gather how large a part the mind played
in the new Way, and how central in it was the doctrine
of causality, which has been well called its keynote.[2]
These men had been companions and fellow-seekers in
the religious life.   Like their fellow-Hindus they must
have been familiar with such teaching; accepting the axiom
that life is evil and that Karma brings rebirth they were
seeking Moksha, freedom from the whole process.   Meeting a Buddhist monk and struck by his calm and radiant
bearing, Sāriputta learned the essentials of the truth in
these simple words:

> Of all things springing from a cause
> The Buddha hath the causes told:
> Of how they all shall cease to be,
> This, too, our Teacher doth unfold.[3]

---

[1] E.g., in the *Sāmkhya-Yoga;* cf. Keith's *Sāmkhya and Philosophy.* Oxford Press,
1921.

[2] M. Anesaki, *Nichiren,* p. 138.   [3] *Mahāvagga* i. 23. 4, 5; *B.T.,* pp. 87–91.

It is difficult to believe at first sight that this doctrine became to so many a real gospel. Even if they had not heard it from their own religious teachers, was it a truth so emancipating ? The answer seems to be twofold: first, that it is one thing to know a doctrine, another to be gripped by it, and to meet men who are radiant with it; and second, that this is what Sākyamuni achieved. Even today men orphaned in the world of faith find in it, as he popularized it, a gospel of salvation; there are groups of European Buddhist monks, for instance, to whom it has given a new meaning in life. Familiar with it as science, in him they find it as religion! And to men haunted by the idea of capricious deities, on the one hand, and beset, on the other, by determinist teachings of a monistic philosophy, here was a great new conviction that the universe is orderly, and that man is free to shape his own destiny. Here is a practical and vital truth: "Put aside these questions of the beginning and the end. This is the Dhamma—that being present this must follow; from the rising of that this arises. That being absent this does not come into being. From the cessation of that this too ceases."[1] Here is reality speaking. Gotama has been called atheist, even by many of his own later followers. However this may be, he made here a notable contribution to an ethical theism; his serene faith in righteousness and in the reality of unseen, intangible values may be called religious; and we may well believe that knowing his people and their genius for religion he believed that he might safely leave them to work out a religious interpretation of this law of causality. What was wrong with most of them was that they were in the bondage of superstition; before they could become truly religious they

[1] *Majjhima Nikāya* 79.

must learn to think of the world as a cosmos of ordered sequences, and not a chaos at the mercy of capricious demons or demigods. Until they were free from such vague fears, on the one hand, and from the fatalism of determinist theories and a vague pantheism, on the other, there could be no true morality or religion; and to give them a sound basis for faith he bent all the energies of his great mind and heart. Thus we find him welcoming all who were ready to accept the doctrine of causality, for example, the Jātilas,[1] and dealing severely alike with determinist teachers who failed to moralize it, and with those who sought by self-mutilation or foolish asceticism to placate the powers of the unseen world.[2]

Let us picture this courageous son of fact with his disciples grouped about him on the Vulture Peak, or some similar height. For twenty-five centuries Buddhists have sought the mountain tops, and these are still the fastnesses of the Dhamma. Master and disciples sit calmly meditating, and after the Indian manner they wait for him to speak. At last a smile lights up his face, and he points to where a peasant is carrying his burden of fagots down from the hillside: "Listen, O monks." "Speak, lord." "I will teach you the parable of the burden and its bearer, of the taking of it up, and the laying of it down." He then proceeds to show that the burden is bodily existence, that the bearer is the individual consciousness, that the taking-up of the burden is Tanhā, that craving to be and to have which brings man to rebirth, and that the laying-down of the burden is the putting aside of such craving.

---

[1] *Mahāvagga* i. 21; *B.T.*, p. 351. They were fire-worshipers of a very intelligent kind.

[2] In *Majj. Nik.* 71, Gotama is made to say: "In ninety-one cycles of rebirth I can remember only one naked ascetic having attained to a heaven. And *he* held the doctrine of the fruits of actions."

And then that they may the better remember it, he sings them a little gātha or hymn:

> This body is of Khandhas made,
> 'Tis man this burden bears.
> Oh! with what joy aside 'tis laid,
> 'Tis taken up with tears.[1]

And all the company, having already experienced something of the joy of laying aside this burden,[2] rejoice with the teacher who has shown them the way. So did Pilgrim rejoice when the load fell from his shoulders. And if it be objected that here was a poor materialistic "gospel," the Buddhist replies: "It is not materialistic: for of the five Khandhas four are not material: Vedanā, feeling; Saññā, perception; Viññāna, consciousness in general; and Samkhāra, a complex including will, attention, faith, and other conative groups."

We may imagine another typical scene. The master and his disciples are seated calm and collected on Gayā Head, a hillside near the spot where he attained enlightenment, when a fire breaks out in the jungle below; they watch it blaze, and then he begins once more to improve the occasion: "All, O monks, is aflame: eye, ear, nose—all the organs of sense. All nature is aflame. What is the cause of this universal conflagration? It is Tanhā."[3] Hate, lust, infatuation—these are the flames. Then, in order that he may help them in their task of teaching a world to extinguish the blaze that is destroying it, he

---

[1] *Samyutta Nikāya*, B.T., pp. 159–60. This little parable was not unnaturally misunderstood in later days, the Sammitiya school interpreting it to mean that man is something more than the Khandhas which make up his "burden." (See Poussin, *E.R.E.*, Vol. XI, Sammitiyas, and note his indorsement of this review as "a good and truly Buddhist one.")

[2] Though still carrying this burden of bodily existence they had got rid of the intolerable obsession of rebirth and of Tanhā.

[3] *Mahāvagga* i. 21; B.T., pp. 351–53.

gives them a new and different chant, a dirge that still resounds mournfully in a thousand monasteries:

Sabbā dukkhā,
Sabbā anattā,
Sabbā aniccā.

Sorrow is everywhere,
In man is no abiding entity,
In things is no abiding reality.

The conflagration, in a word, is to be extinguished by the waters of logic. Face life as it is, sorrowful, transient, and you will no longer crave for it. If the doctrine of causality is the keynote of the Buddhist metaphysic, the doctrine of anattā is the unique thing in its psychology. And both doctrines are applied with an ethical purpose. Like Hume, two thousand years later, Gotama with remorseless logic analyzes the "self" into its component parts. He seeks to get rid of the "ego" of animism in order that he may get rid of the "ego" of egoism. The "self" is unreal because it is compound. Analyze it, and see that it is a stream of consciousness made up of elements of sensation, of cognition, of volition, and you will realize that there is no "soul" in the ordinary sense of a separate entity or "substance," such as that which only a century ago men of science in the West were trying to weigh and to locate. Nor is there even a "substratum" in which qualities inhere. Much less is there an ātman, such as some Hindus conceived in almost physical terms, an in-dwelling microcosm identical with the macrocosm or Brahman.[1] To believe that is to sacrifice moral freedom; and Gotama knew that this is more vital than even intellectual consistency. The self is real enough, because it is a manifestation of Kamma, energy or action, and it is

[1] Buddhaghosa, the great commentator, says authoritatively that the Buddha ana-lyzed man into the five Khandhas "to afford no foothold for animism."

free, in spite of the past, to direct its energies aright in the present. "Self," says the *Dhammapada*, "is custodian of self."

Out of the seeming pessimism of this philosophy of transiency emerges a sane optimism, as is beginning to be recognized by Western writers. Buddhism insists on Dukkham, sorrow, in order that it may show men the way to Sukham, happiness: "One thing only do I teach, O monks—sorrow, and the uprooting of sorrow." Over against the world of birth and death, of Samsāra, it sets the unchanging calm of Nibbāna, beyond joy and sorrow, yet often known as the Supreme Bliss. All religions, as William James has pointed out, are alike in having as their basis an uneasiness and its solution. Gotama has his own solution to offer. "He is a physician; if medicine is pessimistic then he is a pessimist"; says the Buddhist, "having diagnosed the disease he goes on to prescribe its cure."

Even when he wielded the knife it was to cut out the roots of sorrow, and man learned to kiss that strong yet kindly hand. The early Sangha was therefore a happy company; there was "something vernal in the air," and at times a contagion of joy can be seen to pass from these monks and nuns to the people about them. They were in the presence of a beloved leader; they had attained to a vision of the unity and lawfulness of the universe so that they were no more afraid; they believed that they were seeing life steadily and seeing it whole, and they had a purpose great enough to claim their whole energies—to lead the world out of confusion and superstition and fear into a serene peace; out of the transient flux and confusion of becoming to the ordered calm of being. Above all they believed that they would not be reborn to sorrow, and the old obsession was gone forever. Let the student ponder the *Psalms of the Early Buddhists*[1] and he will find himself responding to their joy. This is another hall-mark of the originality of early Buddhism. Much in it was ordinary Hinduism; its spirit was all its own.

During his lifetime it is clear that Gotama encouraged them to put their faith in the Dhamma, or teaching. Like most of the terms he used this was one familiar to his countrymen, but as was his wont he redefined it. Hitherto it had meant the abiding social order, norm, or standard; divorcing it from its connection with social sanction he proclaimed it as the truth of individual existence. Believing that his own enlightenment was a discovery of universal law or order, that all life is a unity, that a moral purpose is at work in it, he saw his task as that of a teacher of these truths. In this lay one of the great secrets of his success; while others seemed to be dealing with vague, intangible things, here was a positivist who insisted upon facing life as individual men and women have to live it, and in whose words there rang the sturdy conviction which comes from personal experience. Men began to say of him, "He knows knowing, sees seeing; he is the eye of the world; he has become knowledge . . . . has become truth . . . . it is he who teaches us, who reveals the hidden truth, who pours out good and gives immortality; he is the lord of Dhamma."[2]

> He hath discerned all this life o' the world,
> In all the world the how and thus of things,
> From all detached and leaning upon naught,
> Who all hath mastered, from all bonds is loosed:
> Touched is for him high peace and blessed calm
> Where no fear cometh more.[3]

[1] C. A. F. Rhys Davids, *Translation of Theratherigāthā*, 2 vols. London: *P.T.S.*, 1909, 1913.

[2] In *Samyutta, P.T.S. Ed.* xiv. 94 f. it is also stated that he is "son of Light, of Wisdom, of Brahmā. . . . ."

[3] Mrs. Rhys Davids' rendering of *Ang. Nik.* ii. 24.

What, in other words, makes him Buddha is that he has found the Dhamma, and having been true to it and identified himself with it proclaims it to the world. In this identification lies the seed for the Buddhology of later ages. The Tathāgata, "he who has reached reality," gives place to the Tathatā, reality itself.

Meantime it is clear that for the first generation of disciples he was primarily an ethical teacher, and that he aimed at showing men a middle path of splendid sanity. This is the central thing in his ethics. If they differ from those of orthodox Hinduism it is in their moderation. While the body must be kept in subjection, it is both vain and painful to torture it, as he and countless others in India had done. On the other hand, family life, and life in the world in general, is a life of confused issues, and though it is not impossible to master one's self while living in the world,[1] it is far easier and safer once and for all to cut out these roots, and to join the monastic order. Yet he provided for a "third order" of lay-people, and there are a score of these upāsikas mentioned in the early books, who are said to have won Arhatship; of them it is claimed that they had destroyed Tanhā, had cut the bonds of rebirth, and realized in this world and in the midst of it an other-worldly peace and joy.[2] In the midst of Samsāra they had been in Nibbāna. Like Brother Lawrence they could practice, while immersed in mundane occupations, an other-worldly peace. And this was to them the guaranty that they would not be reborn. They found themselves masters of the universe, not its slaves.

What did this doctrine of rebirth mean to the Buddhist? All the world is now familiar with the Hindu

---

[1] Hundreds of householders are said to have attained to one of the heavens.

[2] See "Arhat," *E.R.E.*, Vol. I.

doctrines of Karma and transmigration, already established in the time of Gotama Buddha:

> Our actions still pursue us from afar
> And what we have been makes us what we are.

By the sixth century B.C. India accepted the doctrine
that each ātman is reborn into the state it has earned.
But even highly qualified students of Buddhism seem to be
greatly befogged as to how this doctrine can be reconciled
with the Buddha's cardinal doctrine of anattā.   If there
be no "soul" to transmigrate how can there be transmigration ?   Here is a dilemma indeed; and the solution lies
of course in the definition of the terms.   Transmigration
is not what Gotama taught, but rather reindividualization
or, better, a continuation of the ever changing stream
of consciousness in a new channel.[1]   A man is not the
same as he was when a boy.   Yet he is not different.
After death he will be the same yet not the same, as a
river whose content, ever changing, yet remains within the
self-same river-bed.   As a kinema film which through many
minute changes tells a connected story of many reels so
are rebirths continuous yet not identical.

Sākyamuni was primarily a moral teacher, and yet he
had a definite psychology and philosophy.   He was neither
a realist in the ordinary sense, naïvely accepting the current
phraseology and ideas of the time, nor a nihilist as some
of his followers have been.   "Everything is; this is one
extreme view.   Everything is not; this is another."   He
rejects them both.   The "self," he insists, is a part of
the whole phenomenal world, and must be seen through
scientific or analytic eyes.   The old static ideas of it must
give place to a dynamic conception.   It is this individual

[1] This is the actual metaphor of scholastic Buddhism; cf. *Compendium of Philosophy, P.T.S.*, p. 8.

"stream of consciousness" which changes from moment to moment, that is "reindividualized" when the body dies. The change may be more profound; it is only another change.

The best discussion of the whole question from the orthodox Buddhist standpoint is in the *Questions of King Milinda*,[1] a late work of fiction yet of great authority. The man who is reborn, teaches the sage Nāgasena, is neither the same nor yet another. Nothing "substantial" has passed over any more than when one lamp is lit from another—only energy. There is a transference of energy between the two flames. One is responsible for the other. If a spark from my house sets fire to my neighbor's thatch, am I not responsible? A man steals his neighbor's mangoes, but he cannot fool the judge by proving that the mangoes he took are not the same mangoes as his neighbor planted; so by numerous similes and parables the lesson is enforced, and it seems logical enough: Kamma, action, is the energy which passes over from one phase of consciousness to the next. But there are difficulties. What, if nothing but energy passes across, is the thread of continuity? What are the links between one life and the next? They are the same as those between two consecutive moments of our conscious life here and now. Among the senses Buddhist psychology numbers Mano, which is at once a sixth sense, and the "resort, the partaker, the field, and range of them all,"[2]—a *sensus communis*. It is certainly easier to conceive this link between two consecutive phases of the present stream of consciousness than to imagine it connect-

---

[1] I.e., Menander, an Indo-Scythian prince of about 100 B.C. See chap. iii.

[2] *Majj. Nik.* i. 295; *Sam. Nik.* v. 218; quoted by Mrs. Rhys Davids in *Buddhist Psychology*, p. 69.

ing what seem like two different lives, and we are apt to be impatient with this part of Buddhist philosophy.

Perhaps it will help the western reader to tolerate the doctrines of Anattā and Samsāra if he thinks of the unexplained, yet well-attested, fact of telepathy. If one mind can influence another through great spaces, why not imagine that the same mind may be influenced by its own past energies or phases of consciousness, and even kept in action by its own psychical momentum, even when the physical organ which it used has been dissolved into its elements ? Reindividualization may begin at once.

All the habitual arguments by which we buttress our belief in a life after death can be equally well used to support the Buddhist doctrine of Samsāra; and we have to pay our respects to the early psychologists of Buddhism. One of the qualities of consciousness on which they lay stress is Manasikāra, or attention,[1] and this is another link between present and past: we direct our stream of consciousness and determine its direction hereafter as we attend now to this or that range of interests. Another link is memory,[2] that deposit or undercurrent of the stream which may be out of sight and forgotten, but which yet exerts a potent influence. The past, however forgotten it may be, is wrought into the present, and operates in ways which surprise us only because of our forgetful memories. But the saint remembers everything! Near these very hills of Rājagaha the great disciple Moggallāna was foully murdered. Calmly the aged teacher, who seems (perhaps half-humorously) to have claimed something very like omniscience, related the story of how untold centuries before Moggallāna had been an impious son and a parri-

---

[1] Cf. *Majj. Nik.*; quoted in Mrs. Rhys Davids' *Buddhist Psychology*, p. 97, and many passages of the *Abhidhamma*.

[2] *Sam. Nik.* xii. 15.

cide, who, disguised as a bandit, had killed both mother
and father. Thus, in his present rebirth, saint and Arhat
as he was, it was possible, nay necessary, for bandits to
murder him. As for them they had not long to wait
before reaping the harvest of their sin. For the king of
Magadha, a genial despot and a great champion of
Buddhism, buried them up to their navels and then
set fire to them, after which (though it seems rather a work
of supererogation) he ploughed them into the soil.[1]

> Deeds done in envy or in hate,
> Deeds of the fool infatuate,
> Must bear their fitting punishment
> Till Karma's energy be spent.

In such homely ways, by adopting folklore and adapting
it, by snatches of song, and by astonishing claims to remember his own past existences, and those of everyone
else, did Gotama bring home to his disciples the lessons
of Karma and rebirth. And today the simplest peasant
in Buddhist lands thinks inevitably in terms of these
two doctrines. They are the very warp and woof of the
thought of millions who are proud of them and confident,
as one said to me, that "they explain the inequalities of
human life very nicely."

At the same time they long to escape to some state
where these laws no longer hold sway, and the teacher
having enforced these lessons—the ubiquity of the harvest
law, "as a man soweth so shall he also reap," and the
inevitableness of Samsāra—went on to show a way of
salvation:

> As some poor sufferer in prison pent
>   From year to weary year is racked by pain,
> Longs for release and cannot find content,
>   But ever pines and chafes against his chain;

[1] See *B.T.*, p. 221.

> So do thou see in each succeeding birth
> A prison full of untold misery!
> Seek to shake off all chains that bind to earth
> And from existence evermore be free.[1]

Who is the freed man ?   It is he who has snapped the
fetters of ignorance, pride, egoism, lust, hatred—the
Arhat—who "knows that rebirth is exhausted, that he
has lived the holy life, that he has done what he had to
do, and is no more for this world."[2]   That is the stock
description.   He is one who has replaced ignoble craving
by noble desire—one, in other words, who longs not for
rebirth, even as a god, but who longs for the end of rebirth,
for Nibbāna;[3] one indeed who has already attained, and
has realized his true "self."   Arahatta and Nibbāna are
usually synonyms, and in such early works as the "Psalms
of the Brethren" Arhats are "no less Buddha and Tathāgata than their great master."[4]   What then is Nibbāna ?

This doctrine is the *pons asinorum* of the learned.   It
is still gravely debated and strangely misrepresented.
Does it mean annihilation ?   "Yes," says Gotama, "the
annihilation of Tanhā, of sorrow, and of rebirth."[5]   Does
this not involve annihilation of the "soul ?"   "How can
that be annihilated which has no existence ?"   Does the
Arhat in whom craving is annihilated, sorrow and rebirth
ended, Nibbāna reached—does he continue to exist ?
"That," says the Buddha, "is not your affair.   Your
business is with morality."[6]   Could anything be plainer—

---

[1] From the *Jātaka: Heart of Buddhism.* Oxford Press, 1916.

[2] *B.T.*, p. 137.   The Arhat is described in more technical language as one who
has "entered the Fourth Path," "broken the ten fetters," etc.

[3] Cf. *ibid.*, p. 333.

[4] C. A. F. Rhys Davids, *Psalms of the Brethren*, p. xxii.

[5] Cf. *S.B.E.*, Vol. XIII; *Mahāvagga* vi. 31. 7.

[6] Cf. *Sam. Nik.* ii. 223, and *Majjhima Nik.* 63; *B.T.*, pp. 117–22.

or less satisfying to the inquiring mind ? But Gotama is
content, as it seems to me, having himself had a mystic
experience of peace and joy beyond description, to show
others how they too may attain, and to leave it at that.
Not the least admirable thing about him is his reticence.
What if he has opened up alluring vistas, and then kept
silence ? He has only done what all the Mystics must do:

> Oh could I tell ye surely would believe it!
> Oh could I only say what I have seen!
> How can I tell and how can you receive it,
> How till he bringeth you where I have been ?

The highest truth is "ineffable,"[1] above all relativity,
as Buddhist schoolmen later spent themselves to prove,
and though he was not an agnostic in most things, yet like
all men (except spiritualists) he was necessarily an agnostic
as to details of the life after death. But in this life he
could show them how to enjoy the Nibbāna of a quiet
conscience, and of a mind at rest. And though he was
not a Mystic in quite the usual sense, Gotama was of that
august company: he could not describe the goal, but he
could show the way to it; and like other Mystics he
became very definite here, and gave to the world his
famous Eightfold Noble Path. Before we examine this,
let us note here that his refusals to be more definite were
interpreted by Buddhist philosophers in later days as
denials,[2] and that much of the confusion which exists as
to his teaching is due, as Max Müller showed fifty years
ago, to a confusion between the teachings of Gotama

---

[1] Cf. *Dhp.* 218. Nipuna, abstruse; apalokita, unlike this world; anidassana, invisible, are synonyms.

[2] Poussin has shown that the doctrine of annihilation is clearly taught in the *Tripitaka*, but holds that it was not the teaching of Sākyamuni who indeed calls it a heresy. The *Visuddhi magga* calls it a "pestiferous delusion." Cf. "Nirvāna," *E.R.E.*, p. 378.

and those of the schoolmen of later days. "What Bishop Bigandet and others represent as the popular view of the Nirvāna in contradistinction from that of the Buddhist divines was, if I am not mistaken," he wrote in 1869, "the conception of Buddha and his disciples." It was a great forward step to distinguish between the doctrine of the Founder and that of the later schoolmen, and in the following year Childers wrote as follows: "The word Nirvāna is applied to two different things; first to the annihilation of existence, which is the ultimate goal of Buddhism, and, secondly, to the state of sanctification, which is the stepping-stone to annihilation, and without which annihilation cannot be obtained."[1] That later Buddhists have used the word in both these senses is clear, and yet Dr. Rhys Davids[2] is surely right when he insists that the Founder laid all the stress upon the ethical process of sanctification, and refused to answer, except in baffling terms, when men pressed him about the continued existence of the saint after death. He seems indeed on occasion to have indicated that both the annihilationists and the eternalists are wrong, for both are following vain speculations.[3] And yet to many scholars it seems clear that he did himself sow the seeds which developed into the doctrine of annihilation; is not his basal doctrine of anattā such a seed? And is not the whole phraseology of "blowing out," "uprooting," "killing the germ of rebirth," open to misinterpretation?[4] Yet we have always

[1] Trübner, *Literary Record*, 1870.

[2] Dr. Rhys Davids takes a middle course between Burnouf and J. d'Alwis, who are supporters of the nihilistic interpretation, and some who interpret Nibbāna as a kind of paradise.

[3] Cf. *B.T.*, p. 138; *Sam. Nik.* iii. 109; *Points of Controversy*, pp. 32, 62: "The Blessed One would never say that on the dissolution of the body the Arhat is annihilated."

[4] Cf. J. d'Alwis' reply to Max Müller, *Buddhist Nirvāna*. London: Trübner, 1871.

to remember that the records which we possess are the work of later monastic schools and that what their Founder really said is inevitably colored by their own beliefs.

Probably we shall never be able to answer these questions finally; what is clear is that two things are explicitly stated in the canonical books, and in the ortho- dox *Milinda Pañha* to be implied by the term "Nibbāna," first the extinction of craving, and second the extinction of the process of becoming. The first is the means to the second, which is the end. It is well to make a careful study of the synonyms which the Buddhist uses to describe what this ideal means to him.[1] It is called santi, peace; mutti, freedom; it is sītibhūtam, the coolness that allures the pilgrim of a world in flames; it is the dīpam, or island to which he passes from the waters of samsāra; it is saranam or lenam, a refuge from this fleeting show of things; and more negatively it is amatam, that which is not dead; acchuta, that which is not dying; akuto-bhāya, a fearless state; and above all it is tanhākkhaya and dukkhā-kkhaya, the destruction of craving and of sorrow. This is the essence of Buddhism, and in many places occurs the saying: "As the great ocean has but one flavor, so my doctrine and discipline has but one flavor, that of deliverance from suffering." In at least one passage this deliverance is defined as bhava-nirōdho, the cessation of becoming. But this is not necessarily the same as annihilation; and indeed the Mahāyāna soon made Nirvāna a synonym for the Absolute; it is the Ultimate Reality. And if negatives are used to describe it no less are they used in the *Upanishads* to describe the Ātman, the One and Absolute. "Neti, Neti," not so, is the final

[1] See Appendix III.

word in either case, as in all attempts of mystics to define what they experience.

To those who pressed the question: "Does this cessation involve annihilation?" Gotama seems sometimes to have replied that this is not a question which is of practical importance, that it does not concern the holy life, nor lead to insight; but at others he flatly condemned the annihilationists as heretics. And if we who are not Buddhists cannot conceive how a stream of thoughts, emotions, and volitions can persist "when Karma's energy is spent," the modern Buddhist may quite fairly retort: "What is your own doctrine of the soul or self, here and hereafter?" If we refer to the psychologists, they will be found in some cases at least to agree with Gotama that the thinker and the thought are one, and yet that we are free to believe in, even if we cannot imagine, an existence of this "self" after death. And if we turn to the moralists they may well reply with Emerson and Gotama: "Of immortality, the soul when well employed is incurious. It is so well that it is sure that it will be well." And Sākyamuni was first of all a moral teacher—a physician of sick souls.

Yet this statement needs safeguarding. Above the "details of mere morality"—important as they are— he valued his own mystical experiences, for morality must have an authoritative foundation. If the Buddhist cannot say: "Thus saith the Lord," he can and does say: "Thus hath the Buddha told us, and he is King of the Dhamma. Has he not experienced truth? Is he not himself the Truth?"

And the Teacher himself bids men praise him, not for his moral teachings, but because he has "realized and seen for himself other things, profound, subtle, hard to realize and to understand, yet sweet and tranquillizing."[1] "He has found the birthless incomparable Yoga-calm of Nirvāna."[2] And this is beyond the sphere of reason . . . . felt or experienced only by the wise. In a word, he is an authoritative moral Teacher in virtue of his own deep mystical experience. His citizenship is in heavenly places. And out of this other-worldly spring come the wide waters of his benevolence. All sentient life is one—all are companions in the Great Quest, for all are fellow-victims in the toils of Samsāra.

Gotama's ethical system is intimately connected with his more philosophical teaching. It is clearly and closely related to the Hindu systems of his day, and indeed to moral systems everywhere—a fact which still kindles a naïve surprise in many minds. The interesting thing in it is rather that it differs from all other types of ethical theory. Though the Buddha did not deny the existence of the gods,[3] yet he appeals to no divine sanction but rather to an enlightened self-interest. The man who harms another is a fool, for he also harms himself. Vice brings unhappiness as the shadow follows the body. Happiness is the bloom upon virtue. Let each man be a friend to himself and he will be happy; altruism is really an enlightened egoism.

Here, then, is no "thus saith the Lord" of the Hebrew prophet, and no appeal even to social sanction. The "eightfold path" is a moral discipline for the individual, and makes its appeal to the reason. It begins with "right

---

[1] Cf. *Dialogues*, I, 26, and Anesaki, "Buddhist Ethics," *E.R.E.*

[2] *B.T.*, p. 338.

[3] Gotama seems to have accepted the gods of the Pantheon of his contemporaries, and Brahmā in particular engaged his attention; but all were in bondage to Karma and Samsāra.

opinions," for the Teacher realized as few have done that all good or evil begins in the mind, and that people cannot act aright unless they first think aright; and the most popular summary of his moral teachings condenses his ethic in a sentence: "Flee evil, set about doing good, cleanse your inmost thought." Beginning then in the mind, the Noble Path is a carefully graded ascent passing on to right aspirations, right speech, right acts, right means of livelihood, until by right effort and right concentration of mind the high peak of right contemplation and of the four trance-states is reached. Middle Path as it is, it is yet exacting enough to demand a specialization which is only for the few. These are called to break the Ten Fetters and to reach Samādhi, a tranquil, "cool" state of mental equilibrium, and to enjoy the Jhānas. Beginning in a secluded place to meditate upon some subject specially suited to his temperament,[1] the recluse is instructed to concentrate his attention until he reaches a condition of ecstatic joy. Here is a third distinctive feature. This Samādhi is the means to the extinction of Tanhā, to the increasing of religious knowledge, and to the acquisition of supernormal powers, Abhiññā, which include a memory of one's former existences and the power to pass through space, and to work certain other wonders, Iddhi. Here Buddhism owes much to the ancient Yoga, and like it makes faith, energy, wisdom, and other qualities of the moral will prerequisites to these trance-states.

"The ideal of early Buddhism is the equilibrium of morals (Sīla), meditation (Jhāna), and intuitive wisdom

---

[1] There are five principal subjects for meditation:

         Karunābhavana—meditation upon pity
         Mettābhavana—upon compassion
         Muditābhavana—upon sympathy
         Asubhābhavana—upon charnel-house, graveyards, etc.
         Upekhābhavana—upon detachment.

(Paññā)." And this equlibrium is not easily reached. Whether anyone reaches it is difficult to say; the monk is forbidden to make such a claim on his own behalf, and who else can know ? My impression, based on careful investigation, is that in the modern Buddhist world these higher practices are hardly to be found except in some few earnest followers of the Zen school in Japan. That the Founder and some of his immediate followers attained to Samādhi seems clear. That he, or at least the early writers, anticipated that it would become a rare accomplishment seems equally clear. Arhats are not much mentioned after the close of the Pāli canon, partly because of the difficulty of the Way, but more, as we shall see, because it ceased to commend itself to the majority as a true interpretation of the mind of the Founder. The Lohans or Arhats of China are a limited group of eighteen, representing perhaps the "eighteen schools" of orthodoxy, but the Bodhisattvas are innumerable. "Save yourself before you can save others" is the Arhat ideal; "Save others and you save yourself" is the Bodhisattva's creed. In other words: "self-realization" is the former, "self-realization through self-sacrifice," the latter ideal.

From the first it seems clear that Buddhism did emphasize the power of love or compassion, "the unbounded friendly mind," as a means to reach these high states. "All the means available as grounds for right conduct are not worth a sixteenth part of the liberation of the heart through love. That outshines them all in radiance and absorbs them into itself,"[1] so says the *Itivuttaka* or *Logia* of Buddhism, and among the many noble teach-

---

[1] The Buddhist, like the Christian moralist, exhorts us to "put on love" as a girdle which binds together and harmonizes the other virtues; cf. II Peter 1: 5-7. Faith, virtue, knowledge, self-control, patience, godliness, love, have all a place in Buddhist ethics. Six of them are pāramitās of the Bodhisattva.

ings of the early Sangha shines out the poem on compassion so often quoted but always worthy of comment and study:

> As, recking nought of self, a mother's love
>   Enfolds and cherishes her only son,
> So through the world let thy compassion move
>   And compass living creatures every one;
> Soaring and sinking in unfettered liberty,
> Free from ill-will, purged of all enmity!

There are, if we may so express it, two other wings in this early Buddhism besides that of contemplation by which the soul may mount to a life truly sublime. One is the wing of wisdom; the other, less developed as yet, is the wing of love. For it is to the mind, after all, that Buddhism makes its chief appeal, and here lies the unique contribution of Buddhist ethics, that it blends with its practical aim a system of theoretical wisdom. And this wisdom is not the ordinary wisdom of the man in the street, but a mystic insight, an intuition which sees things as they are and chooses the best. Through this insight man realizes the Dhamma as the universal truth, and when he reaches Nibbāna he has realized what was later defined as an all-embracing intelligence, and a love as all-inclusive. Thus the crown and sum of Buddhist morality may be said to be negatively a dispersal of the clouds of ignorance (Avijjā) and positively the dawning of the light of Bodhi. It is morally the thrusting-out of egoism by the awakening of benevolence or altruism. At a later date it was to be religiously interpreted as the surrender of the self to the will of an Eternal Being: for the present it remains a moral communion with all sentient beings. To pervade them with thoughts of love—this is the way to union with Brahman, i.e., to Nibbāna.

Underlying the whole system is this sense of the unity of all things, a germ which was to develop before many centuries into a metaphysical system hardly distinguishable from the Hindu philosophy against which Buddhism was essentially a rebellion; and into a theology akin to that of orthodox Christianity.

And here we must notice the place which faith (Saddhā) plays in the ethical system of Sākyamuni; for his followers in millions today believe in salvation by faith; and in him as Savior, whether they are orthodox lay-Hīnayānists of Burma and Ceylon or followers of the Mahāyāna schools of Japan and China.

The development of such a doctrine is not unnatural. Faith is one of the cardinal virtues of early Buddhism. It is the first of the indriyas, or "organs," energy being the second, mindfulness the third, contemplation the fourth, and wisdom the fifth. In other words, the Buddhist is to have faith in order that he may attain to wisdom. In one passage it is ranked with intuition as the means of salvation. What is the exact connotation of Saddhā, or faith, and what is the object to which it is to cling ?

Much has been written upon the subject, and yet it may almost be summed up in two sayings attributed to Gotama himself. The first is in the *Majjhima Nikāya:* "Whoso shall turn to me with faith and love shall reach one of the heavenly worlds. And whatsoever monk shall conform himself to my teaching, walking in full faith in it, he shall attain to Full Awakening."[1] In other words, faith in the teacher has its reward, but it is a less reward than that given to faith in his teachings. The Buddha is the guide, let the disciple trust in his guidance. It is

[1] *Majj. Nik.* in *Discourses*, Silācāra i. 18; i.e., a heaven for lay-folk by way of pietism; Nibbāna for monks by way of the Dhamma.

clear from other passages that he sought constantly to disentangle the tendrils of devotion which were beginning to cling to his person, and to attach them to the Dhamma: "He that seeth the Teaching, seeth Me," says the *Itivuttaka*.

With this attitude of faith in the teaching should be mentioned that of devotion to the Sangha in which the teaching is embodied: "He that would wait upon me, let him wait upon the sick brethren."[1]

One of the earliest formulas of Buddhism, that of the ordination ceremony, expresses this attitude toward the Three Jewels: "I take refuge in the Buddha, in the Sangha, and in the Dhamma," and these Three Jewels are the objects of orthodox Buddhist faith. This formula is of great importance. The fact that it puts "The Buddha" first in defiance of his own teachings indicates a somewhat late date; as it stands it represents a Buddhist expression of the later Hindu practice—bhakti, devotion to god or saint; knowledge of religious truth; and asceticism. Hinduism put the second first as the most important, and Gotama seems clearly to have done so too. Knowledge of the Dhamma, trust in the Buddha, the mild asceticism of the Sangha—this is the Buddhist substitute for the Hindu ways to Nirvāna. And this "taking refuge" is an act of faith in all three. This faith is a psychological state of mind; the Buddha himself being described as saddhā-hattho, or one who has faith as his hand, and by the words pasāda, mano-pasāda, citta-pasāda, is implied a calm, serene attitude which is produced by the Dhamma as a muddy pool is made clear by a magic jewel.

Faith is moreover "the root of right views,"[2] as doubt (Vicikiccā) is the source of confusion and conflict. "Right

[1] *Majj. Nik.* viii. 6.   [2] *Udāna*, p. 68; Rhys Davids, *Dialogues*, p. 187.

views" says the *Itivuttaka* "are as essential as right conduct."

This attitude soon, however, began to develop into a kind of bhakti, or devotion;[1] the great Teacher could not keep men from loving him; and this love kindled their imagination until they came to regard him as knowing things hidden from the great Brahmā himself;[2] as the only source of truth; "All that is well said is a word of the Blessed One."[3]

Even so, however, the good Buddhist passes on from faith to experience and intuition: "You," says the Teacher to Ānanda, "say this in faith; I know it from experience." And the Arhat is one who has passed on the wings of faith and love to knowledge.

What shall we say as to Gotama's own faith? It is clear in the first place that he believed in the reasonableness of the universe; law is universal. Secondly, he had a conception of law in the moral sphere so thorough-going, so subtle, and intelligent in its workings, as to appear to later Buddhists nothing else than an absolute Mind;[4] and in some undoubtedly early sayings we may find indications that he was no atheist, as some of his followers have believed. In the *Tevijja Sutta* he uses the admirable words: "To pervade the world with kindliness, pity, sympathy, and equable feeling—this is the way to union with Brahmā." This saying is isolated and is of course susceptible of more than one interpretation; it may well be an *argumentum ad homines:* "The devotees of Brahmā are busy seeking union with him: very good; let us redefine the Nirvāna of Brahmā as Nibbāna, and show

---

[1] Cf. *Divyāvadāna*, pp. 360–64; a book of the third century A.D., of Hīnayāna origin.

[2] *Digha Nik.* i. 215.

[3] *Ang. Nik.* xiv. 163–64.   [4] Cf. Poussin, *Bouddhisme, passim.*

them a more excellent way." That this is what the Reformer aimed at doing is clear; but it may well be that it was not Brahmā to whom he objected but the methods of worship employed, and the conception of absorption into the absolute Brahman a kind of chemical fusion. In place of this he offered men an ethical harmony with the universe, and an escape from the flux of becoming to the peace and joy of being. And inasmuch as the ways of Mukti, salvation, offered by the religious leaders of his day were not moral, not related to the human life about them, he did what Jesus did in Judea, and satirized these blind leaders of the blind. They were guilty either of ignoring the real nature of the self or of forgetting the lawfulness of the universe, and the righteousness which is working in it. May it not be that like Jesus the Indian reformer did indeed relate these to a Supreme Being? And that when he used the personal Brahmā and the impersonal Brahman he meant them to be understood in the old way, but with a new and purified connotation? That he came to "fulfil, not to destroy"?

This is what the bulk of modern Buddhists believe, and this was his attitude to the whole Hindu system of his day. Brahmā and Brahman, the Vedas, the Brahmins, Nirvāna, the Dharma, the Ātman, Karma itself—he redefined them all. Early Buddhism, like early Christianity, consisted in a revaluation of values, a transformation of ritual rightness into moral righteousness, a bringing of an other-worldly joy and peace into the midst of a sorrowful world. Gotama like Jesus towers above our vindication of his originality. These gave the people bread; others told them how it might be made! There were, moreover, in Sākyamuni as in Jesus great and sublime qualities which bound men and women to him

by enduring bonds. His magnetism was such that they
were converted in many cases long before their reasons
can have been satisfied, and such was his insight into
human hearts that we find him adapting his method with
so sure a touch as to win the title "Physician of Souls,"
and with so much love that even when he used the knife
his patients loved him no less devotedly. They found
in him one who was intensely interested in them, never
impatient, and in whom was no respect of persons. The
poor sweeper Sunīta, who had seen him moving serene and
majestic among kings and nobles, adored the courtesy
with which he smiled as he greeted him, and to the leper
he gave of his best, discerning beneath his rags and sores
a mind ready "as a clean and spotless robe for the dye,"
and only waiting for the right word to be numbered among
the saints. Men respected the fearless teacher who
redefined so many of their religious and social catchwords,
and who set up a new religious democracy in which worth
rather than birth was the standard, and in which liberty
was sanely tempered and controlled. Here was a new
and reasonable Way, which knew nothing of priestcraft
and yet gave access to divine Truth, which cut at the roots
of religiosity and yet kept much of the mystery and glamor
of religion, which struck a sane balance between asceticism
and worldliness, and between self-culture and altruism.
Here, above all, was an authentic voice speaking of the
things of real experience, however ineffable, and a con-
tagious joy, quiet yet unmistakable, amid the charlatans
and sophists of the day who told men the way to Nirvāna,
but without conviction or enthusiasm, and who handed
out to starving souls either husks or recipes for making
bread. The followers of Sākyamuni might be compared
to these in the words used by Tertullian of the early Chris-

tian church: "Our common people are more virtuous than your philosophers."

They left all and followed him, accepting his simple challenge, "Come, Bhikkhu," as a call to life-long discipline, or if he did not so order it, as laymen served him and his brethren with simple and sincere devotion. So this master of men lived among them, in the world yet not of it, "as a fair lotus unsullied by the mud in which it grows"; so he set up a realm of righteousness and love which in his lifetime centered about him, and when he passed away claimed him as its Eternal King. The story of its growth is one of the great chapters in human history. Not least of the claims of early Buddhism to originality is its missionary spirit. Contemporary Hindu philosophy seems in comparison an arid intellectualism.

CHAPTER II

PĀTALI-PUTRA

The Spread of the Dhamma and Its Safeguarding
(ca. 250 B.C.)

"Greatest of gifts is the gift of the Dhamma."—Asoka Vardhana.

We have seen that the essence of Sākyamuni's teaching was the universality of the Dhamma and of the Law of Causation, and that with this went the conception of the unity of all existence. Kings and emperors, always eager to find a bond of union among the various elements in their domain, soon began to favor this new teaching; thus during the lifetime of Gotama we find Bimbisāra very obviously looking about for a helpful religion, and finally choosing Buddhism, of which he became a devoted champion; and his parricide son, Ajātasattu, later on also became a good Buddhist. Their kingdom of Magadha formed the nucleus of the two mighty empires of the Mauryas and Guptas, aided, no doubt, by the Buddhist religion, which not only unified the people but helped to keep the Brahmins in their place.[1] Pātali-putra, on the northern bank of the Sōn, was the capital of the Mauryas, and though we cannot find evidence of the splendor which made the Chinese pilgrim, Fā-Hian (400 A.D.), attribute its building to genii, yet it was undoubtedly a magnificent city; and Megasthenes, a Greek contemporary, describes it as a fortress with a garrison of a million armed men! A great pillared hall has recently been excavated, and shown to bear a strong resemblance to the Hall of the

---

[1] This was clearly one reason for the success of the Buddhist reform—that its leader was himself a Kshattriya.

29

Hundred Pillars at Persepolis.[1]   Here, two hundred years
after the passing of Gotama, the great Asoka Vardhana
or Piyadassi seized upon Buddhism—or more truly, perhaps, was seized by it—and with his genius for organization used it as a bond of union, and spread its ethical
teachings in a simple lay-form far and wide; for the underlying doctrine of unity had for him political as well as
philosophical meaning, and he realized that it had international as well as national bearings.   In this greatest of
India's kings, "beloved of the gods" and friend of man
and beast, we see what the Dhamma, divorced from its
monasticism, and also apparently from its metaphysic
and psychology, can do for a nation.   Converted about
260 B.C. by the horrors of a great war of aggression,
Asoka became a man of peace and called upon his subjects
throughout India and upon neighboring countries to
accept this "greatest of gifts," the code of filial piety, of
brotherly kindness, of justice and truth, of tolerance and
strenuous endeavor after the higher life.   Setting a noble
example in his own loving care for the temporal welfare
of his people, he urged upon them the pre-eminence of the
Dhamma, set about building glorious Stūpas, com-
memorating not only the life of Sākyamuni but that
of two former Buddhas, and in their honor stimulated
India to produce an art unsurpassed in her history.   By
such means he united his people in the bonds of the
Dhamma, and Buddhism was established as the national
religion.   His guru was, according to northern tradition,
the Bhikkhu Upagupta, known in the Ceylon chronicle as
Tissa, and it is possible that at the end of his reign the
emperor himself became a monk, for the Chinese pilgrim,
I-Tsing, has left us a description of a statue of Asoka

[1] See D. B. Spooner, *J.R.A.S.*, 1912.

THE ANURĀDHAPURA BUDDHA

dressed in the yellow robe, and his younger brother or son, Mahinda, was undoubtedly a monk, who with his sister, Sanghamittā, laid the foundations of a great Buddhist civilization in Lankā, or Ceylon. Asoka is also credited with missions to Suvarna-Bhūmi, or Lower Burma, and in India proper to lands as far north as the Himalaya country around Purusāpura, and as far south as Mysore. Of these missions his edicts, carved on rocks and pillars, are sufficient evidence, and it is likely that missionary envoys were sent also to the Greek kingdoms of Asia and to Egypt, whose rulers are mentioned on several of them. Thus did the benign influence of the Dhamma begin to spread, and its significance as an international bond for the next thousand years cannot be estimated. In Asoka it showed not only what it could do as a nation-building power but also as an international force, and in him we may see the Bodhisattva type prevailing over the more austere Arhat, though he is known to the monks of the Ceylon monasteries merely as an Upāsika, or lay-adherent. The laity of India were not slow to see in him the fulfilment of the old ideal of Cakkavatti, or universal monarch, who united her peoples and bound other nations to her in the bonds of gratitude and peace.

But if Buddhism was to be so great a bond of union, it must itself be united, and already in addition to many minor differences which occasioned no ill-feeling there were by the time of Asoka fundamental points upon which Buddhists disagreed, and already the germs of the amazing divergences of later days are present in the Order. As to what the main differences of opinion were, the texts, which are clearly partisan, give very conflicting accounts.

Orthodox tradition maintains that a hundred years or more before the Asokan period a heresy of the Vajjian

monks of Vesali had been condemned as combining too
great freedom of interpretation with laxity in such grave
matters as sexual continence. However this may be,
no new sect arose for a time, and we should be critical in
accepting the statement of their rivals that it was from
this heresy that the school of the Mahāsanghikas arose in
later days. Yet this school has left us a book, the
Mahāvastu, which indicates that they were, to say the
least, lacking in a sense of proportion. We shall discuss
it later, and merely note here that it contains a small
nucleus of Vinaya, or rules of discipline, overlaid with a
confused mass of birth-stories of the Buddha, and much
other irrelevant matter; and this cursory glance at it will
help us to realize how much Buddhism needed to safeguard
its canon and to insist on maintaining its emphasis on the
sane and lofty moral teaching of its Founder. Whether
Asoka did it the former service or not, he will always be
famous for his championship of this moral law. The
following, one of his later edicts, is typical of all:

> Thus saith his Majesty: Father and mother must be obeyed;
> respect for all living creatures must be firmly established; truth must be
> spoken. These are virtues of the Law of Piety, which must be prac-
> tised. The teacher must be reverenced by the pupil, and proper
> courtesy must be shown to relatives. This is the ancient nature of
> piety, this leads to length of days, and according to this men must act.

Thus, though Asoka confined himself for the most part
to a simple lay-ethic, it seems that he accepted the
Buddhist doctrine of Kamma,[1] and recognized an order of
the universe making for righteousness—not a bad working
religion for an emperor.

It is interesting to think of this great layman convening
a council of the monks, helping them to put their house

[1] He does not mention either Kamma or Samsāra in his edicts.

in order, and advising them on their religious reading; nor is there sufficient reason to reject the large body of tradition which tells us that he did so to fix the canon and to reform abuses. Vincent Smith has made a good case for placing this assembly, which met at Pātali-putra, between 243 and 238 B.C. If it had been earlier, the emperor would surely have mentioned it on the Seven Pillar Edicts set up in the thirty-second year of his reign, to commemorate what he had done for the furtherance of the Dhamma. On the Bhabra Edict he commends seven passages, almost all of which have been variously identified by Winternitz, Kosambi, Rhys Davids, and others; they seem to be portions of the *Vinaya, Itivuttaka, Sutta Nipāta,* and *Anguttara Nikāya;* though "all things spoken by the Blessed One are well spoken," these are of special moment to monks and nuns. Two of his sermons, the famous fire-sermon and his address to Rahula, are specially mentioned. Now it is reasonable to suppose that the emperor, who seems in his paternalism to have been a forerunner of Wilhelm of Hohenzollern, followed up this advice by organizing a council to make some sort of selection from the Sacred Lore, and though the canon was certainly not fixed with any rigidity at this time, nor reduced to writing even according to the Ceylon chronicle for another two centuries, and though some notable additions have been made even after the Sacred Lore was converted into Sacred Books, yet "the Pāli *Tipitaka* may be regarded as not very different from the Māgadhī canon of the third century B.C."[1] How great is the credit

---

[1] Macdonnell in *E.R.E.*, Vol. VIII. Probably Pāli is the literary derivative of Māgadhī akin to Kosali, the dialect used by Gotama. But many other theories may be defended: "the cradle of Pāli has yet to be discovered," says Sylvain Lévi. The edicts of Asoka are for the most part in a developed Kosalan dialect. *Tipitaka*—the three Baskets or collections—passed on from generation to generation like baskets of earth along a line of workmen.

due to the "schools of reciters," mentioned in an Asokan edict and in the *Milinda Pāñha*, and to the faithful scribes whom Fā-Hian found at work in Ceylon in the fifth century, for preserving to the world this wonderful collection of ancient literature! It is their edition that has come down to us. It contains works of real genius, and some of the "Psalms of the Brethren" breathe the freshness and glamor of the dawn, and are yet highly wrought poetry. "In skillful craftsmanship and beauty these songs are worthy to be set beside the hymns of the Rig Veda, and the lyrical poems of Kalidas."[1] Nearly the whole of this great library is now available in Romanized Pāli, and much of it in English and German translations. As its name implies, it is made up of three "Baskets," or collections: (1) *Vinaya*, or "Rules of Discipline," (2) *Sutta*, or "Dialogues," and (3) *Abhidhamma*, "Higher Religion," or explanatory treatises.

I. VINAYA

These rules were gradually evolved, and we can trace their growth in the earliest narratives; as occasion arose, Gotama would make a rule, or establish a practice, sometimes as a result of criticism from without, as when the people of Magadha complained that his monks kept no retreats in the wet season like those of other orders, sometimes to meet schism from within, as in the numerous instances of the unruly monks of Kosambi. After the death of their master the Sangha continued this method of accumulating disciplinary laws for many generations to come, and the *Vinaya* as a whole maintains the directness and precision of the Founder. To students of the monastic life this "Basket" is full of interest, and indeed

---

[1] A. K. Coomaraswamy, *Buddha and the Gospel of Buddhism*, p. 283.

it is not possible to understand Buddhism without it.[1] Yet it almost certainly represents a stage of its evolution later and more monastic than that of the Founder.

2. SUTTA

The second collection, *Sutta*, or "Dialogues," consists of five parts, or *Nikāyas:*

1. The *Dīgha*, or long dialogues, thirty-four in number, dealing with doctrines of special importance, e.g., (*a*) the *Brahmajāla Sutta*, or "Perfect Net," which deals with practices of the Brahmins which are not to be commended, and mentions sixty-two heretical schools; (*b*) the *Samaññaphala Sutta*, which deals with the fruits of the life of a Bhikkhu, and discusses other sects; (*c*) the *Ambattha Sutta*, which deals with the great question of caste; (*d*) the *Sigālovada Sutta*, dealing with the duties of the laity; while others deal with subjects already discussed in chapter i; thus the *Mahānidāna Sutta* has to do with the Law of Causation, and Arhatship is the theme of many.

The collection is clearly of mixed date; amid much that is stilted and conventional it has imbedded in it a rare jewel, the famous *Mahāparinibbāna Sutta*, most authentic of all the Buddhist records of the life of the Founder. In words sublime in their simplicity and pathos it tells the story of his passing, and the characters that it depicts are real human beings, not lay-figures: the fussy and faithful Ānanda is drawn from life, and there are touches of humor in the words of Sākyamuni, which no devout Buddhist would or could invent. Yet even this great

---

[1] The *Vinaya* has three main sections: (1) *Suttavibhanga*; (2) *Khandaka*; and (3) *Parivāra*. The first contains rules of personal conduct for monks and nuns; the second contains the real kernel of the work—*Mahāvagga* and *Cullavagga*; the third is a later appendix probably added in Ceylon. See *B.T.*; *S.B.E.*, Vols. XIII, XVII, and XX.

fragment of a real "gospel" is mixed up with the miraculous, and seems itself to be composite; while another sutta, the *Mahāpadāna*, is clearly late in its entirety, dealing wholly with miraculous happenings, and exhausting itself in honorifics of Sākyamuni. The twenty-sixth dialogue of this collection puts into the mouth of Sākyamuni the prophecy of another Buddha, Metteyya (only mentioned here in the Pāli canon, and in Buddhaghosa's commentary, but a notable figure in the Sanskrit Mahāyāna), who will restore the fortunes of the faith when they have fallen; and unless we are to see in this an utterance of the serene Teacher in a rare moment of depression, it would seem to be a "prophecy after the event"—to belong therefore to a very late era, when the fortunes of Hīnayāna Buddhism were on the wane. The cult of Metteyya seems to have thriven as the Golden Age of Indian Buddhism was passing.

As to the dogmatic contents of this collection, as Dr. Macdonnell says: "It already contains the dogma of six Buddhas as precursors of Gautama, and presupposes the whole Buddha legend."[1] He could, if he would, prolong his existence upon earth for an aeon. In some of its highly elaborated dialogues, too, Sākyamuni is depicted as conversing with heavenly beings, and these may well have served as the model for the Mahāyāna romances which were to become so popular in the first centuries of the Christian Era.[2] The *Tevijja Sutta* contains a notable passage in which directions are given for pervading the whole universe with thoughts of love, for "this is the way to union with Brahmā."

---

[1] "Literature" (Buddhist), *E.R.E.*, Vol. VII.

[2] Cf. Dialogue 14 where Gotama explains his knowledge of former births by heavenly intervention as well as human insight.

2. The *Majjhima,* or *Suttas* of middle length, are one hundred and fifty-two sermons and dialogues, which reveal a more human and less artificial Gotama. But these too are of mixed date, containing a fairly large element of miracle and some ethical teaching like that in the famous "Parable of the Saw," which may well mark a transition stage between Hīnayāna and Mahāyāna ethical ideals, being nearer to that of the Bodhisattva than to that of the Arhat. As to its Buddhology the *Majjhima* is also transitional; its Buddha is a man who has freed himself from passion and delivers others, if they accept his law with unquestioning obedience, for he has attained to absolute truth.[1] He is "the incomparable king of the Dhamma," and as such "the perfect physician," the "captain of the ship of salvation."[2]

3. The *Samyutta,* or mixed dialogues, fifty-six in number, contain some early verse, the famous "Wheel-turning Sermon," said to have been the first public utterance of Sākyamuni after his enlightenment, and some later material, such as the story of Punna, which may well be an echo of the missions of Asoka, and which embodies in an exquisite dialogue the Bodhisattva ideal of resolute and indomitable good-will in sacrificial service. The claim that the Buddha is sinless[3] would also suggest a somewhat late date.

Among the undoubtedly early material in this collection are ballads of great beauty and of considerable dramatic skill, especially those in which Māra the Tempter

[1] Cf. *Majjhima* ii. 173, 1. 265 and 1. 71.

[2] *Ibid.* 92. Cf. Edmunds, *Buddhist and Christian Gospels* (3d ed.), pp. 140–41. The first fifty dialogues of the *Majjhima* have been translated into English by the Bhikkhu Silācāra, and some are to be found in *S.B.E.,* Vol. XI.

[3] *Samyutta* iii. 103. Some of the book is translated into English in Mrs. Rhys Davids' *Book of the Kindred Sayings,* and in Warren's *Buddhism in Translations.*

is defeated by the Buddha or one of his followers, and leaves the stage "cast down and very sorrowful."

4. The *Anguttara*, or "Adding One Collection," is clearly late, recapitulating matter found in early collections, and artificial and tedious in its arithmetical arrangement. Its structure suggests a later development of the catechetical schools. In its Buddhology too it is advanced; Gotama, who has the physical marks of a superman, is sinless—in the world yet undefiled, and is the only teacher of truth; he is, in fact, an omniscient demigod—a position, be it noted, of unstable equilibrium. Either men must go forward and take the Mahāyāna position, or backward and recover that of the earlier Sangha, that he is the wise and loving "elder brother of the world."[1]

5. The *Khuddaka*, or short collection of fifteen books and booklets, mostly in verse, contains prayers and charms, together with some notable poems like that upon Mettam, or compassion, so justly famous. And still more important as a link with the Mahāyāna is its doctrine of Patidanam, or reversible merit, which teaches that merit gained by one may be shared with others—a seed-thought capable of strange and far-reaching developments, as we shall see, and opening the door at once to the ancient ancestor cults of the whole Orient. The doctrine may indeed be an accommodation on the part of Sākyamuni himself, or of the early Sangha, to meet these inveterate beliefs, and certainly the book as a whole is old, containing the *Dhammapada* and *Itivuttaka*,[2] anthologies of *Logia* or

---

[1] German translation by the Bhikkhu Ñānatiloka, Leipsig, and some English renderings in Warren, *op. cit.*; cf. especially *Ang. Nik.* iv. 36, quoted in Edmunds' *Buddhist and Christian Gospels*, p. 135. And in Ceylon Mr. Gooneratne has published an edition of the first three sections (Galle, 1913).

[2] The *Khuddakapatha* for neophytes, translated by Maung Tin, Rangoon; the *Dhammapada*, several translations; the *Itivuttaka*, translated by G. Moore, New York; *Theratherigāthā*, translated by Mrs. Rhys Davids, London; *Jātaka*, translated by E. B. Cowell, 1895.

gnomic utterances, of which the latter was in existence
before the time of Asoka, and many of which may well
be the actual words of the Founder. Gotama is in this
collection a great human teacher whose claim to authority
is self-evidencing, but he has qualified for this position by
a long series of rebirths, having been Sakra no less than
thirty-six times and a universal monarch hundreds of
times.[1] The *Jātaka* book of nearly five hundred and fifty
stories of these former births of the Buddha was already
in process of compilation before Asoka's time.[2]

3. ABHIDHAMMA

The five collections of *Suttas* are all to some extent
brightened and relieved by snatches of verse or by
anecdotes; almost unrelieved in their tedium are the
seven books of the "Third Basket of Higher Religion,"
the *Abhidhamma*. "However," says so kindly a critic as
H. C. Warren, "like the desert of Sahara, they are to be
respected for their immensity."

If the *Suttas* were composed with one eye on the laity,
the *Abhidhamma* is scholastic throughout, and of much
later date. It recapitulates, in the form of a catechism,
the doctrine of earlier books,[3] and its formal logic is clearly
of value to students only, and to them chiefly, we may
suppose, in disciplining the mind and in checking the
inveterate Indian tendency to let imagination run riot.
It is doubtful if there were ever more than a handful who
succeeded in practicing these higher flights,[4] and for the

[1] *Itivuttaka* 22.

[2] Some of the *Jātakas* are illustrated on the Barhut Rail and other monuments of this period.

[3] All that can be safely said is that the *Abhidhamma* as we have it is not known to the older portions of the *Milinda Pañhā*; i.e., it is not earlier than the late second century B.C.

[4] Cf. Mrs. Rhys Davids' translation of *Dhamma Sangani* in *A Buddhist Manual of Psychological Ethics*, London. I think Mrs. Rhys Davids is a little too sanguine as to the early date of this work.

rest of us this work does not add much to our knowledge of Buddhism.[1] Such in outline is the early Pāli canon, "from which," says Professor Poussin, "it would be possible to extract two or three canons all complete, all like one another, and all conflicting!"

It is a library which has had an amazing history, and which is worthy of the devoted labors which scholars of East and West have consecrated to it. With all its repetitions, contradictions, and fiction thinly veiled, in spite of much in its form that is artificial and much in its matter that is tedious, it is a treasure-house, indeed, of the early history of an ethical reform almost unique, of a great springtide of the human spirit, and, may we not believe, of the Spirit of God ? It contains strata of such different dates as to demand long and scientific study, and raises many difficult questions. What, for example, has happened to the original works which must have been compiled in Māgadhī, a dialect akin to that of the Asokan inscriptions ? The Pāli canon is in a later literary diction, and is clearly derived from a different source than the Chinese version.

Very interesting too to the student of religion is the process which he can here watch, by which the historic Gotama is being transformed into a god. All the more impressive because of its naïveté is the growing devotion to him which is revealed. So gradual is it, indeed, that the custodians of tradition, who for centuries handed on these stories with the words, "Thus have I heard," seem quite unconscious of discrepancies and contradictions in the narratives they are preserving side by side. Gradually the beloved Teacher "mounts the throne of Brahmā"

[1] The only early schools which had the temerity to attribute this Basket to immediate disciples of the Buddha were the Sarvāstivādino and their parent-school. This claim Poussin rightly calls "a pious fraud" (*Opinions*, p. 44).

from which his shrewd thrusts have driven this great one among the gods; and the steps are here preserved for us: now he is the infallible teacher; now the sublime being who can, if he will, prolong his life on earth indefinitely; now refusing to do this he leaves a finished work, and turns their eyes to the teachings he has given them, only to find that the human heart is not to be satisfied with such a substitute, and that the empty throne cannot remain for long unoccupied. So the Teacher is hailed as lord and controller of the universe, master of men and gods.[1]

If the canon was fixed in Asoka's reign, one would imagine that the next step would be to transcribe it. But though Asoka's edicts prove that reading was common, this did not take a place for another two or three centuries when, in the reign of Vattagāmini of Ceylon, a Pāli version was made. And that which has come down to us is also due to the Ceylon monks, who, under the leadership of the great commentator Buddhaghosa, in the fifth century A.D., re-edited this earlier version. The *Tipitaka* has therefore undergone accretions and revisions which may well have added to its interpretation of the person of Gotama, but which, being made entirely by orthodox monks, have carefully excluded the "heresies of the Mahāyāna," and which reveal a cautious attitude toward the supernatural which is shared by the Asokan sculptures, but not by those of Gandhāra.

Indeed, it is when we turn from the Scriptures to the monuments of early Buddhism that we can watch the process most clearly. In the first great period of Buddhist art, that of Asoka, there are no images of the Founder, but worship is being paid to his symbols—the empty

---

[1] Cf., e.g., *Anguttara* ii. 23; *Samyutta* i. 67.

throne, the Lotus, the Wheel of the Law, the Footprint; before all these gods and men bow, not only in reverence but in worship. In one of the panels, for instance, of the great Barhut rail we see King Ajātasattu kneeling before the Footprint of the Buddha, and the inscription tells us that he is "paying homage to the lord." It is clear that by the middle of the third century B.C. something very much like worship of Gotama has been established; and numerous scenes from the *Jātaka* are depicted on these railings, and indicate that the Buddha-myth was already well developed. Yet there were no temples but only chaityas, or shrines, with monks in attendance to remind the pilgrims of the limits beyond which worship must not go.

It is not until the second great period of Buddhist art, that of Gandhāra, that images of the Buddha are found, and that he can be described in words of the *Itivuttaka* as "having mounted the empty throne of Brahmā," and become a chief among the gods or even as the *Milinda Pañha* says, "god of all gods." The sculptures of Buddhism seem, indeed, to have lagged behind the Scriptures in this process of deification; they are useful in confirming, and in some cases correcting, the evidence afforded by a critical study of the books.

It may be well at this point to touch upon the schools or sects of the Hīnayāna which now appear, to the great confusion of the student. The best source for a study of these is Buddhaghosa's commentary on the *Kathāvatthu*. The commentary was not written until the fifth century A.D., but the book itself is attributed to Tissa, the king's Buddhist teacher, and parts of it may well belong to his age. Unfortunately it is violently partisan, and scorns even to name the schools which it criticizes, and the commentary is inevitably colored by later developments. Another source is the *Abhidharmakośa*, or "Treasure of Abhidharma," by Vasubandhu,[1] who speaks of eighteen schools; and there are also Tibetan accounts.

Yet much as the traditions differ, they are agreed that at an early date occurred the "Five Points" of Mahadeva's heresy about Arhatship, and that this precipitated an agreement to disagree. The two main schools that resulted were the Sthaviravādino or Theravādino, who claimed to represent the true "School of the Elders," and the Mahāsanghika, or "School of the Great Council," a name allowed them by their adversaries, and suggesting possibly that they came to be a majority. The former school, with its great subsect, the Sarvāstivādino, were realists alike as to the phenomenal world, the self, and the historical Sākyamuni; the subsect differs from its parent in holding that an Arhat can fall from his high estate. The Mahāsanghikas and their great subsect, the Lokottaravādino, held a transcendental view of the person of Sākyamuni which at times became even docetic, holding not only that he had been free from human passions but that nothing but a phantom or apparition had been seen by the men of his day.

The canon of the Elders or their subsect the Vibhaj-jhavādino is substantially the Pāli canon of today. That of another of their subsects, the Sarvāstivādino, was in Sanskrit and little remains except Tibetan and Chinese translations. Of the canon of the Mahāsanghikas we may take as typical the "Book of Great Events," or *Mahāvastu*, compiled by their subsect, the Lokottara-vādino. This book is described by Barth as full of "need-

---

[1] The date of Vasubandhu is much discussed by scholars; Takakusu places him in the fifth century; Péri thinks his death was not later than 350 A.D. and Winternitz agrees.

less padding, two, three, or four accounts and more of the same episode from different sources, sometimes contradictory, sometimes following one another, sometimes scattered through the book, dovetailed into one another, disjointed, lacerated." Among its contents are a number of birth-stories, long lists of Buddhas, and passages of a marked docetic tendency, all of which point to somewhat late compilation. But there is undoubted early material, and a glance at its chaotic contents helps us to appreciate the service attributed to Asoka in calling for the formation of a canon.

The book is interesting, moreover, as helping to bridge the gulf between Hīnayāna and Mahāyāna Buddhism. It had, for instance, a section on the ten Bhūmis, or "fields," of the Bodhisattvas, which is apparently a development of the four stages of Arhatship; and in it adoration of the Buddha is the principal way of salvation. Here, in fact, is a document of the tunnel period between Asoka and Kanishka, which is therefore of considerable value.

The Mahāsanghikas and the Lokottaravādino may be regarded as semi-Mahāyānist in their view of the person of Sākyamuni and in their tendency to deny the reality of the phenomenal world. They prepared the way for the idealistic schools of a later day. The Elders claimed to be more orthodox alike in their insistence upon the reality of the historic Sākyamuni, of the self, and of the world. They agree that the world and the self are unreal in a moral sense, as being transient and in a constant flux. But another subdivision of the Elders, the Sautrāntikas—so called because they preferred to adhere to the *Suttas* and rejected the scholastic *Abhidhamma*—were idealists, maintaining that all that exists is the momen-

tary act of consciousness, and they too began now to sow
the seeds for the subjective idealism of later schools.

As to Buddhology, we may thus summarize the views
of these schools: for Sthāviras, Sākyamuni is a man,
supernormal but not supernatural, though he makes
immense claims upon the faith of his followers; he has
destroyed all germs of rebirth and embodies the Dhamma.
Yet even in this conservative school there are tendencies
at work to claim for him a more exalted position; for
the Sarvāstivādino, for instance, he is a Supreme Being,
worshiped by gods and men. For Mahāsānghikas, he is
lokottara, or supramundane, subject to none of the
passions or pains to which men are subject, yet behaving
as a man to accommodate himself to human needs; by
Yoga he is in union with all truth.

For all these schools alike the belief in his pre-existence
in a long series of sacrificial lives was axiomatic, and
encouraged a tendency natural to Indian minds to relegate
history to the background, and to relate the unimportant
fact to the eternal principle.

We see the Buddhist world, then, busy for some centuries accounting for the great hero who had given it birth,
and finding in some of his own utterances the basis for a
mythologizing process; and in his own principle of the
unreality of the worldly life a germ from which there
grew almost inevitably, first, an idealistic philosophy, and
then a denial of his own real existence as a historic figure.
But until much critical work has been done upon the texts
these can only be accepted as tentative generalizations;
there are crucial questions still to be answered, and among
them the very difficult one as to the Sanskrit texts of
Hīnayāna Buddhism, such as the *Mahāvastu* and the
Lalita Vistara, books which may be regarded as belonging

to the orthodox and yet bridging the gulf between them and the Mahāyāna. Are these translations from works originally in Pāli, or are they original compositions in a mixed dialect coeval with it ? This is a problem which is being attacked by Japanese and other scholars from three sides: their language, the ideas they embody, and the form of their composition. Those books which seem to owe most to Pāli sources are in language most heterogeneous; that is one clue. Another is that where there is a tendency to depart from the double standard of morality of the monastic order, and to substitute for it a single standard, we may suspect an original composition in Sanskrit. For this is the essentially new idea of the Mahāyāna, and was apparently worked out by Sanskrit scholars, such as the group whose work we must now consider. However this may be, there can be no question that the lay-Buddhism of the Asokan period is a link between the old and the new which is most significant; and Buddhists of all schools acknowledge their gratitude to the man who showed on so vast a stage the spectacle of a "theocracy without a God," and who proved that Buddhism is not merely a religion for world-renouncing monks.

Here was a foundation for the new Buddhism, and upon this and two other shafts sunk deep in the Hīnayāna —the transcendental Buddhology of one school and the subjective idealism of another—a new and lofty edifice was now reared.

CHAPTER III

GANDHĀRA AND PURUSĀPURA
(50 B.C.–100 A.D.)

The Birth of Mahāyāna

"I am the Father of the world: All men are my children; all are destined to Buddhahood."—SADDHARMA PUNDARĪKA.

"Then shall it be accomplished that no living thing, no particle of dust shall fail to attain unto Buddhahood."—AVATAMASAKA SŪTRA.

About the northwest frontier of India lie countries which during the Buddhist Era were conquered and reconquered by many races. On the fertile plain to its south was the kingdom of Gandhāra with its chief city of Purusāpura and its University of Taxila, both situated on branches of the Indus. Conquered in part by Cyrus and more fully by Darius Hystaspes, it remained a satrapy until the fall of Persia, when it passed to Alexander and then to the Maurya emperors. It changed hands again several times between the Graeco-Bactrians and Graeco-Indians, until they in turn were driven out by the Sakas, or Scythians, a tribe of whom, the Kushāns, under the great Kanishka, established their sway over Northern India.[1]

These frontier lands were happy in the early missionaries of Buddhism, the gentle and indomitable Punna, whom the Master could not turn from his noble purpose of preaching to the wild frontier tribes, as we read in the *Tipitaka*, and "Kassapa, Majjhima, and Gotiputta, teachers of all the Himalaya lands," envoys of Asoka, who are mentioned in the *Great Chronicle of Ceylon*, and whose

[1] For chronology see Rapson, *Ancient India*, pp. 181–85.

remains have recently been discovered at Sānchi and Sonari.[1] By the middle of the second century B.C. these tribes were strongly Buddhist enough to win the invading Scythians. Their cities of Khotan and Balkh, great centers of trade, were centers also of a new religious syncretism, and in the fourth century of our era, Fā-Hian, first of the Chinese pilgrims, who between 399 and 413 A.D. was visiting India, hails this region as the second Holy Land of Buddhism. It was dotted, he tells us, with a thousand monasteries, and was the home of the cult of Maitri, the coming Buddha. His figure is familiar in the art of Gandhāra, where as a lay-prince he typified the process at work in this region by which Buddhism was being transformed into a less monastic, more picturesque, and more universal religion (a great way—Mahāyāna) and was being fitted to capture peoples less ascetic and other-worldly than those of India. Purusāpura was the capital of Kanishka, a great ruler and a staunch defender of the faith, in the first century A.D.[2] If Asoka is the Constantine of Buddhism, Kanishka is its Clovis, though the comparison in each case does honor to the western ruler. Here at Peshawar a stūpa, the remains of one described by Fā-Hian "incomparable in solemn beauty and majesty," has been recently unearthed, and with it a silver shrine of Greek or Indo-Greek workmanship containing remains of Gotama Buddha. It is not impossible that further search may lay bare a complete commentary upon the Buddhist books, which legend tells us the king engraved upon copper, apparently in Sanskrit.

[1] Archaeological research has several times vindicated the Buddhist chronicles; e.g., at Sānchi, Peshawar, Pātaliputra (Patna), etc.

[2] Some scholars adhere to an earlier date, about 50 B.C. On this vexed question see F. W. Thomas, *J.R.A.S.*, 1913; Marshall, *Punjab Historical Society*, 1913, etc. The Cambridge *History of India* gives 78 A.D. as the year of his accession.

GANDHĀRA SCULPTURE

His coins testify to the vastness of his empire, and some of them to his interest in Buddhism.[1] Beyond this it is difficult to say what was the special service which he did it. Hiuen-Tsiang tells us that in the four hundredth year after the Nirvāna, Kanishka, "king of Gandhāra, at the request of the elder Parsvika, convoked an assembly of saintly men, who were conversant with the exoteric doctrine of the Three *Pitakas*, and the esoteric doctrine of the Five *Vidyas*." It is not possible to be sure that this council ever met, still less that it aimed at establishing a new Buddhism. Indeed, in the Chinese life of Vasubandhu it is stated that Kanishka's object was "to protect the orthodox from hostile schools and from the Mahāyāna," and this is borne out by Fā-Hian, who tells us that the people of the land were mostly students of the Hīnayāna.[2] Some action was clearly called for; indeed, there was imminent danger that Buddhism should lose its individuality; it was beset within and without by tendencies religious and philosophical, which if they did not overwhelm it certainly changed it from a moral reform movement to a pantheistic religion, with polytheistic and almost monotheistic expressions. And about each god or Buddha centered an elaborate worship with liturgies and pomp. "The monks took charge of the cult; so that the old chaitya became a temple and the monk a priest."[3]

To lay this development upon Kanishka, or upon any one man or group is unscientific; it can only be understood by placing the religion of Buddhism in its context, as a part of the complex philosophical and religious move-

[1] Others, however, indicate that he was equally a Hindu and a Zoroastrian! Rulers of India must needs be tolerant, as Akbar found.

[2] Cf. R. F. Johnston, *Buddhist China*, p. 34; James Legge, *Travels of Fā-Hian*, p. 32.

[3] Farquhar, *Outlines of the Religious Literature of India*, p. 113.

ments of the day. Some account should be taken of Iranian and Greek ideas, such, for example, as those of the neo-Platonists, and some of the cult of Mithras, but it is better to look chiefly to India herself, and we may select aspects of five great movements within Hinduism, all of which may well have had their influence upon the development of Buddhist doctrine.

First, we may mention the rationalistic Sāmkhya, which was probably formulated at the same time as Buddhism,[1] aims like it at the removal of misery and like it rejects the monism of the Upanishads. It teaches that from sentient nature there is developed for the sake of spirit a whole universe; that nature (prakriti) and spirits (purusha) are both eternal; the first universal, invisible, and undifferentiated matter; the second, intelligent but passive spectators, incapable of activity. When these two come together the cosmic process begins, and the manifold world appears. Mukti or salvation is made possible by this coming together, because purusha achieves self-realization through it, and so removes or isolates itself once more. In this isolation consists salvation. "The soul of the wise matter ceases to be active, as the dancer ceases to dance when the spectators are satisfied."[2] We can see how readily these tenets might influence the orthodox scholasticism of the Hīnayāna—on the one hand, in its tendency to atheistic interpretations of the teachings of Sākyamuni, for the Sāmkhya, while insisting upon the order of the cosmos, sees no need for a God; and idealistic schools of the Mahāyāna, on the other hand, seem to borrow some elements from the same complex system.

[1] Indian tradition says that the Sāmkhya system anticipated and influenced Buddhism.

[2] "Sāmkhya," E.R.E., Vol. XI.

Meanwhile more popular expressions of Hinduism were also at work, notably the *Bhāgavadgītā*, whose doctrine of Krishna-Vishnu and of his grace in taking the faithful to paradise seems to have exerted a potent influence upon Buddhism in its more popular phases. As we shall see in our study of the "Lotus" scripture, the *Bhagavadgītā*, while it was itself perhaps influenced by the winsome figure of Sākyamuni, helped to work a great change in Buddhism, and to crystallize out Mahāyāna tendencies, until a popular and picturesque cult was produced, able to compete with polytheistic Hinduism for the devotion of the masses.

This Hinduism, whose gods come down partly from the early nature-worship of Vedic times and partly from aboriginal cults, is a pantheism in which the absolute Brahman takes many forms. If they are multiplied it matters nothing; and in any cases the masses will a-worshiping go! One striking example is the famous trimurti, in which the great processes of creation, destruction, and maintenance in being are graphically set forth as the gods Brahmā, Siva, and Vishnu. This conception had undoubted influence upon Buddhism; at this time it returned to the pantheistic philosophy against which it had arisen as a protest, and was ready to compromise with all the gods, demigods, demons, and anti-demons it met in its onward march. In other words, the monism of the Vedānta not only helped to provide Buddhism with a philosophy capable of assimilating new gods but influenced the theological concepts of the Mahāyāna, which begins to surround the Buddha with a veritable pantheon. And in this process it may be that the kings and satraps of the northwest also had a part. Sociological conditions inevitably color theological ideas.

Lastly, though the Yogācāra school of Buddhism did not become articulate for some centuries, yet it nevertheless represents the influence upon Buddhism, which began as we have seen in the days of the Founder himself, of the inveterate Indian practice of Yoga, contemplation, and the practice of trance-states, first as a way to secure magic powers and later as a way to union with the Eternal. With both of these methods Buddhism as it developed had points of contact, and before long established a close kinship. It contains today elements both of magic and of mysticism.

By the first century A.D. Buddhists might be found living side by side in the same monasteries and universities, yet influenced by various combinations of these tendencies and schools of thought; and to this century belongs the crystallization of the new Buddhism from this complex solution. It now began to produce a great literature, much of which seems to belong to Gandhāra, and some to its great University of Taxila, or Taksasilā,[1] which lay in a pleasant valley now being excavated. The *Jātakas* represent it as the seat of the study of the Three Vedas, and Pāli became its language of instruction. Here Indian, Greek, and Persian culture met and mingled, and here Buddhism took on a new and more liberal phase.

We may perhaps trace a beginning of this process in the famous *Milinda Pañha*, which though accepted by the orthodox and written in Pāli, contains the germs of two very important doctrines, which, as they developed, separated the popular Mahāyāna from the more austere Hīnayāna Buddhism. These are the doctrines of salvation by faith, and of the Bodhisattva, a compassionate

[1] Now Rawal Pindi.

being whose ideal is service, and who is less self-centered than the Arhat. Both ideas are, as we have seen, present in orthodox Buddhism, but the *Milinda Pañha* carries them a stage farther. It is an apologia in the form of a series of dialogues upon the main teachings of the orthodox, and may well have been compiled to win inquiring minds of the day away from the allurements, alike of the new Buddhism and of other popular schools of Hinduism. It is on the whole a work of art, "the masterpiece of Indian prose,"[1] eloquent of the skill and genius of its unknown author. We know that King Milinda, or Menander, was a Graeco-Bactrian ruler of Kābul and Punjāb during the second century B.c., and the book must belong within a century of this time, when his memory was still living; for these Bactrian kings were soon afterward driven out of India. But much work remains to be done in sifting the evidence, internal as well as external, before the strata into which it is clearly divided can be dated with any degree of certainty, and we must be content at present to accept the following conclusions: (1) that the original work is represented by Parts 2 and 3 with some of Part 1, where with great animation and brilliance of style old questions, such as the nature of Nibbāna, the Law of Kamma, anattā, and faith are discussed by the sage Nāgasena; (2) that Part 4, dealing with the difficulties raised in the king's mind after his conversion, and ending with his delighted acceptance of the wise if not always logical answers of the sage, is of later date, added by monks in Ceylon; (3) that Parts 5, 6, and 7, with their beautiful if rather fanciful allegory of the City of Righteousness,[2] their similes of the "mental and

[1] Rhys Davids, *S.B.E.*, Introduction, p. xxxvi.
[2] See my *Heart of Buddhism*.

moral treasures" of the Arhat, and their proofs of the existence of the Blessed One, are similarly late: it is significant that they are not included in the Chinese translations made in the fourth century.

These conclusions, tentative as they must be, are borne out by the tendency in these latter parts to present less vital matters in a less notable style. Very important are the facts that the work is almost canonical in authority, that it is quoted by the great commentator, Buddhaghosa, in the fifth century A.D., and that it refers to almost all the canonical books, though only later passages in it refer to the *Abhidhamma*. As to its doctrinal tendency it must suffice to note two points: (1) that the ideal of Arhatship presented verges upon that of the Bodhisattva, an indication of an early authorship in Northern India rather than of late composition in Ceylon, which was the citadel of the Sthaviras for many centuries; (2) that the evasions of Nāgasena which often satisfy the king, but leave us with a conviction that he has been dodged rather than answered, are evidence of a transition period in Buddhist doctrine. Of this transition a good example is afforded by the second question in Part 3, where Milinda asks how it is that an evil man can go to a heaven simply by thinking at the moment of death about the Buddha, and where Nāgasena shirks the real point at issue by asking whether a great load of stones is not borne on the water by a boat; very good, the load of a man's sins is borne by his good deeds! Here clearly is an attempt to disguise what is really a doctrine of bhakti, or saving faith, by calling it a doctrine of works. And when we turn to the Chinese version we are not surprised to find that it contains a more definite acceptance of the doctrine that it is the sinner's "earnest thought" of the

Buddha that carries him across. In Part 2 of the Pāli
text we find faith described in orthodox terms; a crowd
of frightened people are standing trembling on the brink
of a river in flood when there comes along one who knows
his own powers and leaps across; so does the good recluse
"by faith aspire to leap, as by a bound, to higher things."
In much the same way the sage deals, or fails to deal, with
the king's shrewd question: "How reconcile the repeated
assertions of the Buddha that there is no escape from
Death, with his promulgation of the Pirit service, a
magical performance for prolonging life?" To which,
of course, the true answer is that if the Master ever did
sanction any such absurd superstition—well, the less
Master he! But the Sage once more, like divines in all
periods of transition who seek at once to be orthodox and
to appear honest, evades the issue. So instructive are
his wrigglings that they should be carefully studied by
every student of the history of religion, where a true
Mysticism is ever seeking to shake off the coils of Magic.
We may be sure that Sākyamuni himself taught neither
the efficacy of a death-bed piety, nor of a muttered incan-
tation; but human needs are imperious, and human
minds not always logical, and by the time of Nāgasena
these doctrines had clearly established themselves so
firmly as to be regarded as of the essence of orthodoxy.
Here, of course, the question arises, "Which Nāgasena?"
and we can only answer that the first point is taken up
in a part of the book that is of early date, and that while
the second belongs to a later date, yet the doctrine of
Pirit is contained in the canonical *Khuddaka Nikāya*.
Faced with the popular Mahāyāna, perhaps it was too
much to expect of the orthodox that they should adhere
to the austere doctrine of Sākyamuni in all its stoical

purity.   It is barely possible that he himself, as Professor Poussin[1] and all Mahāyāna Buddhists maintain, accommodated his teachings to suit his audiences.   But I prefer to believe that in questions of truth he made no such compromise.   Indeed, he seems to have chosen to be labeled agnostic, rather than pander to human weakness.   And it is one of the strange ironies of history that this great Stoic should become not only a god, but the sanction for strange and wonderful practices of magic and superstition.

Another great literary masterpiece of this period is the *Lalita Vistara,* a Buddha-epic with Mahāyāna tendencies, based on an earlier work of the Sarvāstivāda, which praises the Buddha as Supreme, and reveals him surrounded, as in the sculptures of this period, with adoring Bodhisattvas.

At this time also was compiled the *Sutrālamkāra*[2] of Asvaghoṣa, a collection of ninety stories notable for their fine narrative style and for their wide range of interest. All India and Ceylon are mentioned, but the northwest is the chief setting of these anecdotes, and Kanishka is the hero of two of them.

The *Sutrālamkāra* gives us a valuable picture of Indian life in its many phases as it was during this epoch.   Kings, Brahmins, monks, ascetics, and a whole procession of artisans, sweepers, washermen, courtesans, and clowns, pass before us.   Sixty-four classical arts are enumerated, and keen religious and intellectual activity is manifest;   the author represents Kanishka as punished by a miracle for coquetting with Jainism;   he attacks the Brahmins ruthlessly, and he discusses various heresies;   he refutes the Sāmkhya and Vaiśeṣika philosophies, and claims that the

---

[1] *The Way to Nirvāna,* pp. 136–37.

[2] French translation by Huber.   Paris: Leroux, 1908.   Translated into Chinese in the fifth century.

word of the Buddha has spread in writings all over the world!

Among the many delightful episodes of this collection we may mention that of the conversion of the sweeper, Niti, who is ashamed to meet the Buddha haloed and glorious as he walks through Rājagriha; but the Master pursues him and bids him be of good cheer: "His body may be foul, but his heart is fragrant with the excellence of the Good Law": and when Niti still hesitates, reminds him that the Perfect One is not concerned with caste but with actions past and present, and ordains him monk. This is clearly the story of Sunīta told in the *Theragāthā*;[1] and other tales, such as the "Story of King Longshanks," are taken from the *Suttas*. Another which shows Mahā-yāna influence is that of the Sākyamuni's aunt and foster-mother, the Lady Gotami, who attains Nibbāna through his grace. "I am the Mother of the Perfect One," she says, "but he is my Father; I am reborn in his law. It is I who fed his mortal body (rupakāya) but he has fed my immortal body (dharmakāya); I satisfied his thirst for an instant; he has extinguished mine forever." The Buddha shows his body with its thirty-two marks, and its eighty secondary perfections, and she enters Nirvāna. In this work Asvaghośa shows himself scholar and poet as in his earlier epic, the *Buddha Carita*,[2] an eloquent biography of Sākyamuni. A convert from Brahmanism first to the Sarvāstivādino, then to the Mahāyāna, Asvaghośa was the sweet singer of this period, and wrote his epic in Sanskrit, which now began to take the place of Pāli as the sacred language. Whether or not we believe the legend which tells how Kanishka accepted him in

---

[1] Ccclxii.

[2] *B.N.*, 1351; *S.B.E.*, Vol. XLIX, Part I, translated into Chinese by Dharmaraksha in 420 A.D.

ransom for Pātali-putra, capital of Sāketa, we can imagine this great poet—"one of the greatest of the predecessors of Kalidasa"—leading the Buddhist choirs in antiphonal praise of their Master, now being deified and becoming the type for new divinities in India; "Salutation to the Arhat," it begins, "unequaled, bestower of happiness, surpassing the Creator; vanquisher of darkness, greater than the sun; dispeller of heat, greater than the beauteous moon." Though the poem does not itself go much beyond the Pāli canon in its Buddhology, it was no doubt understood and recited in some monasteries of Gandhāra and Kashmir by those whose conceptions of his person are embodied in the still more famous *Sukhāvatī Vyūha* and *Saddharma Pundarīka*, which seem to have been composed about the same time and in the same north-western region.

The larger *Sukhāvatī Vyūha*, or "Book of the Paradise of Bliss," was translated into Chinese between 148 and 170 A.D., and belongs to a popular and rather unreflective Buddhism, which allures its followers by elaborate descriptions of the Western Paradise, where reigns Amitābha, one of countless Buddhas, and whither, like Vishnu, he conducts the faithful. This Paradise Mahāyāna we shall study more fully in the following chapter, for it was elaborated in the period which saw the rise of the philosophical schools, as a popular offset no doubt to their intricacies. Of the larger *Sukhāvatī Vyūha* there have been at least twelve Chinese translations, the first possibly by Anshikao 148–70 A.D.; the last by Fā-Hian, 982–1001. None agrees entirely with the Sanskrit text.[1] The book is in essence a dialogue between Ānanda and his Master on the Vulture Peak

[1] *B.N.*, 23 (5); *S.B.E.*, Vol. XLIX, Part II.

AMITĀBHA'S SHIP OF SALVATION

before a vast audience of Arhats. We hear from the lips
of Sākyamuni himself of a long line of eighty-one Buddhas
from Dipankara to Lokesvaraja, and of the vow of a monk,
Dharmākara, during the era of the latter that he would
become a Buddha, "equal the unequalled, and be peer
of the peerless."

This prānidhāna, or vow, Lokesvaraja accepted[1] and
under his tuition Dharmākara learned the innumerable
excellent qualities of the Buddha. Emulating those
which seem to him most noble, he shows his own nobility
by a famous utterance known as the King of Prānidhānas,
or vows: "Oh Blessed One," he cries to his teacher, "if
after I have attained Buddhahood all Bodhisattvas living
in these Buddha-lands attain it not as they hear my name
and share my merit . . . . may I not attain to that
perfect enlightenment!" This parināmanā, or dedication of his merit (an important link between primitive
and developed Buddhism), if not quite logical in its
expression, is none the less completely successful, and the
pious monk becomes Amitābha or Amitāyu, Buddha of
Endless Light and Life, whose excellences are inexhaustible
and whose Western Paradise "lacks no beautiful and
pleasant thing"; above all it is free from those hindrances
which make attainment of Bodhi so hard to dwellers upon
earth.

Here, then, we see the Buddhist heart demanding
satisfaction and realizing that all things are possible to
love; and that love is itself the motive, the method, and
the reward of righteous living.

The luxuriance and enthusiasm with which the
Sukhāvatī Vyūha abounds are eloquent too of the hunger

---

[1] This acceptance, Vyākarana, is called by Anesaki a "cosmic response." Unlike
Margaret Fuller, who "accepted the universe," the Mahāyāna monk asks the universe
to accept him.

of Buddhist hearts for a heavenly city, where attainment
and satisfaction are not impossible.   In this apocalyptic
heaven and in the cult of the Maitri Buddha which belongs
to the same era we may see evidence that, the attainment
of Arhatship having ceased, men were constrained to find
satisfaction in contemplating either rebirth in a new era
of enthusiasm or in a Paradise beyond this vale of tears.
And the divine figures of Amitābha and Avalokitesvara
embody no doubt, while they help to inspire, the new
ethical ideal of service and compassion which are one of
the hallmarks of the new movement; men create God in
their own image, but he is also in this very process mold-
ing them nearer to his own likeness.

Striking and significant as is the *Sukhāvatī Vyūha*, it
is eclipsed by the amazing book known as the "Lotus of
the True Law" (*Saddharma Pundarīka*)[1] which also has
apocalyptic elements.   It is nearly as long as the whole
New Testament, and like it is addressed in the main not
to the wise but to the simple.   Yet like the Fourth Gospel
it has a message to the philosopher too, and frees Buddhism by its bold Buddhology from any dependence upon
history.   It is found today in every Japanese temple, and
has had an immense power of kindling devotion, of inspir-
ing art, and of instituting remarkable reform movements
like that of Nichiren, the Buddhist prophet of Japan.
His biographer, Dr. Anesaki, writes:

"The Lotus of Truth" is a rich treasury of religious inspiration
and moral precepts, prophetic visions and poetic imagery, philosophical
speculation and practical admonition.   From this book all ages and
every man in Buddhist countries derived some sort of instruction and
inspiration, each according to his need and his disposition.[2]

[1] *B.N.*, pp. 134, 139; first translated into Chinese in 253 A.D.   The original work
cannot be placed later than the second century A.D.; *S.B.E.*, Vol. XXI.   With the
Sukhāvatī Vyūha and the *Gandavyūha* it is quoted by Nāgārjuna (see chap. iv).

[2] *Nichiren*, p. 31.

Its influence upon the civilization of Japan can only be realized by careful study of that wonderful land.

Today, owing chiefly to the "Lotus" scripture, millions think of Sākyamuni as eternally alive and gracious, seated in splendor on an idealized Vulture Peak:

> A mirage was the smoke of Shaka's pyre
>   That seemed at Kusināgara to rise;
> Death could not bind him, nor might fire
>   Destroy the Teacher of such verities.
> Hark! He yet liveth, and doth speak
> Eternal Wisdom from the Vulture Peak.

Great temple-pictures help the worshiper to visualize the scene, showing the Teacher as he rises triumphant from the bier; and others make real to the Mahāyāna Buddhist the conception of a glorified Master seated in the midst of his five hundred disciples, and preaching the New Evangel. Though modern Buddhist scholars like D. T. Suzuki may see in these representations "the fictitious creations of an intensely poetic mind," yet most Buddhists are neither scholars nor critical, and it is unquestionably true that they accept the teachings of the "Lotus" as the developed doctrine of the historic Sākyamuni at the end of his long career as a teacher.

The book may be said to have three main sections: (1) an Introduction, of which chapter ii is the core, explaining the cause and object of the appearing of the historic Buddha; (2) the main body of the book, of which chapter xv is the core, revealing the eternity of his being; and (3) the conclusion, of which chapter xx is the core, reveals the efficacy of his teaching and his eternal authority. Dr. Anesaki says:

In other words, we have in the first place the actual appearance of the Buddha among men as their Father and the Lord of the World;

then is revealed the original essence (agra) of the Tathāgata, existing and acting from eternity (chiram); in the conclusion we have the assurance of the endurance of his personal influence.[1]

The "Lotus" has often been likened to the Johannine writings, and is clearly the product like them of devout meditation upon historical facts; and like the Fourth Gospel it lays great emphasis upon the three central ideas of Eternal Light, Love, and Life. Written apparently first in metrical form, it was also put later into prose and as in the Apocalypse prose passages are relieved by poems. To the critical eye it is no more historical than the Apocalypse itself. Both foretell a new order of the redeemed. In the prelude "of rather monstrous grandeur," as a Japanese Buddhist has said, "we see the idealized Sākyamuni on a heavenly Vulture Peak and identified with the Eternal Buddha." As he sits there, surrounded by living creatures from Bodhisattvas to the animal creation, "tense with wondering expectation of what the lord Buddha is going to reveal," we feel that he is about to give us one of those "admirable exhibitions" which from time to time relieve the monotony of his age-long silence. We are not disappointed; a vast ray of light pours from the urna on his brow, and like some monstrous searchlight reveals the utmost regions of space—a sign that he is about to speak. Maitri addresses Mañjusrī, the crown prince, or president of the assembly, who as attendant upon many a Buddha may be expected to understand their habits:

Why does this ray sent out by the guide of men shine forth from between his brows? I see the whole universe . . . . with all beings . . . . the Buddhas, those lions of kings, revealing the essence of the Law, comforting many myriads of creatures, and sending out their

[1] "Docetism," *E.R.E.*, IV, 839.

sweet voices . . . . announcing to ignorant and fear-laden men the bliss of rest. "This is the end of toil and pain, oh monks." . . . . I see bodhisattvas in myriads like the sands of the Ganges producing enlightenment as they are able. . . . . Some are giving away jewels and servants, horses and sheep . . . . gladly sacrificing these things to buy for themselves a higher stage of enlightenment. . . . . Some give away wives and children . . . . yes their own hands and feet, their heads and eyes . . . . and aspire to the knowledge of the Tathā-gata . . . . and I see here and there some sons of the great conqueror, their own training completed, preaching the Law to myriads with great joy, arousing many bodhisattvas. . . . . Some there are whose strength is in patience and forbearance, and some who through wisdom reach enlightenment. . . . . Why has the Blessed One emitted this great light ? Oh! how great is his power! How holy is his knowledge! . . . . Is he about to show us the eternal laws which he found upon the terrace of Enlightenment ? Or is he to prophesy and reveal to the bodhisattvas their future destiny ?

To which Mañjusrī replies, having first given some details as to the habits of Buddhas, that the Blessed One is about " to pour forth the good rain of the Law, to beat its great drum, to raise its great banner, to kindle its great torch, to blow a blast upon its great trumpet . . . . the Lion of the Sākyas will declare the fixed principles of the Law. He in his affection and mercy will pour out the refreshing rain upon the expectant multitude."

At last he speaks, but it is only to express the difficulty and profundity of the doctrine. Yielding, however, to their importunity, he consents to reveal it, at which five thousand proud monks and nuns salute him and depart. Congratulating the rest upon having thus been winnowed of the chaff, he proceeds to reveal the central object of his mission on earth; it is for one object only: to show all creatures the true Buddha-knowledge, and to open their eyes. Though there is but one road to Nirvāna, yet in his skilful tact (upaya) he has opened three gates, one for

Srāvakas, or candidates for Arhatship; one for Pratyēka Buddhas, who are inclined to lonely meditation and solitary achievement; one for Buddhas who are sociable and altruistic. There is but one vehicle, the Buddha-vehicle, and even boys who in their play dedicate their little sand-heaps to the Victorious One, even they reach enlightenment; yea, even such as absent-mindedly have made one single act of homage at a Buddha shrine. Great is the skill of the teacher; "Buddhas ye shall all become. Rejoice and be no longer doubting or uncertain!"

Such is the new gospel, and several parables in the next three sections bring home the teaching that men in different ways accept what is given to them; plants take each what they need from the impartial rain; the oculist gradually accustoms the eye to the light; a father rescues his children from a burning house by devices suited to their different understanding—so does this Teacher of gods and men, this spiritual Father of all, adapt his lessons with skilful pedagogy. Let them all teach the Sūtra, which alone reveals the essence of the faith, entering the abode of the Blessed One which is his strong Love, donning his robe which is Forbearance, and sitting in his seat which is the doctrine of Sūnyatā or emptiness.[1] So shall all become Buddhas, winning their way to the positive Nirvāna, as their leader by great and heroic perseverance throughout many ages has won through to it. To each by name he gives a word of cheer, and while all are rejoicing in the good news, there comes an apocalyptic vision of a stūpa containing the faint and emaciated body of the former Buddha, Prabhutaratna; a seven-fold light shines from it, and a voice comes forth praising the work

---

[1] As we shall see in the next chapter, this doctrine of Sūnyatā has two different applications: the phenomenal world is sūnyā, having only relative reality, but absolute reality is also sūnyā—transcendent.

of the Tathāgata, and expounding the "Lotus." All
present salute, and from the utmost confines of the universe, again lit up by a ray from the Buddha's brow,
come the heavenly hosts in worship; the old Buddha
graciously invites the new one to share his throne, and
confesses his own desire to hear the "Lotus" gospel.
Whereupon Sākyamuni reveals that the time for his
departure is at hand, and calls for volunteers to proclaim
the gospel to all the universe. Mañjusrī now modestly
declares that he has already preached it with such effect
that the eight-year-old daughter of the Nāga king has
reached enlightenment, and even false Devadatta has
become a Buddha. Many are ready to preach this good
news for babes and sinners, and are taught the qualifica-
tions of steadfastness and patient meekness under many
trials, of circumspectness in sex and other relationships,
of a practical grasp of the Sūnyatā philosophy leading to
detachment, of a quiet and equable mind, and of a life
of charity and benevolence. There follows a pause of
many million years, and Buddhas from many worlds
appear—great multitudes whom no man can number.
Who are they? They are disciples whom the Buddha
has aroused to perfect enlightenment, his spiritual sons,
of whom he is eternal Lord and Father, self-existent,
supreme Spirit, Creator, Ruler, and Destroyer of the
Universe. The events of his historical life are skilful
adaptations, part of his gracious strategy to win men.
As a wise physician may feign death in order to move his
disobedient children to take the medicine nothing else
will induce them to touch, so by an emptying of himself
the eternal Buddha became man for the sake of the erring
family of men. And as a father departs to a far country
so the great Physician has left the world that his erring

and ailing children may use the medicines he has prescribed.

Such is the Buddhology of the "Lotus," and it introduces us also to figures destined to play a great part in the Mahāyāna, Avalokitesvara, Mañjusrī, Samantabhadra, Bhaisajyarāja, and Maitri. To the first especially an eloquent chapter is devoted; he is revealed under whatever form will prove most helpful, as a woman when women are to be helped, and in many a varying guise.

This most popular of all Bodhisattvas, known to China as Kwanyin and to Japan as Kwannon, is surely a noble conception of the divine nature. Glorious too is the healing King Bhesajyarāja who sets himself on fire and burns through thousands of years to show respect to Sākyamuni and his new gospel,[1] while Mañjusrī and Mahāsthāmaprāpta are incarnations of wisdom, and keep their place even in the highly emotional Buddhism which now begins to come to the fore.

In what sense is the Buddha Sākyamuni Father ? In the sense of spiritual teacher and begetter of men in the truth, with which he is and has ever been one. Even dull and sinful beings may share his eternal life and realize their true nature; for he is Love as well as Light. Supreme Spirit, Creator, Physician, All-knowing, Great Father he appears, another Krishna, whenever unbelief is triumphing.

Such in the barest outline is the "Lotus of the True Law," which has been well called "an undeveloped mystery play"; but which is for the Mahāyānist "the very cream of orthodoxy," the "crown jewel of the Sūtras," and, as Professor Poussin has pointed out, it is

---

[1] *S.B.E.*, XXI, xxi–xxii, deal with Bhaisajyarāja; chaps. xxi–xxvi are probably a third-century addition, e.g., chap. xxi deals with spells and chap. xxii recommends the un-Buddhistic practices of self-torture and suicide.

so carefully worded that like the *Gītā* it is capable of various interpretations—pantheist, theist, or even atheist.[1] "The conception of Krishna-Vishnu as the Supreme is adapted to Buddhist conceptions," says Farquhar.[2]

The "Lotus" is possibly intended to combat certain docetic tendencies of the time. The Sākyamuni of history is its central fact, but he is now related to the Eternal Order, and in this and other ways it resembles the Johannine books of the Christian church. It may well serve as a bridge between followers of the two great religions. He who has seen the Buddha of the "Lotus" is not unprepared for the Christ of the Apocalypse, or even of the Fourth Gospel.

I had recently the privilege of listening to an exposition of Buddhism by a Japanese monk, and my companion asked: "Is this not a modernized Buddhism?" The next day, as I was trying to give my version of Christianity to a group of Buddhist professors, one of them exclaimed: "That is exactly what we believe about God. Is it not neo-Christianity?" I could only give them a copy of the Fourth Gospel, and my revered friend, the Honorable Mrs. E. A. Gordon, whose influence among the Buddhist priests of Japan is very far-reaching, tells me that when she had given a copy of this book to a monk of the sect which makes most of the "Lotus," he changed entirely in his attitude, which had been offensive, and came back exclaiming: "This is a Buddhist book, or I am reading my own ideas into it."

If it were not tragic it would be comic indeed that the followers of the two greatest religions of the world are still sitting for the most part in opposite camps, ignoring

[1] *E.R.E.*, VIII, 145.

[2] *Outlines of the Religious Literature of India*, p. 115.

or misinterpreting one another's beliefs. I would make a plea not only for an attempt to understand one another, but for resolute co-operation in all idealistic enterprises. The enemies today are materialism and militarism, and Christianity and Buddhism, as it has developed in China and Japan, without trying to prove that one has borrowed from the other—an odious phrase when applied to spiritual things—may humbly confess that each has received the truth as a free gift from the Father of Lights, who is indeed a wise physician of souls, and knows best how the truth may be revealed to each nation as to each individual. Impressed and awed by the solemn and beautiful ritual of Buddhist temples in Japan, the Christian student will be deeply moved as he begins to immerse himself in their teachings, and in the Wasan, or hymns, in common use he will find that ideas and titles of the Buddha which seem to him most Christian can be traced back to the *Sukhāvatī Vyūha*, the "Lotus" scripture, and to the later "Awakening of Faith."

From Gandhāra there went out not only these early scriptures of the Mahāyāna but also the famous Graeco-Buddhist art which so clearly links India and the Western World, and both these spread not only southward and eastward into India but also up into the lands of Central Asia. Here many of these masterpieces of the new Buddhism have been discovered by the Stein and Pelliot expeditions, which are adding to our knowledge and appreciation of the great influence which Buddhism exerted over these wild lands. They are known by the general name of Chinese Turkestan, and form a long, narrow tract of upland now almost desert; it is about 1,200 miles long and in most parts less than 400 miles broad, and stretches from the Pamirs on the west to the Chinese frontier on the east.   Legend has it that into these lands of Kashgar Khotan and Yarkand the Emperor Asoka banished certain peoples of Taxila, and that they took with them the Indian culture of their day.   But it is more likely that these lands were civilized during the time of Kanishka, and it is certain that the recent discoveries show not only Indian and Chinese influence but also that of Greek and Roman mythology.   There is little doubt that these lands themselves played a great part in the development of Buddhist art, and in the preparation of Buddhism to fit the peoples of the Far East.

Vast, then, has been the influence and benign the teaching that radiated out from the lands over which Kanishka ruled; notable have been the services to humanity of these anonymous theologians; they are the real fathers of the Mahāyāna, who did for Sākyamuni what Plato did for Socrates, or, as some critics would say, what the Johannine writers did for Jesus of Nazareth.   By their genius they transformed Buddhism into a religion of universal scope, capable of going out and winning lands like China and Japan.   Moreover, though they opened a door for the return of Hindu doctrines and gods into the house which Sākyamuni had swept and garnished, they did the great service of meeting certain docetic tendencies which were seeking to explain him away as an apparition, and they put upon a sound basis the Buddhology without which Buddhism might have remained a creed for the monk and the nun.

CHAPTER IV

NĀLANDĀ AND THE EARLY SCHOOLMEN OF THE MAHĀYĀNA (*ca.* 150 A.D.)

"The doctrine of unreality is the first gate to Mahāyāna."—PRAJÑĀ-PĀRAMITĀ.
"Everything arises according to causation: we regard it all as void."—NĀGĀRJUNA.
"The Buddha sitteth on his Lion Throne, yet dwelleth in every atom."—AVATAMSAKA.

Between the popular Mahāyāna of the "Lotus" and the Paradise Sūtras and the philosophical schools which we are now to study a link is to be found in the *Avatamsaka Sūtra*. Parts of this great book were already in existence by the second century A.D., for, like the "Lotus" and the *Sukhāvatī Vyūha*, it is quoted by Nāgārjuna, and his transcendental philosophy seems to owe much to its idealism.[1] The book consists of a series of Gāthās in praise of the Buddha Sākyamuni, who is introduced to us at the moment of enlightenment, when he is samādhi, and the "universe and all things in it are serenely reflected in his mind as the starry heavens are mirrored in the calm sea." Innumerable hosts of Bodhisattvas, Devas, and other spiritual beings praise him as coexistent with the universe, the sustainer of all things, dwelling equally in the smallest atom and upon his Lion Throne. He enlightens all, and all receive his message, each in his

[1] First translated into Chinese in the early fourth century A.D. by Buddhabhadra. It has greatly influenced the Buddhism of the Far East; the Chinese versions, which are of varying length, contain sections which seem to be identical with the *Gandhavyūha* and *Dasabhūmika* of the Sanskrit text of Nepal. It is possible that part of it was translated into Chinese as early as 170 A.D. and Nāgārjuna's commentary on it in the fourth century. A good abridged translation is appearing in the *Eastern Buddhist*, Kyoto.

70

own way. All worlds are manifested in him, and "his love is boundless as the immensity of space." He is beyond mortal comprehension, yet for the sake of all beings he takes earthly shape and appears to those who seek him, like the full moon rising over a mountain. Let them but think of him for a moment and they will be forever saved from evil and misery; his for all eternity is the task of enlightening the world. Here too we read praises of the Bodhisattva Samantabhadra who "has practiced all deeds pure and holy, and has bathed all beings in the wide waters of his compassion." He in turn extols Vairochana, the Sun Buddha, and his Buddha Land. Knowing him, we know the universe anew as one of complete mutual interdependence and interpenetration. All things are in each and each in all. He manifests his nirmānakāya or adapted body universally, and his creative power is present in every particle of dust. In this world he is known as Sākyamuni, Victor, Savior, and by other great names, but in other worlds he is known by other names— Beloved Father, Path-Finder, Compassionate Lord, Brother of All, and Giver of All. Here, then, is a parallel to the later Pauline theology; the historic teacher is discovered not only to have cosmic significance but to be the source of cosmic life, through whom, in whom, and unto whom are all things.

As to the nature of reality the *Avatamsaka* teaches that things are unreal because they are always changing, yet real because in each this great Buddha and all other existences are present.

From such beginnings the philosophy of the Mahāyāna proceeds, and it takes many forms. It may perhaps most conveniently be grouped around the monasteries of Rājagaha and Pātali-putra, about which there gathered during the next two centuries the great University of Nālandā. Here the doctrines of Sūnyatā and of the Dharmakāya were developed by Nāgārjuna, Aryadeva, and many another subtle thinker. Beginning with the tenet of impermanence, or Sunyatā (the aniccā, anattā, of Sākyamuni), they develop it variously. The Mādhyamaka of Nāgārjuna in the second century teaches that all is unreal except the one great Reality, of which we can neither predicate existence nor non-existence; it transcends experience and is unknowable, the Void. This transcendentalism led on by a natural transition to the idealism of the Yogācāra or Vijñānavāda, which conceives this ultimate unknowable and ineffable reality as Mind. Here, then, we see a transition by natural steps from the teachings of Sākyamuni, who was agnostic as to the Absolute, to a doctrine of the Absolute which differs little from that of the monistic Vedānta.[1] "All is transient," Sākyamuni had said, "for all is causally determined and is composed of elements. Nibbāna alone is the uncompounded, the abiding." As to any other absolute, he refused to speak. His followers of the Theravāda denied what he had ignored, and some of them went on also to deny any substantial existence either in the mind of man or in the phenomenal world. Against this barren doctrine many schools of the Mahāyāna protested that thought, at any rate, is real and that however illusory are phenomena there is an underlying Reality.

Theologically conceived He, or It, is the Dharmakāya, Absolute Truth which manifests itself as the Nirmānakāya incarnate among men in the Buddhas. This doctrine was worked up from the stage at which the *Avatamsaka* left it by the schoolmen of the University

[1] Hindu critics of Vedānta monism accuse it of being Vijñānavāda Buddhism!

of Nālandā.   Of this great university we must gain some
impression before making a further study of its schools.
Fire and the sword of Islam have long since destroyed
the venerable university, and its stones, "long buried by
myriads of little Indian ploughs," are today being un-
covered by the archaeologist.   But for a thousand years
it did a noble work and a detailed history of Nālandā
"would be the history of Mahāyāna from the time of
Nāgārjuna in the second century A.D., or possibly even
earlier, until the Muhammadan conquest of Bihar in 1219
A.D., a period well over a millennium.   All the most noted
scholars of Mahāyāna seem to have studied at Nālandā."[1]
A catholic spirit worthy of a great university seems to
have reigned, and side by side with the scholars of the
new Buddhism worked the "eighteen schools" of the old,
apparently in great harmony.   So we learn from Hiuen-
Tsiang, and from his diary and that of I-Tsing we can
reconstruct a picture of the university at its zenith.[2]   To
travel-worn and weary pilgrims, both of them scholars
and monks, what a haven of refuge it was!   How eagerly
they describe its peace and dignity, its intellectual
achievements, its devotion to the cause they had at heart.
To Hiuen-Tsiang especially it was unspeakably dear, for
he had paid a great price to reach it.   "Take the Master's
tattered robes, let the winds of Gobi whistle through your
sleeve and cut you to the bone; mount his rusty red nag
and set your face to the West. . . . ." Then after this
bitter journey at last "the great ice Mountains loom in
front of you and you crawl like an ant and cling like a
fly to the roof of the world," until "on the topmost sum-
mit still far away from the promised land, you realize

---

[1] Vincent Smith, "Nālandā," *E.R.E.*, Vol. IX.

[2] Hiuen-Tsiang's journey was 629-45 A.D.; I-Tsing's, 671-95 A.D.

two things—the littleness of human life, and the great-
ness of one indomitable soul."

How great a soul it was, "dauntless in disaster,
unmoved in the hour of triumph, counting the perils of
the bone-strewn plain and the unconquered hills as
nothing to the ideal that lay before him, the life-work,
the call of the Holy Himalayas and the long toil of his
closing years."[1]   It is good to think of that long respite
in the groves and lecture-halls of Nālandā.   How lovingly
he lingers on its charms:

The whole establishment is surrounded by a brick wall, which
encloses the entire convent from without.   One gate opens into the
great college, from which are separated eight other halls, standing in
the middle (*of the Sanghârâma*).   The richly adorned towers, and the
fairy-like turrets, like pointed hill-tops, are congregated together.
The observatories seem to be lost in the vapours (*of the morning*),
and the upper rooms tower above the clouds.

From the windows one may see how the winds and the clouds
(*produce new forms*), and above the soaring eaves the conjunctions of
the sun and moon (*may be observed*).

And then we may add how the deep, translucent ponds, bear on
their surface the blue lotus, intermingled with the Kie-ni (*Kanaka*)
flower, of deep red colour, and at intervals the Amra groves spread
over all their shade.

All the outside courts, in which are the priests' chambers, are of
four stages.   The stages have dragon-projections and coloured eaves;
the pearl-red pillars, carved and ornamented, the richly adorned
balustrades, and the roofs covered with tiles that reflect the light in a
thousand shades, these things add to the beauty of the scene.

The Sanghârâmas of India are counted by myriads, but this is the
most remarkable for grandeur and height.   The priests, belonging to
the convent, or strangers (*residing therein*) always reach to the number
of 10,000, who all study the Great Vehicle, and also (*the works belonging
to*) the eighteen sects, and not only so, but even ordinary works, such
as the Vêdas and other books, the Hetuvidyâ, Śabdavidyâ, the Chikit-
sâvidyâ, the works on Magic (Âtharvavêda), the Sañkhya; besides

[1] L. Cranmer Byng in Beal's *Life of Hiuen-Tsiang*, Introduction.

these they thoroughly investigate the "*miscellaneous*" works. There are 1,000 men who can explain twenty collections of Sûtrâs and Sâstras; 500 who can explain thirty collections, and perhaps ten men, including the Master of the Law, who can explain fifty collections.[1] Sîlabhadra alone has studied and understood the whole number. His eminent virtue and advanced age have caused him to be regarded as the chief member of the community. Within the Temple they arrange every day about 100 pulpits for preaching, and the students attend these discourses without any fail, even for a minute (*an inch shadow on the dial*).

The priests dwelling here are, as a body, naturally (*or spontaneously*) dignified and grave, so that during the 700 years since the foundation of the establishment there has been no single case of guilty rebellion against the rules.

The King of the country respects and honours the priests, and has remitted the revenues of about 100 villages for the endowment of the convent. . . . .[2]

From I-Tsing's *Buddhist Records of the Western World* we get a later, but not less enthusiastic, account:

The priests, to the number of several thousands, are men of the highest ability and talent. Their distinction is very great at the present time, and there are many hundreds whose fame has rapidly spread through distant regions. Their conduct is pure and unblamable. They follow in sincerity the precepts of the moral law. The rules of this convent are severe, and all the priests are bound to observe them. The countries of India respect them and follow them. The day is not sufficient for asking and answering profound questions. From morning till night they engage in discussion; the old and the young mutually help one another. Those who cannot discuss questions out of the *Tripitaka* are little esteemed, and are obliged to hide themselves for shame. Learned men from different cities, on this account, who desire to acquire quickly a renown in discussion, come here in multitudes to settle their doubts, and then the streams (of their wisdom) spread far and wide. For this reason some persons usurp the name (of Nālandā students), and in going to and fro receive honour in consequence.

[1] I.e., Hiuen-Tsiang himself.   [2] Beal, *op. cit.*, pp. 111-12.

We learn too that heresies had arisen "like clouds of ants and bees"; so it may be imagined that occasional heresy-hunts kept life from stagnation, and gave point to the labors of the orthodox.

Such was the University of Nālandā, a very haven of refuge to the pilgrims. How good to find one's self again in the haunts of learning and to exchange the brandishing of intellectual for that of material swords—to defend the faith instead of one's own life—to exchange spiritual gifts instead of delivering one's goods to the footpads of the hills. It was a haven indeed: "Here ten thousand priests sought refuge from the world of passing phenomena and the lure of the senses."

No wonder that the Scriptures increased in volume, and that art and sculpture developed; we read of a student painting a picture of the coming Buddha Maitri or Metteyya, whose cult throve in the northwest; and of the worship of Avalokitesvara and of Tāra.

But these are later developments, and we must return to the early schoolmen of the university. Let us look first at the *Prajñā-pāramitā* literature which now begins to be edited. Those who enjoy the brandishing of metaphysical swords will perhaps enjoy the endless negations of these books; but their essence is contained in a famous leaflet, the *Prajñā-pāramitā-hridaya-Sūtra*, or "Essence of Transcendental Wisdom," which has had an immense influence and is still repeated daily by multitudes in the Far East. A word as to its title: Prajñā is the Sanskrit form of the Pāli paññā, which early Buddhists used to denote intuitive transcendental knowledge as contrasted with the plodding of the discursive intellect. It is a distinction familiar to Mystics, and therefore of the essence of Buddhism. Pāramitā means perfection, and the title of these books is a claim that they reveal Bodhi, or final enlightenment. This shortest of them, containing their essence or heart, is a later summary, which runs as follows:

Adoration to the All-wise! Thus have I heard. Once the Blessed One was dwelling at the Vulture Peak near Rājagriha, attended by a company of monks and bodhisattvas. Seated thus He became absorbed in a meditation known as Deep Enlightenment. Then, too, the great Bodhisattva Aryavalokitesvara was practicing the deep prajñā-pāramitā; and he perceived that the five constituents of being are empty, and so was saved from misery and suffering. "O Sāriputra," he cried, "material form is emptiness and emptiness is material form." So is it with the other skandhas; all are empty, sensation, consciousness, the samkhāra all are empty. They are not born nor are they destroyed; they are not tainted nor untainted; they neither increase nor decrease . . . . there is therefore neither ignorance nor wisdom, no birth, nor age nor death, no suffering, no path of escape from suffering, no attainment, nor anything to be attained. The bodhisattva who relies on this prajñā-pāramitā frees his mind of obstruction; and because he has no obstruction he is freed from fear, and goes beyond perverted and unreal thoughts to final Nirvāna. All Buddhas, past, present, and future, reach perfect wisdom depending upon this prajñā-pāramitā.

This famous booklet is used by all Mahāyānists, though perhaps not one in a million understands its meaning. This is, however, not very obscure; the essence of the matter being that there is an ultimate Reality compared with which all things are empty. But many Buddhists prefer to use it as a magic charm or formula which is believed to have immense potency. About this *Prajñā-pāramitā* literature the Mādhyamaka school of Nālandā centers.

Chief among the new group of Buddhist philosophers is Nāgārjuna, its editor and chief exponent. A Brahmin by birth, he was converted after a dissipated youth to the Hīnayāna and later to the less austere Mahāyāna, now growing rapidly in power. A native of South India, he seems to have found his way to the Himalayas, and to have met there with the cult of Amitābha, for the larger *Sukhāvatī-Vyūha* was taken to China about this time, and he quotes it in his writings. Far less probable is the legend of his meeting in the south with an aged teacher dwelling in an iron tower, who revealed to him the supremacy of Vairochana, and gave him the mystic rite of abhisekha, or baptismal ordination. The story suggests, however, that he knew the *Avatamsaka Sūtra*, and indicates the zeal of heretical schools to claim the authority of the august name of Nāgārjuna, who came to be venerated as a second Buddha "without marks," and for whom it is claimed that he is Ānanda, reincarnated in fulfilment of a prophecy of Sākyamuni himself.

Nāgārjuna's great achievement is an attempt by his Mādhyamaka, or Middle Path, to reconcile the doctrines of realism and nihilism—"being" and "not being." "The phenomenal world," he teaches, "*is* unreal; to realize this is to enter the first gateway to Mahāyāna,"[1] yet living in it we can reach Reality. This, itself, is Sunyatā or the Void, because it is ineffable and transcends all relativity, and the phenomenal world is suñyā because in it relativity holds sway. The *Mādhyamaka Sāstra* begins with the statement of eight negatives, the famous "Eight Noes":

"No production nor destruction; no annihilation nor persistence; no unity nor plurality; no coming in or going out." Between these extremes his Middle Path steers its course, just as earlier Buddhism aimed at avoiding alike the extremes that all is and that all is not. Sākyamuni had refused to encourage either the naïve realists or the too skeptical nihilists; and even in the

---

[1] *Mahāprajñā-pāramitā-sāstra, B.N.,* 1169.

vital matter of the "soul" he steered a middle course; for, on the one hand, were animistic theories, and, on the other, the annihilationists. Nirvāna itself is ineffable, beyond the crudities of our every-day speech.

Early Buddhism, in fact, contains the germs of most of the chief tenets of the Mādhyamaka; and even its distinction between relative and absolute truth is foreshadowed in the Pāli books, where philosophical truth (paramatthasacca) is distinguished from popular or everyday truth (sammiti sacca).[1]

This distinction is developed by Nāgārjuna and made the basis of his school, which has the practical aim of taking its followers to Absolute Truth; Paramārtha Satya, Bodhi or Sūnyatā. To do this the school teaches that all things are causally related and have only relative existence. The very notions of "being" or "not being" are relative:

> Thy light shines bright,
> And murky night
>   Is straightway fled!
> Yet night's not dead
> Though light is shed,
>   And drives it far.
> This lamp of thine
> Doth dimly shine,
>   Save in the night;
> So dark and light
> Unreal quite,
>   And empty are.[2]

In popular jingles of this kind did the wise schoolmen embody their philosophy; and the purpose was the very practical one of calling men from the garish light of day to the serene moonlight of Absolute Truth, to Nirvāna.

[1] Cf. *Sutta* i. 263, and C.A.F. Rhys Davids, "Reality," *E.R.E.*, Vol. X.
[2] *Kāsyapa Parivarta* (*B.N.*, XXIII, 57–58); cf. Suzuki, *Outlines*, p. 391.

This is well expressed by the Japanese poet, Akazome
Emon:

> If I that sing am nothing, nothing they
> That are about me—men and things—then pray,
> How shall I fail in mind to press
> To that One Goal of Nothingness ?

For Nāgārjuna, as for Heracleitus and many another, the
conclusion is that since sense-knowledge is relative we must
find absolute truth within: and this truth is Bodhi. The
phenomenal world is denied, that Nirvāna may be realized.

The world, Sākyamuni taught, is transient, aniccā:
it is unreal, unsatisfying, and empty of abiding worth.
"Look on it as a mirage," says the *Dhammapada;* and the
same book opens with an aphorism which has been taken
to indicate that the Founder favored subjective idealism:

> All that we are by mind is wrought
> Fathered and fashioned by our thought.

It is unlikely that Sākyamuni concerned himself with
this question; in fact, it is clear that he was a common-
sense realist so far as the phenomenal world is concerned;
but the Mādhyamaka even in its more conservative phases
is idealist, and in its more extreme form goes over to sheer
nihilism. Which position Nāgārjuna himself took is uncertain: some commentators maintain that he admitted
the reality of the phenomenal world, but taught that it was
unreal from the absolute point of view; in other words,
sammiti satya is relative truth, not sheer untruth. This
would seem to be the teaching of words attributed to
Nāgārjuna:

> All things that are from causes spring,
> This is the Middle Path we sing:
> All all unreal save the Void,
> For all save That with mind's alloyed.

So runs a Kārikā or couplet of the *Mādhyamaka kārikās*.

The *Prajñā-pāramitā* has similar passages which seem even truer to the teachings of early Buddhism:

> Thus shall ye think of all this fleeting world
> A star at dawn, a bubble on a stream,
> A flash of lightning on a summer cloud,
> A flickering lamp, a bubble and a dream.

All these things are real enough, however transient; but according to Chandrakirti and others, Nāgārjuna went much beyond this, and taught that the phenomenal world has no existence whatever; that it is unreal, as a flower in air, a hare with horns, or the child of a virgin carved in stone!

> An artist once a picture painted
> Of such a monster that he fainted:
> Thus endlessly men transmigrate,
> By false ideas infatuate.

The mind, according to this view, not only colors and distorts all we see; it creates it. The phenomenal world is "like hairs that a monk with diseased eyes thinks he sees in his almsbowl."[1] They are not there; the way to know them is not to know them. Nay, more; there is no monk, no almsbowl—nothing except the Absolute Void. Silence is the best and only way to attain it.

This nihilistic teaching had its effect, of course, in ethical matters, the very citadel of Buddhism; and it has done harm to the Buddhist cause, first, by its insistence on the relativity of every-day truth, and second, by undermining that altruism which is the essence of the Mahāyāna. But the conscience of the earnest Buddhist finds a way out of the dilemma. If my neighbor does not exist, to help him is impossible. Yet to do so is none the less the mark of a true Buddhist.

[1] Poussin, "Madhyamaka," *E.R E.*, Vol. VIII.

"Let the Bodhisattva, as he offers his gift, realize that it has no existence; limitless shall be his merit."[1] Let him cherish his little blind sister Karunā or Pity, let him realize that she *is* blind and his gift will be "perfumed." Moral conduct is "laukika," mundane, when the agent believes in the reality of agent, act, and object; it is "lokottara," other-worldly, fragrant with transcendent truth, when he believes in the reality of none! Such other-worldliness seems pale and unreal. Its "perfume" is a little sickly! If neither the monk nor his almsbowl, neither the almsgiver nor the alms, are real—so might the worldling retort—why bring these unrealities together in a fresh entangling relationship? No doubt, however, when it came to daily bread, the doctrine of absolute truth gave place to that of relative or practical truth; man cannot live on pure idealism alone; and even in monastic circles we find the doctrine severely criticized, especially among the practical Chinese; the wise Tsung Mi, for example, asked, as we shall see below: "If mind as well as the objective world be unreal, who is it knows that they are so?" And men of the world may well have asked: "If all life be a delusion, why this emphasis on the high calling of the monk?" "It is true," Nāgārjuna would no doubt reply, "that all is a dream. Yet the dream of the monk is more seemly and less unreal than that of the worldling and ends at last in Reality"; and the laity must needs be content to leave the monk-philosophers to dream, while with dream-coins and fantasmagorial food they kept alive these dreamers of dreams only less empty than their own.

That this doctrine of the Mādhyamaka held sway in Nālandā for several centuries is clear; we learn from

[1] *Vajracchedikā Sūtra.*

Hiuen-Tsiang, through whom it spread to China and Japan, that it was known as the "Three Period Doctrine," and that he learned it from the great logician, Silabadhra, who maintained that the Buddha had himself taught in three successive periods: (1) that the ātman is unreal, but the phenomenal world of dharmas real—this is the Hīnayāna view; (2) that all phenomena are unreal, but the mind is real—this is the subjective idealism of the Yogācāra and other Mahāyāna schools; (3) that neither is real—this is the nihilism of some followers of the Mādhyamaka school, which finds its most characteristic utterance in the paradox, "Delusion is wisdom; the flux of Samsāra is Nirvāna." These are but different names for the same thing: two aspects of one Absolute. The world of Samsāra is the realization of the Ideal, a fleeting expression of the Eternal.

This classification is, of course, pure propaganda. The Yogācāra is a later development than the Mādhyamaka, and, though both are developments of germs in the teaching of Sākyamuni, neither was ever formulated by him.

Significant as was the philosophy of the school, it made an even more important contribution to Buddhology. Applying its doctrine of relative and absolute truth in this sphere, it worked out the Duākāya doctrine of the *Avatamsaka*, and put the Amitābha cult on a sounder theological basis. "The Buddha," says Nāgārjuna, "has two bodies, one is the body of miraculous transformation, and fills the ten regions of space, limitless and immeasurable, serene, majestic, radiant, infinitely eloquent. The other is his human body, subject to mortal limitations."[1]

In other words, the Dharmakāya, absolute or real existence, empties itself at times, and a Jātakāya, Rup-

[1] *Commentary on the Prajñā-pāramitā.*

akāya, or Nirmānakāya, which is relatively real, or unreal, makes its appearance in the phenomenal world. This is a concession to the naïve realism of ordinary folk. But philosophers know better.

The Dharmakāya is the Absolute Truth or Norm behind all its fleeting manifestations, to which there is no limit. Amitābha, Vairochana, Sākyamuni, are notable examples of such manifestations, and each in turn, or all side by side, may be the central object of worship. This doctrine opened the door wide to all the pantheons of the new lands into which Buddhism was rapidly penetrating. A polytheistic cult with a basis of pantheistic idealism, it was now ready to adopt and adapt any deity—a sun-god, or a god of war, or some less reputable figure—who had a hold upon the allegiance of its converts. Yet this polytheism had in it, like that of the *Rig Veda*, the germ of a true monotheism; the claims of individual gods for a supreme place in the Pantheon now begin to be urged upon the faithful. And as in the *Rig Veda* Varuna almost achieves the supremacy, so in the Buddhist Pantheon Amitābha now makes a bold bid for the allegiance of the faithful. Gods many there might be—indeed, Gotama himself seems to have had a bowing acquaintance with them—but was there not one lord whom all should worship, accessible, and indeed seeking to bring multitudes to his Paradise ?

Here then were laid the foundations of a pietistic as well as of a philosophic Mahāyāna: the latter universalizing the Buddha-nature and finding in the Dharmakāya, which is his essence, the true meaning of the universe; the former making of the historic Sākyamuni and of the mythical Amitābha adaptations of the Eternal.

The cult of Amitābha is studied best in the *Amitāyur-dhyāna Sūtra*,[1] which contains instructions as to the practice of meditation leading to visions, more or less hypnotic, of the Pure Land of the Western Paradise, and a more developed theology than the *Sukhāvatī Vyūha*. The book opens, as is usual in Mahāyāna sūtras, with a Prelude, in which we see the Buddha on the Vulture Peak accompanied by a host of Bodhisattvas with Mañ-jusrī at their head. But unlike the Buddha of the "Lotus" it is no glorified being with whom we have to deal but the historic Teacher. He appears to the Queen Mother Vaidehi in despair at the conduct of her unnatural son Ajātasattu, who has imprisoned his father, and threatened her with his impious sword. Having in one pregnant sentence raised the problem of suffering, she does not stay for an answer but pours out her plea: "My one prayer," she cries, "is this: Tell me, I pray thee, of worlds where there is no sorrow, where the wicked cease to trouble and the weary are at rest: where I may be reborn in peace." The response is immediate and effective: from his brow there flashes forth a light which reveals to the Queen the ten quarters of the pure and admirable Buddha-lands. She chooses that of Amitābha, the Pure Land of Bliss.[2] Then, in response to her plea, he shows her how to cultivate "a threefold goodness," and to be reborn in this land "which is not very far off." This goodness consists in three groups of pure actions, including, besides ordinary Buddhist morality and beliefs, the observance of due ceremonial and the study and recitation of the Mahāyāna sūtras. Works as well as faith are demanded of the candidate for that Pure Land: yet it is

[1] *B.N.*, 198; *S.B.E.*, Vol. XLIX, Part II.

[2] Here we actually see what Max Müller calls Kathenotheism at work—one of many gods is chosen for worship.

by the power of the Buddha, not by one's own effort, that
one may see it.   One must become as a child, and he will
reveal it.   The Queen is thus brought to a state of calm
resignation;   and telling her frankly that she is a very
ordinary and rather stupid person, the Blessed One proceeds to give her lessons in meditation which form the
second main section of the book.

"All save the blind can see the setting sun.   Do thou
then with due ceremony and concentrated effort gaze into
the western sky, especially at the time when the sun hangs
in it like a suspended drum."[1]   Then follow instructions
as to meditation upon water, ice, and *lapis lazuli* until
there shall arise the vision of the golden banner on an
azure background, with strains of music and voices cry-
ing: "All is suffering, all unreal, all impermanent."
Gradually a dim picture of Sukhāvatī will be formed,
and will free multitudes from sin and suffering.   There
follow ten other meditations upon the features of that
delectable land, upon the bodily marks of its heavenly
King and of his spiritual Sons, Avalokitesvara and
Mahāsthāmaprāpta.   The third section of the book
defines the threefold thought as true, deeply believing
and full of longing for rebirth in this Paradise, and teaches
that there are three classes who will attain it—the compassionate who follow the precepts, the faithful who recite
the sūtras (especially the *Vaipulya Sūtras*), and those who
practice the sixfold remembrance.   If for one or for seven
days any man practice one of these, he will be reborn in
that Pure Land, and to him will appear the Buddhas and
Bodhisattvas of the West, with monks, inquirers, and

[1] Nāgārjuna himself is said to have died with his face turned to the Western Paradise.   The first teacher of this cult of Amitābha seems to have been his teacher Saraha.
Could he have been a Jew or an early Christian missionary?   The name does not
sound Indian.

gods innumerable, and will give him the hand of welcome and a diamond throne. And, as is fitting in a heaven designed in India, the retinue allowed will be proportionate to the merit acquired.

The book concludes with a vision granted to the Queen in which all this splendid heavenly kingdom is shown to her. "Behold," she cries, "the half was not told me," and the officious and practical Ānanda winds up a book, which would have made his Master gasp, by asking what it is to be called. So amid scenes of ecstatic joy in heaven and upon earth the curtain falls.

One very significant passage deserves special comment:

> If there be any sinner, even of the five deadly sins . . . . and he be about to die and repeat the words, "Praise to Buddha Amitāyus," ten times without interruption and with continued thought fixed upon the Buddha . . . . he will by the merit of this deed expiate at each repetition the sins whose punishment is rebirth for eight millions of ages.[1]

Akin to this teaching is that of the larger and smaller *Sukhāvatī Vyūha*.[2] But it is noteworthy that though these three books are all equally authoritative, they differ in this point: the two former insisting that while this faith in Amitābha is indeed most potent, yet some merit on the part of the faithful is needed, and the smaller *Sukhāvatī Vyūha* denying that rebirth in the western heaven can be achieved by merit. Again the larger of these two *Sukhāvatī Sūtras* expressly denies what the *Amitāyur-dhyāna Sūtra* teaches, that those who have sinned any of the five deadly sins may be reborn in the Western Paradise. In these three books of the Paradise Mahāyāna, which may well have expressed and molded the devotional life of Nālandā, we may then trace the

---

[1] *S.B.E.*, XLIX, 197–98; *Amitāyur-dhyāna Sūtra*.

[2] *B.N.*, 23 (5), 27, 199, 200.

gradual development of the doctrine of faith at the expense
of the old doctrine of merit.   Nālandā was the home of
theologians as well as philosophers.   As we saw above,
the Chinese pilgrim found there a great statue of Avalokitesvara, and an artist who was busy painting a picture
of Metteyya Buddha.

From these indications we may reconstruct something
of the religious life of the great university, and it will help
us to remember that Buddhism is a religion and not
merely a philosophy, and to note the inevitable stages
by which it was popularized and universalized in preparation for its great achievements as a missionary religion.
At Nālandā it was equipped with a philosophy, a principle
of pedagogy, and practical methods of devotion, all of
which were needed if it were to appeal to the peoples of
trans-Himālaya, and yet to keep its self-respect.

What are the links between these theistic and polytheistic schools and the ethical reform instituted by
Sākyamuni ?   Some we have already discussed.   Another
is to be found in the elaboration of the Bodhisattva ideal.
Either at Nālandā or at similar centers of literary activity
the parabolic method of Sākyamuni was developed; some
Indian Aesop used the current folklore of India and wove
into it the Buddhist ideal of the Bodhisattva and the
theory of reincarnation, providing a veritable storehouse
for the teacher of simple folk.   We know from the monuments of Asoka that part of this work was done by the
second century B.C., and by the first century A.D. we find
the legend of Sumedha worked out.   In the dim distant
past he took a vow in the presence of the reigning Buddha,
Dipankara, that he would not enter Nirvāna until all
creatures were saved; his vow was accepted and it was he
who finally became the historical Sākyamuni.   In such

ways was developed the elaborate succession of Bodhi-sattvas, who, by their sacrificial life and often by their death, have made a bank of merit upon which the faithful may draw; and by the fifth century A.D. the great Ceylon commentator, Buddhaghosa, is able to exclaim: "More than the ocean has he given of his blood, more than the stars of his eyes!"[1]

Fā-Hian records that when he visited Ceylon in the early fifth century it was the custom at the annual procession of the Tooth Relic for a royal herald, mounted upon a richly caparisoned elephant, to proclaim the sacrificial acts of the Blessed One: during untold ages he spared not himself, gave away wife and child, plucked out his eyes, and cut off his head as an alms, until he won to Buddahood, turned the wicked from sin, and gave the weary rest. After this recital the king would exhibit the effigies of the five hundred bodily forms which had lodged this sacrificial spirit, and they were greatly honored by the crowds which then as now gathered for the festival of the Tooth of Gotama. This Bodhisattva ideal, as it was fully developed in the Mahāyāna, is nobly set forth in the *Sukhāvatī Vyūha*, and may be compared with the Arhat ideal set forth, for example, in the *Dhammapada*. While there is much that is similar in the two types, they differ in very noticeable ways,[2] and the transition between them is to be found, as we have seen, in the *Milinda Pañha* and in these *Jātaka* tales, which are at once fables and popular theology, an attempt to account for

---

[1] In his famous *Visuddhi Magga* composed at Anurādhapura. To Buddhaghośa also is attributed the familiar prayer which embodies the longings of millions in Buddhist lands: "May I meet Metteyya when he comes to lead multitudes to the haven of salvation. May I see the Lord of Mercy and be wise in the three scriptures."

[2] The ideal of the Bodhisattva is higher and more arduous than that of the Arhat; he pledges himself by a solemn vow (pranidhāna) to put out every effort and dedicates to others his merit (parināmanā).

the historic Sākyamuni. But Amitābha, incorporated
into Buddhism about this time, had also to be accounted
for. And the new Buddhism had to depict a new and
more arresting series, and to pile up even more extrava-
gant claims if it was to win its way. Or perhaps the shoe
was on the other foot! It may be that the Theravāda
schools, being put upon their mettle by the winsome figures
of the Mahāyāna, developed such tales as those of Vessantara and Sumedha, and added them to the growing list
of the *Jātakas*.

The Bodhisattva of the Mahāyāna is certainly an
arresting figure: charming, gentle, and compassionate,
full of tender and affectionate thought, unbiased, serene;
he is zealous, and ever girded for the duties of his high
calling; and has no thought that is not pure and wise.
He rouses others to good deeds, and stirs them up by his
activities to realize that the phenomenal world is "empty."
Himself walking in the highest perfections (pāramitās)
of knowledge, meditation, strength, patience, and virtue,
he rouses others to a noble emulation, so that in countless
multitudes they are established in enlightenment, and
provide for innumerable Buddhas the gifts in which they
delight.[1]

Such is the description of the Bhikshu Dharmākara,
whose perfect prayer or vow to save all beings brought him
to the Western Paradise as Amitābha, Light infinite in
brilliance and power, surpassing that of Sun and Moon,
whose Pure Land is prosperous and good to live in, filled
with physical delights, like every apocalyptic heaven,
but also radiant with spiritual joy and free from sin as
well as from pain. In it there mingles with the musical
cries of peacocks, parrots, and geese the sweeter music

[1] Cf. *S.B.E.*, Vol. XLIX, Part II, pp. 25–26.

of Buddhist philosophy, and voices are heard, beloved,
sweet, and pleasant alike to ear and heart, like the sound
of many waters murmuring "unreal, transient."[1] Very
interesting too are the ethical notes of this heavenly
music; Karunā, pity, Kshanti, patience, Maitri, love, are
prominent among them. The ethical system of the
Mahāyanā, as embodied in these popular tales of Dharmākara and his vow, is clearly almost the same as that of
the Hīnayāna, as embodied in the *Jātaka* tale of Sumedha,
who promises to practice the virtues of charity (dāna),
morality (sīla), resignation (nekkhamma), wisdom
(paññā), exertion (viriya), forbearance (khanti), truth-
fulness (sacca), persistency (aditthāna), love (mettā), and
equanimity (upekkhā), and who by this noble path
arrives at Buddahood, and is born as Sākyamuni. We
may imagine the two tales being worked out side by side
in the vihāras of Nālandā. The great difference between
the two schools is this: that whereas only lofty souls like
Sumedha could tread the lonely path of these perfections,
and so long as they followed the way of virtue, the multitudes could not attain, all could become Buddhas by
following the Mahāyāna; and a minor but yet noteworthy
difference is that in the latter system a more prominent
place is given to altruistic virtues. This is, however, a
matter of emphasis rather unfairly pressed by Mahāyānist apologists.

But as Dr. Anesaki has pointed out, momentous consequences followed from this change of emphasis, and
sympathetic benevolence developed into spiritual communion as the ideal of the new school, until in Japan and
China perhaps the most characteristic note of Buddhism
is the sense of the unity of all things and their mutual

[1] *Ibid., passim*, especially pp. 39–40.

sympathy.[1]   From such a sense springs the practice, now universal in Buddhist lands, known as parināmanā, or parivarta, the dedication of one's spiritual and material gifts to the salvation of others, the "turning over" to them of merit.   The little mother offering a strand of her hair at the Burmese pagoda, the Sinhalese monk reciting Pirit, the priests of China and Japan saying masses for the dead—all are imbued with this belief.

So too for all the ultimate Goal is the same, Nirvāna, Bodhi, or enlightenment, though their immediate purpose be the securing of material benefits in this life or in the underworld for themselves, for their clients, and for the dead; and though almost all are more eager for a paradise than for Nirvāna.

From the increasing emphasis upon the Bodhisattva ideal sprang this doctrine, and the germs of both are in the Pāli books.   For the example of Sākyamuni himself is nearer to the Bodhisattva than to the Arhat ideal, and he himself seems to have found in such devoted sacrifice as that of the saintly Punna as acceptable a type as the rigid self-culture of the recluse;   and even in the earliest accounts the two ideals are seen side by side, and the practice of parināmanā is adumbrated.   But the Mahāyāna, by its courageous doctrine of the Buddhahood of all, cut at the roots of the dual morality of Hīnayāna monasticism, which has undoubtedly put the celibate monk on a much higher plane than the layman.

Perhaps the first indication of an attempt to break away is in the Gandhāra sculptures of Metteyya as a prince in lay costume, and it is, as we have seen, to Gandhāra that we may attribute the "Lotus" teachings which so clearly and boldly assert this truth of the One

[1] Cf. "Buddhist Morality," *E.R.E.*, and other papers by Dr. Anesaki.

Way for layman and for all sentient beings as well as for monks. But at Nālandā and elsewhere the doctrine was worked out until Buddhism was fitted to capture the allegiance of China, Korea, and Japan.

The *Amitāyur-dhyāna Sūtra* is more than a popular treatise on Paradise. Belonging, on the one hand, to the Paradise Mahāyāna, it is also a link with the Yogācāra school which we have now to study, for it is a textbook for the Mystic, instructing him how he may experience the truth of his religion, and escape here and now the sorrows of the world.

This is the aim of all Buddhists, but some schools lay special stress upon it. The Yogācāra, as its name implies, is one of these; notable for its philosophical distinction, it has won its way because of its practical aim, which is nothing else than the achievement of the Mystic Union, even if it has often contented itself with magic. The metaphysical contributions of this school are great. Under its leaders, Asanga and Vasubandhu, Brahmin converts of Northwest India, it developed at about the beginning of the fourth century of the Christian Era three notable doctrines.

1. It elaborated the doctrine of twofold knowledge as follows: There are, it said, three lakshana, aspects or stages of Truth; first comes the ordinary naïve realism (parakalpita lakshana); but things are not what they seem to our deluded sight, and a second stage is reached when we realize the relativity of all things, and come to know that there is no abiding Reality in them; this stage is paratantra lakshana, and from it we must pass on to full and perfect knowledge, parinishpanna lakshana, and realize that the world in which we live and our own minds spring from a Supreme Mind. Having pierced the

clouds of illusion and scaled the heights of relative knowledge, the Mystic soars at last into the pure ether of Bodhi,
perfect enlightenment, and has transcended the dualisms
of subject and object, Samsāra and Nirvāna.

2. Of this ultimate reality the new school had its own
interpretation.   It is more positively conceived than by
the Mādhyamaka as a Supreme Mind.   The school is, in
fact, idealist, and its conception of the Ālayavijñāna,
the nidus, or foundation of all things, and the ground
and basis of thought, is a remarkable one.   It is called
Citta, mind, and is distinguished from Manas, human intelligence and will, which arises when Karma acts on the Ālaya
and calls it into being, or rather to the delusion of being.

It is this Manas which sees and apprehends the objective world, and the school has its own elaborate and not
very convincing psychology.   As in early Buddhism it is
"ignorance" which causes the production of a new self
or delusion of self; and even the Ālaya is itself only relatively real.   The absolute Reality is Tathatā, or "suchness," which seems hardly distinguishable from the Void;
this true nature of all things is free from all characteristics.
But the name, Tathāgata-garbha, or "Buddha-womb,"
is given to it as a concession to those who cannot rest
satisfied with so barren an absolute.   What really matters
is to recognize that the self and the world are unreal;
that thought—blank and without characteristics—is the
fundamental reality; and to have no attachment to this
transcendent goal.   To this extent all of us may be good
Buddhists!   But it is expressly stated that only "higher
men" can apprehend this teaching, and it may well be
that it is here misrepresented.

The whole doctrine of the school is condensed in
Asanga's *Mahāyānasamparigraha-Sāstra*, which begins

with a statement of ten points in which the Mahāyāna is superior to the Hīnayāna, and goes on to expound the Ālaya as "that which sustains and upholds, deep and subtle, wherein the seeds of being flow eternally." It is, in other words, the substratum of all things, and holds together the elements of which they are composed. It is also called Ādāna, or receptacle—a storehouse in which the seeds of Karma are preserved until the time comes for them to sprout and bear fruit. Each conscious being leaves behind him an energy, which remains latent in this receptacle and finally acts and reacts with it, bringing about a new regrouping of Skandhas. The Ālaya remains tranquil until it is "perfumed" or contaminated by Manas; till then, though it is in ceaseless motion, it is unconscious.

3. The Yogācāra proceeded to systematize the rather undeveloped Buddhology of earlier schools. Some concept was needed to link together the two "Bodies" of the Mādhyamaka. How was the historic Founder, for example, to be linked with the Dharmakāya? The Yogācāra school added the new concept of the glorified body, or Sambhogakāya, who becomes henceforth the object of interest in the Mahāyāna. This glorious being was the reality incarnate in the accommodated body, or Nirmānakāya. In this way the historic is linked to the eternal, and Indian distrust of history finds a way to substitute eternity for time.

Such are the three contributions to theological and philosophical thought made by the Yogācāra school. Even more important is its practice, for it met the needs of hungry human hearts for a religion of experience. It is not to be supposed that the arid abstractions of the schoolmen satisfied ordinary humanity, and of the charm-

ing pictures of other-worldly joys drawn by the theologians many must have asked: "Do they correspond to
objective fact?" To such the new school offered the
practice of Yoga, long familiar to India and clearly influencing Buddhism from its earliest times, but now frankly
accepted as the heart and essence of the whole matter.
The Supreme Reality is Bodhi, compared with which the
Ālayavijñāna itself has only relative reality; and to attain
to Bodhi all the stages of the Bodhisattva must be
practiced.

The *Lankāvatāra Sūtra*[1] is a standard work of this
school and teaches that the Bodhisattva will reach his
goal if he realizes that all things are mental creations:
that they exist only as a mirage, or a nightmare, and are
produced by the mental impulse of a former time which
operates upon the Alayavijñāna to produce a new illusion
of being. This will cease when he goes on to grasp the
true nature of ultimate reality; and to help in this quest
a series of meditations is laid down for him; beginning
with the jhānas of early Buddhism he is to go on and
enter farther and farther into the mysteries of unreality.

Thus we see the Mahāyāna conception of the Bodhisattva—often so admirable in its altruism—degenerating
into what seems as futile and selfish a pursuit as that of
any Arhat; and Buddhist scholasticism, whether at
Nālandā or in the Vihāras of Ceylon, is at work in the
fourth and fifth centuries of our era to the undoing of the
Buddha's way of virtue. It is difficult to believe that so
negative a mysticism is worth while: to toil upward, step
by step, and at last to arrive faint and weary at one last
Negation—such seems the idealism of the Vijñānavāda
no less than the franker negativism of the Mādhyamaka.

[1] *B.N.*, pp. 175-77.

The seventeen stages of this long ascent Asanga set out in the *Yogācārabhūmi Sāstra*, and in a volume of verse with a prose commentary, the *Mahāyānasūtra-lamkara*, the philosophy of the school may be studied.[1] The former work is ascribed to the Bodhisattva Maitreya, and it is noteworthy that he has largely superseded the historic Gotama in this school; his cult for several centuries becomes very prominent, and its traces are widespread today from the sculptures of Gandhāra to those of Korea. On Kōyasan the saints of the Mantra or Tantric Buddhism, a development of Yogācāra, await his coming, and his fat and genial smile greets the visitor at the entrance to every Chinese shrine.

Clearly influenced by Asanga and Vijñānavāda philosophy is another famous book, the *Mahāyāna Sraddhot-pādasāstra*, or "Awakening of Faith in the Mahāyāna."[2] Attributed by tradition to the poet-minstrel, Asvaghosa, it is clearly of much later date; its style has nothing in common with the *Buddha Carita*, and that poem has no hint of its ruling ideas.[3] The "Awakening" centers about the doctrine of Tathatā—absolute reality beyond all comprehension and expression, yet immanent in all. It claims that the Mahāyāna is great in essence, for the essence of it is the mind and store of all; great in attribute, for it embraces endless potentialities of Buddhahood; great in work, for these potentialities develop when duly disciplined.

[1] *Ibid.*, pp.1170, 1085, 1190; the latter translated into French by S. Lévi. Paris, 1907.

[2] *Ibid.*, pp. 1249, 1250.

[3] Nor has his other epic, the *Saundarānanda Kāvya*. Moreover, I-Tsing, who writes about him, makes no mention of the "Awakening," and other books have been wrongly attributed to him. For able discussion of Asvaghosa see M. Anesaki in *E.R.E.*, Vol. I; Sylvain Lévi in *Journal Asiatique* (July and August, 1908). Dr. Anesaki calls him "the Buddhist Origen." His colleague, Dr. I. Takakusu, supported by Drs. Sylvain Lévi and Winternitz, is opposed to the tradition of Asvaghosa's authorship of the "Awakening." D. T. Suzuki now believes that it is a Chinese work (*Eastern Buddhist*, Vol. I, No. 2, pp. 103–4).

It is a concise and well-compacted treatise, idealist like the Yogācāra and practical like it in its purpose, which is to awaken faith in the Mahāyāna, and to set forth the One Reality as an absolute mind of which individual minds are parts—as the waves on an ocean.

This Absolute is more satisfying than that alike of the Yogācāra and of the Mādhyamaka, which the "Awakening" may well intend to reconcile, for it is set forth as a Tathāgata-garbha, or "Womb of the Buddhas" from which all things proceed.

The term, Ālayavijñāna, is applied to it, but it is conceived as less relative and more absolute than the Ālaya of the Yogācāra.

For ordinary folk this concept is set forth as the Bodhi-Citta, one universal, perfect mind, loving as well as wise, who has compassion on all; let them put faith in him. Such faith "is upright, having right thoughts of this Eternal; profound, rejoicing to study and practice whatever is good; greatly compassionate, anxious to deliver all."

For the more philosophical the Bodhi-Citta is described as the essence of all things, alone real, and therefore indescribable, yet known to men under the conditions of their phenomenal life. This, the highest truth (paramartha satya), is ineffable, and beyond definition, neither "empty" nor "not empty"; it alone is the Real, the Eternal, and may be translated either "suchness" with Suzuki, or "the True Model" with Timothy Richard, for Tathatā means "that which is," the "thing in itself." This under another aspect is the Dharmakāya,[1] and under another represents the Nibbāna of the Pāli books,

[1] From Dharma, "law, teaching," but also "nature," "thing," to Dharmakāya, "the body of law," but also that which is the essence of nature, the foundation of existence—this is an evolution natural to the human mind. Behind phenomena is the Absolute, behind the norm the Norm.

that Supreme Truth of which Sākyamuni is alike discoverer and embodiment. For this is still the goal of Buddhism, even if in some Mahāyāna schools it is almost forgotten in the joys of Paradise.

In these two doctrines the "Awakening" is developing the teaching of Sākyamuni; first, that this highest Truth is ineffable; and second, that the Dhamma is the truth underlying all things. The Dharmakāya, it teaches, is this Absolute, which reveals itself either in human form, such as that of Sākyamuni, when it is called the Nirmānakāya or Buddha in *Kenosis,* or as the Sambhōgakāya, or Buddha in bliss.

The Christian theologian will at once see the resemblance between this attempt to account for the historic Gotama and to relate him with the Eternal Order, and the early Christology of the church; the Nirmānakāya may be compared with the historic Jesus, the Sambhōgakāya with the glorified Christ, while the Dharmakāya resembles the eternal God-head.[1] For the theologians of both religions the problem was to do justice at once to the absolute authority of the Teacher and the contingent circumstances of his human life. Both solved it by a theory of *Kenosis,* or self-emptying.

What then is faith ? It is belief in this threefold nature of the Buddha who saves us by his grace, grasping us as the tigress grasps her cub; belief in his Dharma, or teaching, and in his Sangha, and with this belief joy in them all. This faith, however, seems to be about to cling to some Being more personal and less abstract.

Whether the "Awakening of Faith" in its early form definitely taught that this faith should center in Amitābha

---

[1] So the absolute Brahman is revealed in the transfigured and in the human Krishna of the *Bhagavadgītā.*

is not clear; there are passages which seem to imply such a personification of the Dharmakāya, and in the Chinese versions in common use[1] the doctrine is explicitly taught in at least one passage at the close of the book, but these versions belong to the sixth and seventh centuries and the passage may be a gloss. It refers to an earlier work called "The Sūtra," possibly the *Sukhāvatī Vyūha*, and exhorts the faithful to think of Amitābha, and to direct their good deeds toward his Western Paradise. They will then be reborn in it and will be confirmed in their faith in the Buddha.

Side by side with faith goes enlightenment (for we are still dealing, after all, with Buddhism); this consists in transcending subjectivity, and in realizing that the Absolute is the real, "that the mortal is with the immortal blent." So only is ignorance annihilated, and man's essential nature realized. In other words, the Bodhi-Citta, or Buddha-mind, latent in all men, awakes when they realize their true nature as parts of the Eternal. All are capable of Buddhahood, and this note is struck with emphasis, for the author realized that men are saved by hope as well as by faith, and that if so many early Buddhists had reached Arhatship all men might become Buddhas.

Such, in essence, is this remarkable book which has been a gospel of hope and comfort to countless millions, and which helped to lay the foundations for a universal Buddhism. It is accepted, in fact, by all schools of the Mahāyāna, of which it is in many ways the crowning achievement.

How did this notable development of doctrine take place ? It is not sufficient to urge the claims of the human

---

[1] One translated in 553 A.D. by Paramartha, one in 695–700 A.D. by Sikshānanda.

heart, nor even the demands of human reason, though here is the nucleus of a true answer; man needs a conception of the Divine, he *will* argue back to a First Cause, and in it he will always postulate compassion as well as wisdom; he cannot well get along without belief in a Creator and Savior. But there is also the historic fact that converts, trained in Hindu philosophy, brought back into the main stream of Buddhism doctrines which the Buddhist reformation had, for the moment, submerged. The "Awakening of Faith" may seem unorthodox Buddhism; it is "good Krishnaism," and in it we may see Hindu philosophy taking a noble revenge. So there appears in Buddhism a formulated pantheistic idealism, and a universalistic note which has made it a gospel for the many.

As Mahāyānist scholars claim, here was a legitimate development; from the very first the historical Gotama had tended at once to emphasize faith in himself and, paradoxical as it may seem, to remove himself behind the Dharma; how natural that this Dharma, which stood for universal moral law, should itself first tend to take on a cosmic significance, and then be embodied in a personal savior. The Dharma emanates from the Dharmakāya; the Tathāgata is the embodiment of Tathatā.

Like the "Lotus," the "Awakening of Faith" may serve as a useful link between the Christian and the Buddhist, as let the following incident attest. Dr. Timothy Richard, a veteran missionary in China, has put it on record that when the latter book first came into his hands he sat late into the night reading it, and was again and again constrained to exclaim to his companion: "Listen to this; it is a Christian book," only to be told by that champion of orthodoxy: "Go to sleep. You are reading your own thoughts into it." Yet the doctrine of an Eternal Being whose nature is love, and whom to trust is to be saved, is common to both, and the great bulk of the worshipers of the two religions are simple folk who do not trouble their heads as to whether this Eternal is personal or not. In the "Awakening of Faith" we see Buddhism becoming a religion whose idea of God has nothing in it which is unworthy, and whose philosophy is closely akin to much Christian idealism. Yet, like other Mahāyāna books, it lays Buddhism open to the dangers of pantheism, because it does not sufficiently emphasize the transcendence of the Tathatā, or Absolute. This was one reason why Buddhism was later reabsorbed into Hinduism, and the great University of Nālandā fell as much through internal degeneration and compromise with Tantric Hinduism as through the iconoclasm of Islam.

Yet from the second to the ninth century it remained a great center of learning, and especially of the two great schools of the Mādhyamaka and the Vijñānavāda, whose textbooks went out from its halls to China and Tibet, many of them in the possession of the great pilgrim with whom we started out on our investigation; it must have been a great university which won the enthusiasm of Hiuen-Tsiang.

Other great and notable names on its roll of honor are Chandrakirti and Santideva. To the latter we owe an admirable, if not very original, compendium of doctrine, the *Sikshā-Sammucaya*,[1] in which the Bodhisattva ideal is set forth as one of real beauty, and here we see the positive side of the *via negativa* discussed above.

[1] Rouse and Bendall, *E.T.* London: Murray, 1922.

How shall I seek the goal to gain
While others live in fear and pain ?
Should I this self of mine preserve
And fail those other selves to serve ?

asks its first Kārikā, or stanza, and it is answered:

O thou that wouldst that goal attain
And find for all the end of pain—
Make firm the root of faith within,
Set thine own mind the Light to win.

This is as orthodox as the *Dhammapada,* and the book
goes on to show that the Bodhisattva regards others as
himself—nay, above himself: "It is better that I alone
should suffer than that others should sink to torment."

More original and full of fine fervor is the *Bodhicārya-
vatāra* of the same author, written "for his own satisfaction," perhaps as a result of his patient and devout edi-
torial work on the "Compendium." As he muses the
fire kindles, and he begins to glorify the Bodhi-Citta,
and to implore Bodhisattvas to become servants of all.
"May I be medicine to the sick . . . . their physician
and nurse . . . . a guide to the lost, a ship to the voyager,
a lamp in darkness, a couch to the weary. . . . . The
sorrow of the stranger I must destroy as my own. . . . .
I must serve others because they are beings like myself."
Yes, this beautiful dream ends in the stark unreality
of nihilism. "Who can be honored, who reproached ?
Where are joy and sorrow, the loved and the hated,
avarice and liberality ? Search as ye will ye may not
find."

"It seems," says G. K. Nariman, in his excellent
account of Sanskrit Buddhism[1] (which has reached me

[1] *Literary History of Sanskrit Buddhism.* Bombay, 1923.

as this goes to press), "to be the curse of Indian mentality that whenever it soars too high it lands in absurdity."

Alas! The schoolmen of Nālānda fell into worse depths, and it is one of the tragedies of history that this great university, alike in her too great tolerance and in her oversubtlety, deserted the Middle Path of Sākyamuni.

About the sixth century began the penetration of his austere house by Sakta Hinduism, a process which we shall study in a later chapter; and even in the Tantric Buddhism which resulted Nālānda was before long overshadowed by the new University of Vikramasila on the Ganges, and at last went down before the furious onslaught of Islam, that scourge of degenerate faiths.

CHAPTER V

MIHINTALE, ARIMADDANA, AND SUKHŌTHAI

Fastnesses of the Theravāda in Ceylon, Burma, and Siam (250 B.C.–1400 A.D.)

> "*As is the sowing so is the harvest . . . .*
> *The monks are the harvest-field of merit.*"
> —SĀKYAMUNI.

Amid a sea of scrubby jungle that shimmers in a perpetual haze of heat rises the rocky knoll of Missaka; it is today known as Mihintale, and on its three peaks are dāgobas and vihāras, where a few monks of the Theravāda keep alive the monastic form into which early Ceylon Buddhism was cast by the great Mahinda, while his father, Asoka, was making it a religion for the masses of the people of India. Here today one may visit the rock-hewn study or cell of the royal missionary from which there went out the emissaries of the Dhamma. Seven miles to the west is the sacred city of Anurādhapura, which more, perhaps, than any relic of Buddhism captures the imagination of the student, and reveals something of the splendid civilization which grew up about the Sangha. Its vast dāgobas, its ancient trees and pleasant parks, its slender stone pillars and great carved lintels remain to tell of a noble city, where kings once vied with one another in honoring the Sangha, and where monastic Buddhism, withdrawn yet watchful, overawed the throne and nerved it to fresh devotion. The island chronicles, *Dīpawamsa* (fourth century A.D.) and *Mahāwamsa* (early fifth), are in their main impressions borne out by Fā-Hian, who spent some time in Lankā. He contrasts its triumphant championship of the order and their activity with the shameful neglect of the Buddha's Holy Land, and he returned to China inspired by the picture of what a Buddhist kingdom might be, and thrilled by its gorgeous ceremonial and elaborate worship. Even as early as the Asokan era there is evidence on the great gateway at Sānchi of the coming of Sanghamittā, the sister of Mahinda, bringing with her a branch of the sacred Bo-tree. It stands today in the Meghavana Park, a citadel of the orthodox. It seems to totter, yet life still courses in its ancient veins—at once a relic and a symbol of the amazing vitality of the Dhamma. And the mighty cities of Anurādhapura (third century B.C. to seventh century A.D.) and of Polunaruwa (eighth to thirteenth century A.D.), ruined though they are and half buried by jungle, are equally eloquent of its powers of recovery, and of the close alliance of church and state in the island. Even Kandy, the capital of a later and degenerate era, has its royal palace and its Temple of the Tooth practically under one roof.

The history of the kings of Ceylon from Tissa, the friend and ally of Asoka, onward is intimately bound up with that of Buddhism; and sometimes the alliance benefited the people, as in the noble instance of Dutthagāmini of the house of Tissa, who, leading out his armies to crush Elara, the Tamil usurper, was seized by the truly Buddhist conviction that battles are vain and disastrous. Halting his armies he rode forth alone on his great elephant, challenged Elara to single combat, slew him, and erected a monument to his memory. Dutthagāmani is perhaps the Asoka of Ceylon, and eleven chapters of the *Mah-*

āwamsa tell us of his pious works, among them the Ruanweli Dāgoba, greatest of Anurādhapura's great pagodas, to the founding of which came Buddhists from lands as far off as Alexandria[1] and Kashmir; for the Dhamma was already far flung. Another patron and builder was Vatthagāmani, who reigned in the first century B.C. He built the Abhāyagiri Dāgoba, and in his reign we hear of the first heresies, none of which, however, amounted to a breaking away from Hīnayāna, though as Huien-Tsiang tells us, Mahāyāna was also studied in some of the vihāras of Ceylon. Here, especially at Abhāyagiri, dwelt the schismatic Vetulyas. They were strong enough to maintain a separate existence for twelve centuries, refusing to be reconciled to the great and orthodox Mahāvihāra.

As we read of the great building activity of the kings, and visit the colossal remains of their ancient cities, we cannot but realize that the Sangha was not an unmixed blessing; by the end of the fourth century Fā-Hian tells us there were over 50,000 monks in the island, and today one-third of its arable land is monastic property. At the head of the thousand steps leading to Mahinda's retreat are two well-wrought marble slabs which tell of the gifts of various kings, and lay down regulations for the management of the vast estates belonging to the monastery. Such records are common in the island, and the gradual conquest of it by Indian invaders and by the encroaching jungle suggests a people worn out by the exactions of an aristocratic and austere religion, which throve most when kings smiled upon it. Some of these kings, however, inspired by its true spirit—that of the Bodhisattva—built

---

[1] The "Alasanda" of the chronicle may be an Indo-Greek town, or it may be the Egyptian Alexandria. Asoka sent a mission to Tulamayo or Ptolemy of Egypt.

roads and irrigation tanks, and the monks for their part
have laid upon the world the debt of having transcribed,
edited, and preserved the *Tipitaka*. It is possible that
the whole *Abhidhamma* is their work. This literary
activity went on from about 20 B.C. until the fifth
century A.D., when the great commentaries were composed.
The greatest of these monastic commentators, Buddhaghosa, a convert from Hinduism, is said to have proved
his fitness for the task by writing the great work, *Visuddhi
Magga*, "Path of Purity or Salvation," a systematic
exposition of the Theravāda. After this, with amazing
energy and erudition, he produced a series of notable
commentaries on the chief Pāli books: "In these works,
while the life of the Buddha as a monk is still clearly
realized, he is also thought of as a sort of divine being
exercising cosmic powers as in the Mahāyāna."[1] In this
state of indecision as to its Founder's real nature Ceylon
Buddhism has remained to this day, and Buddhaghosa is
largely responsible for this crystallization of the religion
at a stage of suspended judgment. Insisting that Pāli
was the language for the canonical books,[2] he further
safeguarded their integrity by his admirable commentaries,
of which we may note especially the *Visuddhi Magga*.

It has three main divisions: (1) chapters i and ii, dealing with Sīla, conduct; (2) chapters iii to xii, dealing with
Samādhi, meditation; and (3) chapters xiii to xxiii, dealing with Paññā, intuitive knowledge of religious truth. In
other words, it consists of a commentary upon the three
great disciplines of meditation and the transcendental
knowledge which are based upon right behavior, and it has

---

[1] J. N. Farquhar, *Outlines of the Religious Literature of India*, p. 155.

[2] About 400 A.D. Mahadhammakathi had translated the suttas into Sinhalese.
There is little evidence for the tradition that Buddhaghosa destroyed the Sinhalese
version of any of the books.

served to keep the monks of Ceylon, Burma, and Siam
true to the dictum of early Buddhism, "No paññā without
samādhi, no samādhi without paññā." It has also kept
before them the far-off goal, Nibbāna, and though to
this day they differ among themselves as to its exact
nature, they all agree as to the way of reaching it, and
turn austerely and resolutely away from the less stoical
devotion of the Mahāyāna. Hopelessly, yet with dogged
endurance, they cling to the forty subjects of meditation,
and if none attains to the six High Powers, or abhiññā,
yet for the most part they abstain from worldliness, and
some reach a certain wise and gentle patience which is
true to type.

With Buddhaghosa Pāli became the classic language
of the island, and the copying and recopying of the *Tipitika*
on palm-leaf strips has become one of the main activities
of the monks. They have remained the champions of
Theravāda orthodoxy as against the Mahāyāna, of which
some traces are found in the island, and against Hinduism,
which has been an ever present rival, between whose champions and the Bhikkhus debate and controversy have been
frequent and bitter. Of one such debate, which took place
in the ninth or tenth century, we have a record in the life
of Mānikka Vāchagar, the Tamil poet. With his face
veiled so that he should not see their "ill-omened counte-
nances," the poet met a Buddhist delegation which had
been summoned to the king's court at Madura in South
India. In the presence of the two kings, their backers,
and of innumerable deities who regarded with a jealous
indignation the deification of Sākyamuni, the poet is seen
challenging the Buddhists to show reason for their presence. They are no whit abashed. "To tell the city
are we come that there is no god but him whose worship

we celebrate, our lord Buddha." "Can a hare become
an elephant? Who is this god of yours?" "Can one
reveal the sun to the blind? Yet he is revealed in our
books, and has been born in many a loving shape." The
Buddhist champion then went on to expound the Eightfold Noble Path and the doctrines of Anattā and Aniccā.
The former the Saivite rejected as having nothing original
in it, and the latter called down his scornful indignation:

> Since all is transient and without substantial entity, where is the
> knower, the knowledge, the object known? Where is the lawgiver
> and deliverer himself? How does he continue to deliver and to teach?
> He is by your own showing annihilated; and annihilation is your
> creed.

He went on to taunt the Buddhists with hypocrisy, for
with all their special emphasis on ahimsā, or not killing,
they naïvely eat the flesh of that which has been killed;
and the Buddhist champion is represented as having
retreated, unable to rebut some, at any rate, of these
arguments. It seems clear that scholastic Hīnayāna *was* at
this time largely annihilationist in its doctrine of Nibbāna.

About this time, driven ignominiously out of South
India, defeated both by Hindu and Mahāyāna polytheism,
orthodox monastic Buddhism was gaining a powerful hold
in Burma. According to Burmese tradition it was Bud-
dhagosa himself who first established it there. Yet it is
certain that it waited until the eleventh century to become
in any sense a national religion, and as in Asokan India and
in the Ceylon of many centuries it was the throne which
raised it to this position. The ancient capital, Arimaddana
or Pagān, had been for hundreds of years familiar with
Buddhism, but it was Anawrata who in the middle of the
eleventh century was converted by a wandering monk
to the Theravāda and became its zealous patron. Send-

ing to his neighbor the king of Thaton (Sudhammapura), he demanded a complete edition of the *Tipitaka,* and being refused, sacked the town and carried books, monks, king, and people to Pagān, now a veritable city of pagodas, which he and his successors built. The library was housed in a splendid building, and Pagān became a fastness of Pāli scholarship, especially in grammar and syntax.[1] As in Ceylon, the *Abhidhamma* has especially attracted the attention of the monks of Burma, and in the twelfth century Anuruddha compiled a commentary upon it covering much the same ground as the *Visuddhi Magga,* but more psychological in character.[2]

While, however, Burma is now, and has been since the time of Anawrata, a fastness of the Theravāda, archaeology is revealing traces of a degenerate Mahāyāna mingled with magic and tantric practices, and there was also a constant tendency to fuse with the ever present animism, which is still so strong among the Burmese. In spite of the efforts of Anawrata and others to rid Buddhism of both, the religion of the Burmese is by no means free from them today, and the cheerful, sunny temperament of the people and their naïve propitiation of the spirit-world contrast strangely with the sad refrain of the monks: "Dukkhā, anattā, aniccā." Burmese Buddhists have, moreover, a vague, pantheistic philosophy of life which is more akin to the Mahāyāna than to the Hīnayāna, and their worship of the pagoda and of the images, their sharing of merit, their prayers for material and other blessings, and their ardent desire to be reborn in a paradise would all seem to indicate that the Buddhism of the Burmese masses is

---

[1] The *Karikā* of Dhammasenapati (eleventh century) and the *Saddaniti* of Aggavamsa (twelfth century) are well-known examples of Burmese grammatical works on the Pāli language. See M. Bode, *The Pāli Literature of Burma,* chap. ii.

[2] The *Abhidhammatha Sangaha;* see "Compendium of Philosophy," *P.T.S.,* 1910.

somewhere between the Hīnayāna and the Mahāyāna. The great pagoda platform at Rangoon has indeed been likened to "the bazaars of Paradise," where the people throng for social as well as religious purposes, and the shrines are somewhere between the old chaitya of the Hīnayāna and the temple of the Mahāyāna. Lights and incense burn before innumerable images of the Buddha, and here one sees what can only be described as worship. It may well be that in its cheerful seriousness the religion of the lay-people has not changed much since the days of Sākyamuni. Now as then it has made great concessions to human needs, which the more stoical and often rather unsympathetic monk himself has had to tolerate; yet there is much in it, such as its mechanical conception of merit and its magic practices of exorcism, which the Founder strove to banish. It is, however, by such concessions, and by seeking to adapt itself to the social life of the people, from festive marriages to no less festive funerals, and from the birth of the child to the welfare of the dead beyond the grave, that Buddhism has made itself a national religion in Burma, and is known as "Burma custom"; and for these the monks are responsible.

Yet life within the monastery itself has changed but little; the monks are still monks and not priests, and the more learned of them regard these popular manifestations as sideshows, necessary concessions to human frailty; most honored among them is still the austere and ascetic Arhat.

The student of conservative monastic Hīnayāna will find in the monasteries of these lands of Southeastern Asia a Buddhism which has kept true to type since the days of Buddhaghosa and the early champions and formulators of the Theravāda.

In Siam as in Burma Buddhism owes much to the Sangha of Ceylon. Though earlier missions had been at work from the fifth century A.D. onward, some from Burma and some from Camboja, yet it was not until the fourteenth century that Siamese Buddhism took its present form. King Suryavamsa Rāma, following the example of Anawrata, sent to Ceylon for a teacher. He received him in great pomp at Sukhōthai, appointed him Sangharāja, a title which his successors have kept, dedicated a golden image of the Buddha, and prayed that the merit of this act might bring him to Buddhahood. To hasten this consummation he himself entered the order, and once more we see the age-long struggle of the monastic ideal against the secular. It soon took dramatic form, for the king's example spread and the affairs of state languished until the people took alarm and insisted that he and his court return to their proper spheres. The Siamese Sangha pulled hard in the opposite direction, but the Ceylonese abbot, who had seen similar conflicts in the history of his own people, wisely bade the king return to his throne, while he himself would remain king of the order. As in Ceylon and Burma, therefore, a division of function was arranged, the king and the laity supporting the monks and winning merit by their gifts of buildings, food, and clothing. The Buddhism of Siam is specially worthy of study because it still basks in royal favor and its Sangharat is still a member of the ruling house. Here, in fact, is a Buddhist medieval kingdom with much of the glamor of the days of Dutthagāmini and of Anawrata still upon it. Slowly along the river wind splendid barges of state in which the king and his court ride to offer at the principal Wats the gifts of clothing which their women have been busy preparing; this is the old Buddhist practice of Kathina, the preparing of robes for the monks, to which the whole country gives itself every October. Within the monasteries also, the spirit of devotion is alive. The yearly examination of candidates for degrees in Pāli learning has been lately restored, and is making for higher standards.

All these lands of Southeastern Asia are indeed fast-nesses of the Hīnayāna; the yellow robe of the monk and the bizarre roofs of pagodas and monasteries are the most striking features of a tropical landscape. Here Buddhism flourishes; Siam has over fifty thousand monks and ten thousand novices; Burma has nearly sixteen thousand monasteries, and those of Ceylon own a third of the arable land of the island. Though the great strongholds Mihintale, Arimaddana, and Sukhōthai lie in ruins, and the jungle struggles to reclaim them, yet the life of the monks goes on unchanged, and the people are well content with Buddhism so long as it tolerates their superstitions and continues to provide religious junketings and elementary education. Its moral code too they know and appreciate, even if, like the rest of us, they select from it those things which are not too high and difficult. The great lesson of compassion, for example, they admire even when they let it peter out to a one-sided emphasis on taking no life; liberality they conceive in a truly liberal spirit as their gifts to monastery and pagoda and their hospitality to strangers bear witness. In these ways sīla and dāna are observed by most. The third great pillar of the Buddhist system, jhāna, or meditation, they leave for the most part to the monks; but in certain old people there are to be seen a wistful striving after this high goal and a conviction that Nibbāna, though it is very far off, is an alluring ideal, and that when Metteyya Buddha comes their feet will be guided along that steep road. In the meantime they can win merit alike for themselves and for their families, and they aspire to the honorable title of "pagoda-builder." In all these lands too it is common for one son to become a monk; and in Burma all boys are admitted for a period to the Sangha.

To enter the monastic life is easy, and the Pabbajjā, or act of leaving the world, is dramatically represented by putting off the rich apparel, shaving the head, and donning the yellow robe; it is followed by the Upasampadā, or ordination, a simple ceremony in which the candidate is examined and sponsored by his tutor, and then repeats the ancient formula: "I take refuge in Buddha, the Sangha, and the Dhamma."

Undoubtedly many world-weary men and many unsuccessful in worldly callings find their way into the order, and the vocation to the monastic life, as in all religions, is a rare one; but criminals and other undesirables are usually kept out.

The orders are Samanēra, Novice (Burmese, Shin; Siamese, Samanen), Bhikkhu, Monk (Burmese, Pyit-shin; Siamese, Phikhu), and Thera, Elder (Burmese, Pōngyi; Siamese, Phra), and there is in addition in Burma a tendency to a hierarchy, culminating in the Superior, or Thāthanabaing, who, under the Burmese kings, wielded a power like that of the great abbots in the palmy days of the Ceylon monarchy. In Siam the king's brother is head of the order, Sangharat, and under him are four chief abbots nominated by the king and called Somdetchao.

The monks of all these countries are on the whole well versed in the scriptures, some of them knowing whole books by heart, and special fame attaches to scholars of

the difficult and abstruse *Abhidhamma;* the inscription at
Mihintale referred to above lays down the regulation
that a monk who can repeat this Higher Religion is to
receive twelve measures of rice as against five for the
repeater of the *Vinaya*, and seven for the repeater of the
Sutta. In other words, the third Basket is as valuable
and as difficult as the other two put together! The most
fruitful and the most arduous of the monkish exercises is
the practice of the various forms of meditation prescribed
in this collection, and in such commentaries as the
Visuddhi Magga we find a description of forty Kam-
matthānas which include: (1) ten recollections (anussati)
upon the Three Jewels, morality, liberality, the gods,
death, the body, the Yoga practice of deep breathing, and
calmness; (2) ten Asubhabhavana, or contemplations of
unpleasant states of the dead and decaying body, which
lead to disgust and detachment; (3) the Brahmāvihāra,
or spiritual abode of the sentiments of benevolence
(Mettam), compassion (Karunā), cheerful sympathy
(Muditā) and equanimity (Upekkhā), which Buddhism
took over from the Yoga of ancient India; (4) ten Kasina,
practices of concentrated attention upon such objects as
earth, water, space, air, primary colors, etc.

These practices lead to a unification of consciousness
(cittassa ekaggatā), and to serene mental states in which
the schoolmen distinguished four Jhānas, or stages, and
the experience of the austere pleasure of these states of
Samādhi is, as we have seen, the kernel of the whole
Buddhist religion, interpreted in its highest manifestation
as the realization of Nibbāna and the cessation of Samsāra.

It is the attainment of some measure of success in these
high exercises which keeps the Sangha alive and expectant;
and when any monk shows promise of becoming expert

in them his fame spreads rapidly, and hope revives that an Arhat is once more to be found among men. He will be recognized by possessing the abhiññā, which are the divine ear which can catch all sounds, the divine eye which can see to the utmost confines of space, the power of working miracles and of reading the thoughts of others, and memory of former existences.

About this hope, forlorn and precarious as it must seem to us, the life of the Sangha is organized, and in the daily round of the monks of Ceylon, Burma, and Siam we have undoubtedly a picture of Theravāda Buddhism as it has been preserved for at least two thousand years.

Their Patimokkha ("Cuirass," or code of discipline) was almost certainly forged in ancient days, and is accepted by all schools of Buddhists. In its shorter form, that of the Pāli language, it contains 227 rules, and in the Chinese and Tibetan form 250 and 259, respectively. These rules are recited in Southeastern Asia twice a month. Gathering in one of their central halls, the brethren of the yellow robe sit in solemn assembly, and as each regulation is recited, are admonished to confess if they have broken it. But, as in the Christian church, such public confession is almost always replaced either by secret confession to one another, or by silence.

More familiar is the pindapātika, or collection of food from the laity. Solemnly, in the early morning, a file of monks is seen to pass down the village street, stopping without a word at each house with downcast eyes, begging bowls held out; no word of thanks is spoken, for it is the donor who gains the merit; and in most monasteries it is the dogs who benefit in material things, for a more palatable meal is usually prepared for the mendicants by those who remain within doors. The letter of the old

law is kept also in the practice of the Pamsakulika, or
Kathina.   The Founder having enjoined upon his monks
that they should go clad in rags, new cloth, often specially
woven and dyed for the monks, is cut up by the laity into
small squares and then sewn together again.

A day in a monastery of one of these lands passes leis-
urely and not unpleasantly, with a reasonable division of
function: the younger to attend to the wants of the elder;
all to do their share of meditation; while some are set
apart for the teaching of the primary school.

What do they teach the laity of religious truth?
Clearly the *Abhidhamma* is too high for them; the *Vinaya*
is for the monks alone; and strangely the *Suttas*, so rich
in biographic material, are not so much used as the
Jātakas, or myths, among which that of the Vessantara
is most popular.   Very well known too is a summary of
the ethic for laymen, the *Māha Mangala Sutta* (Burmese,
Mingala thōt), and a "Song of the Eight Victories,"
which tells how the Blessed One vanquished his foes,
physical, intellectual, and spiritual.[1]   These runes are
used as Pirit, a magic ceremony, which the laity have come
to associate most with the monks.   If snakes are to be
driven out, or a pestilence stayed, the monk is called in,
and he often improves the occasion by preaching upon
the cardinal tenet of ahimsā (not killing).   The villagers
may want to drive out a nest of cobras, or the government may urge the extermination of the rat and the mos-
quito, but there stands the monk, an embodied conscience.   "Let them not harm their little brothers, but
trust to the power of spirit, and give gifts to the Sangha."
The doctrine of merit (kusalam) won by such gifts, or
by building shrines, has become the warp and woof of

[1] See my *Heart of Buddhism*.

lay-religion in Ceylon, Siam, and Burma. "The laity to make offerings, the monk to meditate; thus both win merit" is the accepted division of labor. It is perhaps not unfair to say that the former plays the game more honorably than the latter. After all, it is easier to part with a coin than to keep a vigil.

The Buddhism of Southeastern Asia is not troubled much by denominations. They are of minor importance, and do not lead to serious friction. In Ceylon, for example, the Siam sect is more aristocratic and exclusive than the others, admitting only members of the upper castes—a course to which it may well have been driven by competition with Hinduism. In Burma again the Sulagandi lay more stress than the Mahāgandi upon free will, and in Siam the Dhammayut is a reformed and more rigorous sect. But the hospitality of the monastery is not denied the visitor of other sects, and at great national festivals, such as that of the Buddha's Tooth at Kandy, one may see a striking demonstration of the fundamental unity of the Sangha. Here, bowing low before the reputed relic of their great leader, respected by the laity as custodians of his Dhamma, we may leave them, joining, before we go, in the cry which goes up from the assembled multitude: "Sadhu—Well done!" for we too are debtors to the brethren of the yellow robe!

CHAPTER VI

LOYĀNG, CHANG-ĀN, T'IEN T'AI

Buddhism in China (ca. 100–600 A.D.)

"Confucian China would never have accepted the Idealism of India had not Lao-tze and Taoism towards the end of the Chow dynasty prepared a psychological foundation for the development of both these extremes of Asiatic thought."—OKAKURA.

"The Way of Confucius and the Way of Sākyamuni are two wings; without either China cannot fly."—WEN LI.

While Gotama was preaching in the Ganges Valley, Confucius and Lao-tze were grafting upon the ancient Chinese stock of animism, or naturism, their own distinctive teachings. And while in India and adjoining countries the exclusive Hīnayāna was being transmuted into the universalist Mahāyāna, this great parent-stem of Chinese religion was being shaped to receive the new graft.[1] Here is material of vital interest for a philosophy of history which must some day be written, and in it we may note these stages: (1) sixth century B.C.—(*a*) Sākyamuni in India, Confucius in China, teachers differing radically in purpose, and yet agreeing on certain great fundamentals of morality; (*b*) Sākyamuni in India, Lao-tze in China giving a general background for such teachings in the idea of a Dhamma, or Tao, a Norm, natural "order," or "road" following which men attain to righteousness; and both essentially Mystics; (2) the

---

[1] Cf. De Groot, "Confucian Religion," *E.R.E.*, Vol. IV, and his "Religion in China," pp. 2–3; cf. his comment: "It is a remarkable coincidence that this greatest moment in the development of religion in China was synchronous with the birth of Christ and Christianity."

leaven at work in both lands, moralizing the ancient faiths, bringing order and harmony to men's thought, and adding a mystic tinge to moral endeavor; (3) second century B.C. to second century A.D.—the grafting of the new teachings upon the ancient faiths until they become the main branches; and (4) the gradual shaping of the Indian branch and of the Chinese trunk for the grafting of the former upon the latter. Such, in bare outline, are the stages of a long and remarkable process for which the metaphor of grafting is too simple; another from the same science, that of cross-fertilization, would be more appropriate; but for our purpose that used will suffice to indicate the great event in Chinese history which we have now to study—the introduction of Buddhism.

So well was this grafting done that by the sixth century Buddhist monuments show the Buddha attended by Confucian and Taoist gods, and we meet the scholar, Fu Hsi, dressed in a Taoist cap, a Buddhist stole, and Confucian shoes, and pointing to each in turn when the emperor questioned him as to his religious beliefs. It is interesting to reflect that we in the West are nearly two thousand years behind the East in the comparative study of religion, and early in the ninth century the scholar, Tsung Mi of Kwei Fêng, published his famous *Origin of Man* in which the teaching of the three schools are compared, criticized in detail, and reconciled.[1] The Chinese is not unreasonable nor superficial when he refuses to say that he belongs exclusively to any of the San Chiao, the "three which are one"; nor is it indeed possible today to divorce Confucian ethics from Buddhist philosophy and religion, with which Taoism is inextricably interwoven.

[1] B.N., *Yuen Jan Lun*, 1594. "The teachings of Kung-fu-tsz, Lao-tsz and Shakya are different . . . . each supplementing the other." For a translation of this important work see K. Nukariya, *Religion of the Samurai*.

It is no more possible to say when or how the first Buddhist mission in China began; yet an early chronicle records a mission in 217 B.C. when Li Fang and seventeen others arrived at Hsi-An;[1] and there is every reason to suppose that the great caravan roads allowed interchange of ideas as well as of merchandise. And the great Han dynasty (202 B.C.–220 A.D.) may well have used such help as Buddhism affords in consolidating its rule. Such may be the meaning of the famous dream of the Emperor Ming-Ti (58–76 A.D.), that a high, shining "golden God" appeared to him and entered his palace; such dreams do not come "out of the blue"; there must have been some basis for the vision in thoughts already in the emperor's mind, and in some Buddhist image or Buddhist teachings already circulating in China. Nor could Ming-Ti's dream be interpreted unless a knowledge of Buddhism already existed in China. Indeed an image is said to have been brought back by an expedition in 121 B.C. And when the emperor obeyed the vision, sending an embassy of eighteen, and summoning the missionaries, She Moteng (or Kāsyapa Matanga) and Ku-fa-lan (or Gobharana), in 65 A.D. from Khotan, they succeeded so well that we may believe that they were sowing on soil previously prepared. They both came from Central India, but had worked in the land of the Yuehchi; and now in 67 A.D. they settled at the capital, and the one work assigned to them which has come down to us was a handbook of moral teaching which could give no great alarm either to Confucianists or to Taoists, and which might be claimed equally well by Hīnayāna and by Mahāyāna Buddhists.

[1] The legend that they were sent by Asoka if not exact (he died about 231 B.C.) may yet have some truth in it, for the impetus he gave to Buddhist missions lived on.

The scene of their labors was the ancient city of Loyāng,[1] now once more the center of a splendid civilization, for the great dynasty of Eastern Han had chosen this peaceful yet busy capital in the valley of the Hoang-ho, where great trade roads met. And here the missionaries found a cosmopolitan society, and were given a cordial welcome by the emperor.[2] Weary with their long journey, they would enjoy the wide prospect over lake and river, and not far away were mountains dear to the Buddhist heart. Here in the Royal Library they worked, and their first apologetic is still an honored classic, a proof of the tact and skill with which they approached the Chinese mind. An early record tells us that they "concealed their deep learning and did not translate many books"; if they did nothing but give to the Chinese this *Sūtra of Forty-two Sayings*, their mission was amply justified. It seems to be a compilation from larger works, intended as a manual for the use of the emperor and other inquirers, and is wisely cast in a Confucian mold. Each paragraph begins after the manner of the Analects, "Thus saith the Master," and most of the more controversial things of Buddhism are omitted.

First comes a brief statement of the facts of Sākya-muni's life, a reference to the two hundred and fifty rules for monks, and then the ten precepts and the four stages of Arhatship. Next is a discourse on compassion and patient meekness which is very Taoist; let the sage remember that whosoever insults him is like one who spits against the sky, his spittle returns upon his own head!

[1] Modern Honan-fu.

[2] While Kāsyapa and his colleague were being welcomed to the Chinese capital, SS. Peter and Paul were being put to death in Rome. This is an illustration at once of the superiority of Chinese tolerance, and of the less revolutionary character of Buddhism as compared with Christianity. It seems to have supported the imperialism of the Han dynasty at least.

The Way is difficult, yet the pure in heart and single in
purpose can understand it, and it is a Way of joy and
power—the power of meekness, which is restful and pure.
By it ignorance is vanquished, lust is cast out, and freedom
attained. Let all be benevolent but avoid attachment,
which clouds the mind and dulls the keen edge of the
spirit. He who is bound to wife and child is more closely
a captive than he who lies manacled in prison. Better
be thrown to a tiger than submit to such bondage.

Here is the usual monastic teaching of Buddhism,
which even in so careful an apologia will out, and we cannot wonder that it met with opposition in a land of filial
piety like China. But, as if to disarm criticism, the
Sūtra goes on to suggest a sublimated family life; if the
monk meets women he is to treat the young as sisters or
daughters, the old as mothers.

There follows sane advice upon the discipline of mind
and body which should be as a well-tuned lute, and some
characteristic questions and answers as to the real nature
of the life of man; a passage of especial interest, no doubt,
to the Taoists. The Buddha asked his disciples: "What
is the life of man?" "It is the span allotted to him on
earth," said one; "Thou knowest not the Way," said the
Master. "It is the (energy of the) food we eat," said
another; "Nor thou," replied the Master. "It is the
sequence of many single moments," ventured a third.
"Thou," exclaimed the Master, "art not far from the
true Way!"

All this is typical Hīnayāna Buddhism, with perhaps
rather more emphasis on the Bodhisattva than on the Arhat
ideal; but there are two passages which suggest that the
compilers were looking toward a more developed doctrine
of the person of the Buddha, and which at a later date

helped to transform Buddhism in China from a way of
conduct to a way of devotion: "Rely not on thine own
will," and again, "You may be far from me, O my children! Keep my precepts and you will be as in my
Presence."

The two pioneers did not long survive their arrival at
the capital, but they left a tradition of sound scholarship
and earnest work, and their monastery of the White
Horse, Pai MaSsŭ, became the model for many of its
successors. "Toil on as the ox plods through deep mire,
his eyes fixed on the goal that lies ahead"; in these words
of their Sūtra we may find perhaps an echo of their resolute
endeavor, and their fitting epitaph.

Seventy years went by before a second mission arrived
to carry on their work. In 148 A.D. came the "Parthian
Prince," Anshikao, whose birth and education had fitted
him to develop the work of adaptation they had begun,
and who for twenty-two years toiled in Loyāng at the task
of translation.[1] No less than one hundred and seventy-
six works are attributed to him, of which fifty-five remain,
the majority being translations of books of the Pāli canon,
but some being apparently independent works; and to
him is due the first introduction into China of the
Amitābha sects, which have run so victorious a course.

That the historic Sākyamuni survived and was not far
from his faithful disciple—such might be the pious inference from the *Sūtra of Forty-two Sayings;* that behind
him stood the Eternal Father—such was the explicit
doctrine of the *Amitāyur-dhyāna Sūtra* which Anshikao
and his Indo-Scythian colleague, Lokaraksha, known to
the Chinese as Leou Kia Tchang, now made accessible

---

[1] Meanwhile Antoninus Pius and M. Aurelius were ruling in Rome, Papias and
Polycarp were being martyred, and Justin Martyr was defending Christianity.

to them. It seems clear that from the first the masses of the people were not attracted by the monastic type of the new religion; in fact, four centuries passed before Chinese were admitted to the order, and the ideal of a family life in the Paradise of Amitābha Buddha (Omito Fō) attracted those whom the lonely peace of Nirvāna left cold. There was, moreover, as we have indicated, a strong and venerable theistic cult which perhaps predisposed the hearts and minds of the Chinese to Omito Fō; already for more than two thousand years the emperor had offered prayer and sacrifice for the nation on high places like Tai Shan to Shang Ti, whose name is used by Christian missionaries today as the name of God, and is universally revered in China.

With Omito Fō came another deity already familiar to us; known in India as Avalokitesvara he is beloved in China as Kwanyin or Koan-cheu-yinn, an attempt to translate his name, "the god who looks down or hears the cry of man." It is as Avalokitesvara that Amitābha comes to earth. Of these compassionate beings Anshikao had no doubt himself become a worshiper, and we may picture him as he turned in worship to the setting sun, filled with poignant memories of home and dear ones, whom he would one day meet in the Western Paradise. Did visions of Omito Fō come to him ? If so he is one of a great company in China of whom it is believed that their devotion has been rewarded by radiant manifestations of this Lord of Bliss; and at such places as Puto Shan the pilgrim still strives to see the Lady Kwanyin (for she is the most popular form of Avalokitesvara), shining in the spray of sea or waterfall. Nor has this cult lacked devotees among the sages; as early as the sixth century we find the great Indian scholar, Bodhiruci, who translated the *Amitāyus-Sutropadesa* into Chinese,[1] chiding a Taoist alchemist for his vain search for the elixir of life:

> How vain these prayers for five-score years
> Of such poor life as this!
> When Life is yours in endless stores
> Of Amitāyu's Bliss.

With these two missions at Loyāng begins the first great epoch of Chinese Buddhism—an epoch of translation lasting for four centuries, during which leaders from foreign lands were patiently educating a Chinese church and forming a Buddhist mind in China. That there was opposition is clear, for the Han period was strongly Confucian,[2] and a steady production of polemical and apologetic works went on, of which we may cite the defense of Buddhism, by Moutzu, a contemporary of the Christian apologists Tertullian and Clement of Alexandria, and a convert from Confucianism, who with considerable skill uses his knowledge of the three religions to show that the Buddhist doctrine of impermanence is truer than the Taoist attempts to prolong life, and that, on the other hand, the mere morality of Confucius is not enough, though it is a good basis of government. Buddhism faces the facts of life, yet offers a mystical satisfaction to the yearnings of the human heart. It is difficult and austere, yet by no means unnatural, as its critics aver.

That Buddhism sometimes descended to the miracle-mongering of the later Taoists is evidenced by the work of Fo-t'u-cheng, who had a vast number of disciples and is credited with the founding of nearly nine hundred monasteries, and whose pupil, Tao-an, was one of the leading Buddhist thinkers of the fourth century.

---

[1] *B.N.*, 1204.

[2] China has never ceased to be so, and in 555 A.D. an imperial edict enacted that every provincial city should have its Confucian temple.

At Loyāng also worked Ku Fā Hu or Dharmaraksha (266–313 A.D.), of Chinese Turkestan, translating many of the scriptures, among them two which have played a great part in the popularizing of Buddhism in China—the "Lotus of the Good Law"[1] and the *Ullambana Sūtra*. The "Lotus," with its glorified Sākyamuni and its note of universal salvation, was a gospel to satisfy the Chinese, and the *Ullambana Sūtra* gave a place within Buddhism to the Chinese veneration for the dead, providing masses and other ceremonies by which filial piety may further the well-being of the departed. Here was a triumphant answer to Confucian and other critics: "You neglect filial piety" was their charge; "On the contrary," the Buddhist could now reply, "we practice it even beyond the grave." Modern China spends millions yearly on masses for the dead, and it is a common sight to see some layman kneeling devoutly before the abbot of a great monastic house while services on behalf of his dead are intoned by choirs of monks.

In the tantric and some other sects the Buddhist pantheon is classified as guardians of the soul, each having his appointed period of service, and there are regular festivals of the dead, such as the Bon Matsuri of midsummer, so well known to visitors to Japan. In all Buddhist countries the pre-Buddhist animism has been blended in such ways with the cult, and indeed with the philosophy, of the new faith. In the *Ullambana Sūtra* it is recorded that the great Moggallāna, having attained the celestial eye of the Arhat, used it to investigate the present condition of his dead parents. Seeing his mother toiling at some penitential task in the dim underworld, he asked the Master how he could help her. The reply was unhesitating:

---

[1] Chinese *Kan fa hwa kin*. See *B.N.*, 138.

Nothing can help thy parents, except my monks. They only can work on her behalf. This must thou do. On the fifteenth day of the seventh month go offer a rich gift of food and drink, of garments and other choice offerings to the Brethern. They are a field of merit, in which if thou sowest thou shalt reap a rich harvest, and shalt help thy dead even to the seventh generation.

This is true to the earliest Buddhist teaching; why weep for the dead when you can help them in such a practical way ?

> What boots for them your wailing and your tears ?
> Mourning ye do but plough the desert sand!
> But offerings to the Brethren surely bring
> Rich harvests to the hungry Spirit-land.
>
> For there's no farming in the Spirit-world,
> No tilth, nor herds nor any merchandise;
> Alms of the faithful are their only hope:
> Your charity alone the under-world supplies.[1]

So teaches the Buddha, or his monkish chronicler,[2] and perhaps the finest flower of this devotion is seen on the sacred mountain Kōyasan, where stands a monument to all who fell in the war with Korea, friend and foe alike. He who would understand the spirit of the East will not pass lightly over these inveterate beliefs, but may, if he will, learn here some lessons which will enrich life:

> One long deep breath, a sigh from sleeping earth,
> As though in troubled dreams her spirit stirred,
> And all is still. No call of wakeful bird,
> No lift of leaf on trembling wave of air,
> But soulful silence brooding everywhere;
> The stars are veiled, and from their heights are heard
> The noiseless sweep of spirit forces, stirred
> As at the moment of some wondrous birth.

[1] From *The Heart of Buddhism*.

[2] It is interesting to note that offerings to the dead were prohibited in the Deuteronomic reforms in Israel, and that the priests there too benefited by the practice!

Before each household shrine the candle gleams;
The food is spread for guests that come unseen;
And human faith in simple ways is fed.
The air is filled with lucent, mystic beams;
They come indeed, the loved and lost, I ween;
And human hearts by lowly ways to God are led.[1]

Such are the beliefs and practices, childlike perhaps, yet sprung from deep roots of human love, which express themselves most finely in the Bodhisattva; if merit is "reversible," let me turn it over to all who need it. Such is the resolution of the Bodhisattvas:

May these, our deeds of merit, all
The universe of life pervade:
And may we soon to Bodhi win
And with us take the souls we aid.

Here then at Loyāng by the end of the third century A.D. Buddhism was proving its power to appeal to the masses as well as to the philosopher. With the fall of the great Han dynasty its center now shifts to the capital of the eastern Chins, Chang-ān, where for a hundred years it basked in the favor of the court, until the Tartar invasion drove it south to Shien-yeh, now called Nanking.

Situated on the Waiho River, a tributary of the Hoang-ho, Chang-ān[2] was a wonderful center of intellectual and artistic life. Here six great trade roads converged, thronged then as they are today with an endless and varied stream of traffic. And with the caravans came a steady succession of Buddhist missionaries. As a prisoner from Kharakar came Kumārajiva, in 383, a man of loose life but of profound scholarship, who had been converted from the Theravāda to the Mahāyāna; and we read of

[1] Translated by Dr. Lombard, quoted in *The Faith of Japan* by T. Harada.
[2] Later called Singan-fu.

embassies from Persia, of Zoroastrians, and of Manichees, all mingling in the great city. Here later came Nestorian missionaries and received a cordial welcome as teachers of a doctrine at once "pacific, mysterious, and free from verbosity," until soon the land was filled with their "Temples of Joy" and it seemed as if a new international bond were to link China with India and the West. In the seventh century also flourished Shan-tao, leader of the Amitābha sects, and he and the Nestorians had much in common. The place and the era alike favored the exchange of ideas. Now in the fourth century began the travels of the Chinese pilgrims to India. While Kumārajiva was settling at Chang-ān, Fā-Hian (399–413 A.D.), first of Chinese Buddhist pilgrims, was making his famous journey to India, and his *Record of the Buddha Land* is a priceless document,[1] and tells of great intellectual activity in Buddhist India and Ceylon. In the Far West Augustine, Chrysostom, and Jerome were doing yeoman service to Christianity. East and West alike, this was an age of devotion as well as of acute speculative thought, and now perhaps for the first time, with Taōan in the south and Kumārajiva and his colleagues at Chang-ān, Buddhist philosophy won for itself a firm hold upon the thinkers of China. So excellent too was their rendering of the Sanskrit texts into Chinese that their works are still read as models of classical expression. Kumārajiva gave special attention to Asvaghośa and Nāgārjuna, whose biographies he translated, and of the philosophical works he made available to the Chinese we may select three whose influence has been immense. First may be mentioned Nāgārjuna's *Commentary on the Avatamsaka*

[1] *B.N.*, 1496; *Fo-Kwo-Ki*, French translation by A. Rémusat (1836), English by S. Beal (1869), H. A. Giles (1877), J. Legge (1886), and T. Watters (1918).

Sūtra (*Hua Yen*)[1] which has molded the philosophic thought, and the *Fan-Wan-King*,[2] or "Net of Brahmā," which has guided the monastic life of China, Korea, and Japan. The latter is rather strangely called by De Groot, "the most important of the sacred books of the East," and "the principal instrument of the great Buddhist art of salvation." It opens with an apocalyptic vision of the usual Mahāyāna type: Seated at the heart of a gigantic lotus is Roshana, a Buddha whose colossal (and very ugly) image is familiar to visitors to Nāra, but who plays a minor part in the religion. The lotus on which he is enthroned has a thousand petals, each of them a world, and about the central figure throng the Bodhisattvas of the universe, to whom he preaches the high and difficult way of renunciation, patience, zeal, joyous endeavor, meditation, and enthusiasm for the welfare of the world. Let them press forward to the high peaks of achievement, and they will arrive, albeit by steep ways, at the goal of Nirvāna. All the worlds are, as it were, beads upon the great net of Brahmā, who as Creator has set them in their appointed station. At this point appears Sākyamuni, returning from a visit to Siva, the destroyer of the Hindu pantheon, and declares that he is in communion with the gods as well as with the Buddhas, claiming that authority is given to him in this age, as it was to Roshana in the past, and that the rules and regulations have now been made more detailed and precise. He then sets forth the forty-eight rules of Mahāyāna, and declares that the Hīnayāna is a slow and tedious path, and that it is possible by obedience to become without delay a Bodhisattva or even a Buddha. This is, of course, orthodox Mahāyāna doctrine, but the situation is made piquant

[1] *B.N.*, 1180.   [2] *Ibid.*, 1087.

by putting it into the mouth of Sākyamuni himself, who, as Father Wieger says, "is made to anathematize his own teachings, and to recommend things to which he had given never a thought."[1] Here clearly Hinduism has begun the peaceful penetration of Buddhism, and it is not surprising to find this amazing book, like the Chinese version of the "Lotus," go on to prescribe the cruel branding of the scalp which is still largely practiced in China—though tapas, or austerity of this sort, is condemned, with murder and butchery, by the Founder. Here, however, we find the usual admirable exhortations to benevolence toward all living things; but the motive is more Hindu than Buddhist. "Are they not all bound up in the one great bundle of life, in the meshes of the net of Brahmā?" "All," said Gotama, "are your kindred and your fellow-pilgrims"; "All," adds the *Fan-Wan-King*, "are children of the same creative Power."

Side by side with this rather popular theology Kumārajiva gave to the Chinese the doctrine of the Void, translating the *Satyasiddhi Sāstra*[2] of Harivarman (of whom we know only from Chinese sources), and his translation is known to the Chinese as the *Khang-shih-lun*. It is a text of the Sautrāntikas, and deals with the nature of the self, maintaining that there are two kinds of "emptiness" which can be predicated of it. It is empty as a basket is empty, it is also unreal or empty as the withes or strands of the basket are empty—an illustration which cannot be said to add very much to our enlightenment! But fortunately we are already familiar with this idea, that because the self is compound it is unreal, and because the elements which make up the self are compound

---

[1] *Histoire des Croyances Religieuses et des Opinions Philosophiques en Chine*, p. 450.
[2] *B.N.*, 1274.

they too have no reality. Yet the Buddha speaks of the "I," and of the rewards of virtue; if there is no self to be rewarded, why persevere in contemplation and self-sacrifice? The wise will give up philosophy, and be content to leave the dilemma unsolved. So ends the *Satya-siddhi Sastra*, on a note of faith or suspended judgment. Not so the great Nāgā-juna, whose transcendentalism Kumārajiva now proceeded to give to China in the *Three Sastras*, the authoritative scriptures of the San-Lun sect.

With the coming of this Indian scholar then and the rapid multiplication of the scriptures, Chinese Buddhism enters upon a complex stage; a catalogue published in 518 A.D. mentions over 2,000 volumes, and one two centuries later contains 2,278 works in over 7,000 volumes; and, as we have noted, the books do not all agree. Can they be reconciled? What is the essence of the matter? How is it to be made available to ordinary folk? To these questions significant answers were given by three great schools: that of the Indian Bodhidharma in 520,[1] that of Chi-i a little later, and that of the Mantra school in the eighth century. They have made Chinese Buddhism the complex and comprehensive thing that it is today.

The first of these schools was introduced, or at least popularized, in the neighborhood of Loyāng by Bodhidharma, or P'utiTamo, a prince of South India, who was the twenty-eighth patriarch of the Sangha. While the Chinese lay-pilgrim, Sungyün,[2] was visiting Udyana and Kandahar, Bodhidharma, disgusted perhaps at the course of things in his own land, where Buddhism was becoming

---

[1] "One account has it that at the beginning of the sixth century the number of Indian refuges (*sic*) in China was more than 6,000."—A. K. Reischauer.

[2] Translations of his *Travels* into English by S. Beal (1869), into German by Neumann (1833), into French by Chavannes (1903).

BODHIDHARMA

(A portrait of the Zen School)

a tantric Hindu cult, came by the sea-route to Ningpo. He was a picturesque figure, and has laid a strong hold upon the Chinese mind, influencing such original thinkers as Tsung Mi (eighth century) and Wang Yang Ming (1472–1529). His swarthy, bearded face, staring eyes, and gnarled limbs are a popular motive in Japanese art, from the kakemono of temple and teahouse to the sword-hilt of the Samurai; and he is still the beau ideal, if the paradox be allowed, of every monk in China! In Korea I felt that I was really making progress when I was greeted as a "Tamo" from the West!

A Japanese disciple says of Tamo:

He was, however, not a missionary to be favourably received by the public . . . . entirely different in every point from a popular missionary of our age. The latter would smile or try to smile at every face he happened to see, and would talk sociably: the former would not smile at any face, but would stare at it with huge glaring eyes that pierced to the innermost soul. The latter would keep himself scrupulously clean, shaving, combing, brushing, polishing, oiling, perfuming; whilst the former would be entirely indifferent as to his apparel, being always clothed in a faded yellow robe. The latter would compose his sermons with great care, making use of rhetorical art, and speak with force and elegance, while the former would sit silent as a bear, and kick off any who approached him with idle questions.[1]

We might perhaps more fitly contrast Tamo with Columba, his great contemporary in the Far West, "from whose gentle nest at Iona the doves of peace and good will were soon to wing their flight to all regions," or, indeed, with the gentle Punna and Mahinda and other pioneers of the Sangha.

Yet Tamo was not less devoted, and his influence to this day is in many ways unique. His Master, Gotama, embracing poverty, writing no book and trusting in no

[1] K. Nukariya, *The Religion of the Samurai*, pp. 5-6.

organization, has won the enthusiastic admiration of mankind; Tamo without speaking, except to be rude, has laid a strange spell upon the East. It captured first the Emperor Wu-ti at his capital K'ien-K'ang. Receiving the strange traveler with courtesy, he began to tell of the service he had rendered to the Faith: "We have built temples, multiplied the Scriptures, encouraged many to join the Order: is there not much merit in all this?" "None," was the blunt reply. "But what say the Holy Books—do they not promise rewards for such deeds?" "All is void. There is nothing holy." "But—you yourself—are you not one of the holy ones?" "I don't know." "Who then are you?" "I don't know."

"The elephant can hardly keep company with rabbits," says Mr. Nukariya. And indeed the books are full of exhortation to the wise to wander lonely as the elephant, and Tamo was of the Arhat rather than the Bodhisattva type; but the Emperor Wu-ti was no rabbit,[1] and there is surely more than mere rudeness in Tamo's reply. First he tried to show that merit and truth are within, as Mr. Nukariya has so clearly and forcibly argued, then he goes on to prepare his pupil for the doctrines of anattā and anicca. Unless we are ourselves enlightened, observances and the scriptures themselves are of no avail; and the first step in enlightenment is to realize the unreality of the "ego and of the world." "To seek aught outside thine own heart and mind is to grasp the air. Prayers, alms, learning, zeal, what good are they? All are unreal."

That this is the meaning of Tamo's reply to the emperor seems clear from another very popular story of him. A Confucian inquirer[2] came to him, and stood silent before

---

[1] Already a staunch Buddhist he later persisted in taking the vows of a monk.

[2] Shang Kwang or Eka, who succeeded Tamo as second patriarch in China.

him; the sage took no notice and so a week went by, until the seeker, as his tears dropped frozen on his breast, to prove his sincerity drew his sword and cut off an arm. "Well, what is it ?" "Master, my soul is sore troubled. Help me pacify it." "Where is it ?" "I cannot find it, though I have sought it earnestly for years." "There, I have pacified it for you," said the sage, and a flash of intuition revealed to the seeker, faint though he was with loss of blood, the truth discovered by Gotama and forgotten by the masses of his followers. Tamo came to call them back to orthodoxy, and the effect of his teaching, or absence of teaching, was profound: "It was the introduction, not of the dead Scriptures . . . . but of a living faith; not of any theoretical doctrine but of practical enlightenment, not of the idea of Buddha but of the spirit of Sākyamuni."[1]

Yet the Buddhism of Tamo was different indeed from the Buddhism of Gotama, and has been called a kind of Vedānta. It finds a cosmic significance in the Buddha-nature, immanent in all men and things. If there is no ātman the Atman is Reality itself; it is the sole reality, and gives a meaning to the world, and to men an understanding of its true nature. By intuitive rather than discursive reason man grasps this truth, and it can only be imparted from mind to mind and from heart to heart by intuition. So it has come down in unbroken succession from Sākyamuni to all the patriarchs, of whom Kāsyapa was first, Ānanda second, Parsva tenth, Asvaghośa twelfth, Nāgārjuna fourteenth, Vasubandhu twenty-first, and Bodhidharma twenty-eighth—to name only those of supreme eminence. The school relates the story of

---

[1] Nukariya, *op. cit.*, p. 5. Yet the Chan school bases itself on the *Prajñāpāramitā* books and makes much of the *Lankāvatāra Sūtra*, which emphasizes the inner light.

Kāsyapa's appointment: Master and disciples were seated on the Vulture Peak, when the god Brahmā drew near and offered a flower to the Blessed One, requesting him to preach the Law. He kept silence, and while all looked expectant, Kāsyapa alone smiled in understanding. Are not the greatest things ineffable ? So began an apostolic succession of which every name is treasured in a school that lays little stress on the scriptures, and therefore must vindicate the authority of its verbal teachings. That of Tamo is accepted by all, and from his day the patriarchate descended to his Chinese followers.

A discourse purporting to be that of Tamo at the court of Wu-ti has been translated into French by Father Wieger,[1] and though it is most unlikely that he ever delivered so full and rounded an exposition of his doctrine, and quite doubtful if he knew Chinese, it is worth study as a summary of the Dhyāna teaching. It says:

> The heart is Buddha. Outside of it there is no reality. Apart from thought all is unreal. There is neither cause nor effect apart from the mind and heart. Nirvāna itself is a state of heart. See in thyself the true Buddha-nature, know that thou art Buddha, and canst not sin. There is neither good nor bad, but only the heart, and this is Buddha and impeccable. . . . . One sin only is there, to ignore thine own Buddhahood. . . . . This ignorance it is which makes the wheel of transmigration to rotate: it is enlightenment which destroys the power of Karma. The enlightened can neither sin nor be reborn. O heart of man, so great that thou canst embrace the world, so little that thou canst not be touched by a needle's point—thou art Buddha. That is my word to China.

It might be Vivekananda or any other Vedāntist speaking, and it is possible to hold with Father Wieger that Tamo was asked to leave by the Buddhists of South

---

[1] *Tamo Hsu Molun, op. cit.*, p. 520. It is not known, I am told by Mr. R. F. Johnston, to most Chinese scholars, though it is included in a supplement to the Chinese *Tripitaka*.

India; but those who could digest the tantric vagaries of a few decades later were not squeamish, and this Dhyāna teaching accords well enough with Mahāyāna pantheism, on the one hand, and with the mysticism of the Founder, on the other, while the emphasis on enlightenment and of contemplation, as the way to it, is a clarion call to the pietist to "leave this chanting and singing and telling of beads," and to return to the rock from which he was hewn.

The odious teaching, however, that good and evil are alike, is not Sākyamuni's, nor is it probable that Tamo pressed his pantheism to this conclusion. His followers, even where they have held this strange view, have done much to ennoble Chinese and Japanese life by attuning the mind to Nature in her loveliest moods, and have blent the quietism of India with the poetic intuitionism of Southern China, until a Japanese authority can say with conviction: "There is hardly a form of thought or a duty that Zen has not touched and inspired with its ideal of simple beauty."[1] In the first place, by its pantheism, which finds the Buddha-nature in all things, it brought religion into all life:

> The golden light upon the sunkist peaks,
> The water murmuring in the pebbly creeks,
> Are Buddha. In the stillness, hark, he speaks!

This poetic quietism has laid its spell for more than two thousand years upon world-weary men and women; seeking the mountain-tops they have since the time of the Founder possessed their souls amid the beauties of Nature. But the Dhyāna school has appealed also to soldier and statesman in the midst of strenuous days. What has been its secret ? In the first place, it has developed a joy in

[1] M. Anesaki, *Buddhist Art*, p. 54. Zen is the Japanese form of Chan; both = dhyāna.

simple things, and has helped them to retreat, for a time
at least, into a quiet kingdom of the mind, and to be free
from life's trammels:

> Unanchored, riding free
>   On the still clear waters, see
> In the calm cool air of night
>   Doth float
>   A tiny boat,
> All bathed in silver light.

Here, as it were in a cameo, is crystallized the coolness of
the enlightened mind, calm and serene; like the moonlight
beautifying all it touches; free as the little boat that
rides unanchored on the waves.

Here was a genuine religious experience, an intuition
of the unity of all things and often of the presence of the
Buddha.   There are many stories of sages of this school
converted or enlightened by the croaking of a frog in the
silence, the ripple of a stream, or the fall of autumn
leaves.   In all these the Buddha-nature is immanent:

> A score of years I looked for Light;
>   Passed many a Spring and Fall;
> But since the peach-bloom came in sight
>   I nothing doubt at all.

We find blending in these lovers of Nature something
of the delicacy of the blossom and the ruggedness of the
mountain.   With poetical insight went a Spartan simplicity and an ascetic rigor of life, and in their hymns there
is nothing of the somewhat effeminate pietism of the
Amitābha schools.   They are thinkers imbued with an
idealism which transfigures Nature, and to them images
and scriptures are alike unnecessary; Nature is at once
their scripture and the embodiment of their God.   We
read, in fact, of sages of this school warming themselves

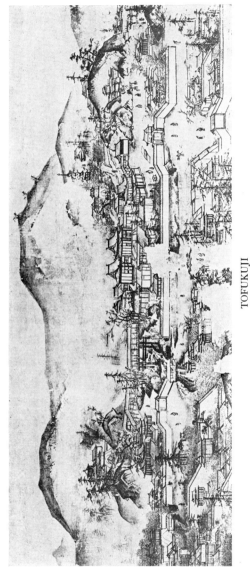

TOFUKUJI

(A temple of the Zen Sect, Kyoto, built in 1236 A.D.)

at a fire made of a wooden image of Buddha, or giving
away the halo of a golden one to feed the poor.

> I have a Buddha image, aye
>   Though people see it not!
> Not made of cloth or clay,
>   Nor carved in wood, I wot.
> 'Tis not by artist drawn,
>   No thief it steals;
> One from Time's very dawn
>   Itself reveals
> In myriad form
> This Buddha norm.[1]

From their quietism too and counteracting the danger of
their pantheism, they drew moral inspiration, for they
read Nature in the light of Buddha's teaching.

> Ye who seek for purity and peace go to Nature. She will give you
> more than ye ask. Ye who long for strength and perseverance go to
> Nature. She will train and strengthen you. Ye who aspire after
> an ideal go to Nature. She will help you in its realization. Ye who
> yearn after enlightenment go to Nature. She will never fail to grant
> your request.[2]

For man and Nature are alike filled with the same
universal spirit: "Unchanging and pure, eternally bright
and clear is the Tathāgatagarbha," says Tsung Mī of
Kwei Fêng.

To be in unity with Nature is to be in tune with Eternal
Truth. Why, then, are so many folk foolish and perverse?
They are like the drunkard who ignores the precious gems
which he has in his own pocket. Drunk with egoism, they
forget the true nature of the "ego," which is Buddhahood:

> Within me dwells my "self";
> Yet ere this little "I" awoke,
> Came the free Buddha-self
> And dwelt within.[3]

---

[1] From the *Zen-gaku-hō-ten:* "Religion of the Samurai," p. 93.
[2] K. Nukariya, *op. cit.*, p. 74.   [3] From an anonymous Japanese poem.

They are like the prodigal son of the "Lotus," who deserts his own rich heritage and goes to dwell in a far country; but at any moment they may "come to themselves," to find a larger self than they had dreamed of, "the eternal Buddha-mind, which makes them one with nature and mankind."

The school is neither absolutely idealistic nor absolutely nihilistic. For if the mind be unreal, who is it who knows that the world of phenomena is unreal ? And if they be unreal what causes them to appear ?

We are witnesses that there is no one of the fleeting and unreal things of earth but is made to appear by something real. If there be no real ocean, how can there be the transient and unreal waves ? If there be no real mirror, how can there be images unreal and transient reflected in it ? If the dream be unreal, does it not at least imply a dreamer ?[1]

So argues this school against the nihilists.

The Chan school, in fact, teaches a pantheistic realism, and on this basis builds its systematic mind-training. By careful practice the mind may be purified alike from destruction and from lust and egoism, and in this lies the secret of bodily as well as mental health. Being asked the secret of his own amazing vitality at the age of one hundred, an eighteenth-century master of this school replied: "Keep your mind and body pure for fourteen days, and I will tell you the secret." This injunction he repeated until he felt that the time had come to whisper in the inquirer's ear: "That is the secret. Keep free from passion. Keep that rule even at the cost of life."

There is something whimsical in the school, derived no doubt from the quaint figure and methods of Tamo himself, which has endeared it especially to the Japanese,

[1] *Yuen Jan Lun*, or *Gen-Nin-Ron*, of Kwei-Fêng Tsung Mi, refuting the nihilism of the *Mādhyamika Sāstra*.

who never weary of stories illustrating the unorthodox manners of the Zen masters; they test the spiritual progress of their pupils by a sudden blow or an insult, and the sincerity of an inquirer by some gross bit of rudeness. Samurai, gathered about the camp fire, would love to tell of Tokiyori, who, having invited a Zen master to visit him, and having welcomed him with charming courtesy and an elegant poem, received in reply only a stunning blow; yet, equal to the occasion, replied with a smile: "Your blessing, O Master, makes my whole body thrill and tingle with joy!" And as they prepared to die on the field of battle, they would compose terse and charming poems which often express with a simple elegance the ideals of Zen. Of this tradition the latest and most notable exponent is the late General Nogi, who met the news of the death of his two sons with calm resignation, and immediately composed a poem in their honor; and who not long afterward sought his own death with the same stoical detachment.

Of the more intricate things of the mind-culture of this school it must suffice to note the system of Ko-ans which are its unique feature: dark sayings or paradoxes, by which the mind, puzzled at first, learns to desert the ordinary processes of thought, to acquire a new point of view, and to develop its powers of intuition.[1] In an exquisite room in the midst of a peaceful courtyard where no sound entered except the murmur of the brook, I consulted a Zen abbot as to how one might set about practicing the mind-culture of the school. "No one can help you," was his reply, "You must find enlightenment yourself." This is, of course, the answer I expected. The Mystic cannot explain. As a Chinese textbook of the

---

[1] The answer to these Ko-ans must be given in a word, which adds to their difficulty.

school says: "Only he who has tasted salt knows what salt tastes like. If you want to know, taste! . . . . There is a teaching which cannot be taught." . . . . As Lao-tze used to teach, "The Tao that can be tao-ed is not the true Tao." And not unlike this phase of Buddhist mysticism is the great saying of a Christian contemporary of Tamo: "By love He may be gotten; by thought of understanding, never." But the abbot went on to give me one of the first of the Ko-ans: "Listen," he said, "for the sound of a single hand";[1] and when I smiled, "You had better go," he said, "to one of the simpler and more popular sects." I felt, be it confessed, that the abbot was true to type, and entered into the feelings of many an inquirer who has received a shrewd blow in return for his importunity.

Another such elementary Ko-an is the question, "What is your original face, even before you were born?" and like all such questions it aims at "laying the axe to the root of our everyday experience in order to build up a new order of things on the basis of Zen," as D. T. Suzuki expresses it. Other Ko-ans are in the form of anecdotes of Zen masters, whose replies to inquirers are unintelligible to the ordinary mind. In answer to the question, "Why did Tamo leave India and come to China?" the Master Joshu (778–897) replied, "The cypress tree in the courtyard," which served also as his statement of the ultimate principle in Buddhism! When asked "Has the dog Buddha-nature?" "Non-existent," was his answer. Similarly, Tungshan (806–69) being asked, "Who is the Buddha?" answered, "A pound of flax." If we attempt

---

[1] This famous Ko-an is attributed to Hakuin (1685–1768). When it has been mastered it is followed by another: "Hark to the sound of a single hand on Mount Fujiyama"; and a third: "If you are dead and without form, produce the sound of a single hand."

to rationalize these statements, we receive another slap! "Under no circumstances," says Dr. Suzuki, "ought Zen to be confounded with philosophy." Abandon logic and reasoning, let intuition have free play, all ye who would enter its quiet haunts, for consciousness is clogged with the rubbish of our daily life, until the Zen physician has given us his drastic purgatives; then only is the subconscious free to send up its truth.

Such is the system as practiced in Japan, and though Chinese Chan Buddhism has not so fully developed the system of Ko-an or Kung-ang, yet its followers are trained by these and by Zazen—systematic contemplation and reverie, in which while many need to remember the word of Sākyamuni, "Torpor is not the same as Aryan silence," yet there are some who soar on the wings of intuitive insight to Truth, and to such many miracles are attributed. Like Tamo they can walk upon the waves and "know all mysteries."

Tamo then stood for a Buddhism simplified, mystical, and austere.[1] His younger contemporary and pupil, Chi-Kai or Chi-i, attempted the more difficult task of harmonizing the complex elements, devotional and philosophical, which Tamo rejected.

In the province of Chekiang is the beautiful range of T'ien-t'ai, and here in the latter part of the sixth century Chi-i studied and travailed to bring forth a new and comprehensive Buddhism, subordinating philosophy to devotion, yet giving it due recognition. He was indeed a mighty thinker, whose masterly if arbitrary genius brought order out of the chaos of the schools.[2]

---

[1] It is noteworthy that his school, while it failed to win the less poetic north, established itself firmly in the south of China, where it gave rise to five subsects in the eighth century.

[2] For his works see *B.N.*, 1510, and twenty-one others.

As we have seen, their philosophical teachings ranged from a naïve realism to an absolute nihilism, and it is the glory of the T'ien-t'ai school that it reconciled in a Middle Path the imperious demands at once of common sense and of idealistic thought. It is true that the knowledge we have is colored by our mind, yet the phenomenal world is real, for immanent in it is the tathatā, or Absolute. Here is a pantheistic realism, in which both relative and Absolute are parts of an eternal process, and causally related. The relative is at once identical with and different from the Absolute, which is self-dependent.

Here Chi-i is blending the idealism of "the Awakening" and of the Mādhyamaka of Nāgārjuna, whom he regarded as his Master, with the devotional teaching of the "Lotus," that all have inherent in them the Buddha-nature. He seized on this identification of the Bodhi with cosmic truth, and worked it out as a systematic and devotional creed.

Though the Absolute is unknowable, yet it is attainable in meditation, and is the underlying reality, or Dhammatā, which alone gives meaning to this empty world. The historical Buddha is the embodiment of this universal Reality which, though it is eternal, is dependent upon them for its realization: "The Truth (tathā) is a mere abstraction, a dead name, unless there appears a tathāgata in concrete human life."[1]

Thus the historical Buddha is the adaptation of the Eternal Truth to human needs, and in him is represented the trikāya. Chi-i now drew out what is implicit in the "Lotus," and argued that there is in all men a corresponding triune nature; for each is a "son of man" in whom the universal truth is particularized, and in whom

[1] M. Anesaki, *Nichiren*, p. 151.

there is a glorified body representing the spiritual influence which passes out from him. So too with all sentient beings, from demons tormented by their own vices to Buddhas who by their virtues lead many to Truth, in all is this threefold nature inherent.

In addition to the "Lotus," Chi-i makes much of the *Nirvāna Sūtra,* and of the *Prajñāpāramitā Sāstra,*[1] seeking by an ingenious but quite fanciful division of the life of the Founder into five periods to account for their diversities of doctrine. It is one thing to hold that there was some development of doctrine during the Founder's own lifetime, and quite another to follow the ingenious harmonist as he works out his "Five Periods," and it is interesting to discover a Japanese higher critic, Tominaga, as early as 1744 pointing out the arbitrariness of the arrangement.

The first period was a few weeks after the enlightenment, when the Buddha was busy instructing gods and a limited circle of other celestial beings, who alone could understand him. The *Avatamsaka Sūtra* contains these teachings and this is the name given to this period.[2]

Next came a time of accommodation to human needs, which lasted twelve years, during which the Hīnayāna teachings were given. It is known as the Āgama period.

The Vaipulya is a period of eight years, when men had grown in the Faith and were ready for the Bodhisattva in place of the Arhat ideal.

Then to reconcile these Mahāyāna doctrines with those of the Āgamas, the wise Teacher spent twenty-two

---

[1] Many of the schools select three scriptures from the vast Library of the Mahāyāna; e.g., the T'ien-t'ai chooses these three, the San Lun chooses the three chief works of Nāgārjuna, the Paradise schools the three Amitābha books.

[2] This Sūtra is certainly not milk for babes; it contains, however, valuable metaphysical statements of the One who alone is himself undifferentiated, yet dwelling in all and working in all to bring them to Nirvāna.

years, the Prajñāpāramitā period, arguing that there is no real gulf between them; they are stages of one journey.

Lastly, in the fulness of time, when he was seventy-two years old, he revealed the sublime truth that all may attain Buddhahood. This period lasted eight years and its doctrine is to be found in the "Lotus," and *Mahāpāri-nirvāna Sūtras*.[1] With its completion the Teacher's work was done and he was free to enter Nirvāna.

As to its moral teachings, T'ien-t'ai Buddhism is not so original. Chi-i wrote a commentary on the Bodhisattva, and accepted the usual moral system of Mahāyāna, but to the twin foundation-stones of Prajñā, wisdom, and Dhyāna, meditation, he gave a new connotation. The true wisdom is to realize that passion is itself enlightenment, and that Samsāra is itself Nirvāna; to meditate on this is the fruit of meditation on the "Three Truths," that all is empty and the world unreal, that the dharmas of the phenomenal world are real because they are a manifestation in time of the Eternal, and that they are neither real nor unreal, for being conditioned they are real and yet unreal in the sense that their existence is empty of real worth and meaning. So by the Middle Path Chi-i follows Nāgārjuna, only to arrive at the same barren paradox of the pantheist that good and evil, transmigration and its end, passion and enlightenment, are identical; all are real because all are manifestations of the universal life, and only real when so viewed *sub specie aeternitatis*. It is to the credit of Chi-i that he refused to take a step which some of his followers took, and to go on to obliterate all moral distinctions. Indeed, though he did not make sīla, morality, fundamental, yet he laid great stress upon it.

[1] *B.N.*, 113. To be distinguished from the famous Pāli scripture of the same name.

As to the method of progress toward enlightenment there are six stages: (1) Men are ignorant of the "Three Truths"; (2) they know them, but do not meditate upon them; (3) they begin to meditate upon them; (4) they attain to insight, but their passions are not subdued; (5) they reach a negative illumination by destruction of ignorance; (6) they reach full and positive illumination by grasping the doctrine of the Middle Path.

So only are they distinguished from the other dharmas, of which Chi-i enumerates three thousand. All contain the Buddha-nature; it is only enlightened men of this sixth stage who realize it, and claim it for themselves. In them only does cosmic truth come to self-consciousness. But as it is embodied in each it is present in its fulness in a single thought, and even a hungry spirit in hell has in his every thought the full three thousand dharmas of the universe.

Such is the system of Chi-i, which in its view of the Absolute coming after a long process of evolution to self-consciousness, anticipates Hegel, and is saner in maintaining that it is only enlightened human nature as seen in the Buddhas, which can be regarded as the true revelation of the Eternal.

Is this Tathatā personal? "Such terms," Chi-i would answer, "are all relative; words limited by our human experience cannot describe the Absolute." But, like Kant, he would distinguish between the practical and the pure reason, and leave the devotee free to conceive of his Supreme as personal. And the two great scriptures of T'ien-t'ai speak in such language: "All living beings are my children," says the "Lotus," "I alone can save them." "The love of the Buddha," says the *Nirvāna Sūtra*, "is equable towards all. But as a father, though he has

seven children yearns over one that is sick, so doth the
Buddha hover about those who are in sin."

Just as Gotama taught of a Karma so exact and just
as to seem like a Providence, so the later schoolmen of
the Mahāyāna, themselves not anthropomorphic in their
thinking of the Eternal, speak of the loving heart, the
supreme wisdom, and even the eternal fatherhood of the
Dharmakāya.

Immanent in the world of things and in the mind of
man, the Dharmakāya is yet transcendent, greater even
than the revelation of himself manifested in the Buddhas.

In 597, as Augustine was setting up the standard of
the Cross at Canterbury, died Chi-i, mystic philosopher,
harmonist, may we not say theologian, on his beloved
mountain, and left about a score of works to carry on his
teachings. His posthumous name is Chih-che-ta-shih
"the great wise teacher," and his influence has been
great indeed. His three most important works are a
commentary on the "Lotus," an introduction to it, and a
work on meditation and knowledge.[1]

An important factor in the building up of the Buddhist
pantheon was the deliberate attempt of certain Hinduized
Buddhists to make it available to the masses. Neither
the intuitionism of Tamo nor the comprehensive and difficult system of Chi-i could expect to win the allegiance
of the many, and there is ample evidence to show that
they did not seek it; theirs was a monastic Mahāyāna.
In this, at any rate, it was true to type. But in South
India Bodhidharma must have met the degenerate popular
cult of a Buddhism that was paying the price of compromise, and by permitting the worship of Hindu deities was
losing its soul. It may well be for this reason that he

[1] B.N., 1534, 1536, 1538.

left his own land and went to China, though some critics
hold that he was driven out by the orthodox because he
was himself becoming too much of a Vedāntist!

However this may be, the Yogācāra school of Asanga
seems to have opened the door to other Hindu practices,
until almost all that distinguishes Buddhism from Saivite
Hinduism was sacrificed.   The men responsible for introducing this mongrel cult to China were Subhakāra,
Vajrabodhi, and Amogha, all from Southern India.[1]   But
the way had been paved by the magical practices of
Taoism, by the teachings of part of the "Lotus" itself,[2]
by a treatise of Asanga translated in the sixth century,
and negatively by the failure of Confucian ethics and
Buddhist philosophy to satisfy the religious needs of
the masses.   We must not take too dark a view of this
Mantra school.   It has done much for art,[3] and if its
pantheism has, on the one hand, lent itself to sensuality,
it has, on the other, kept alive the sense of a Divine Order
penetrating and animating the world.   It has in it something of a cosmotheistic idealism, seeing all things as a
sacrament.

Some of the new deities, too, were worthy of a place
in the devotion of this heart-hungry people.   Vairochana,
for instance, was identified with the Sun, who has long
held an honored place in the "Naturism" of China;
and now he begins to compete with Omito Fō for the
presidency among the gods.   His mūdra (gesture)—the
fingers of one hand encircling the index finger of the

---

[1] Vajrabodhi came to China in 719, and his nephew, Amoghavajra, in 746.

[2] E.g., chap xxi of the version of Kumārajiva teaches the use of magic spells.

[3] As Dr. Anesaki has shown, this school is noted at once for its "delicate painting
and vigorous sculpture" (*Buddhist Art*, p. 36).   The art of the Heian period of Japan
(800–1100 A.D.) is characterized by a unique sense of intimate communion with the
gods, by a remarkable symbolism, and a marvelous precision.   Cf. Okakura, *Les Ideaux
de l'Orient*, pp. 131–33.

other—typifies the union of the individual with the cosmic soul, and the idealistic schools had prepared the Chinese mind for this teaching.

Vairochana, the Cosmic Lord, is not a mere spirit. His body is the whole of material existence, and even a grain of dust partakes of his spiritual life and owes its existence to him. The whole world is a living organism, manifesting its life everywhere and endeavouring to attain full self-consciousness in every particle.[1]

Another great figure popularized by the Mantra school is Bhaisajyarāja, or Yao Shih Fō, the healing Buddha, who, like Vairochana, is a dhyāni-Buddha revealing hidden truth, and familiar to the student of Chinese temples as one of the Great Buddhas who are seated upon the high altar. Among the titles of Sākyamuni is that of "Physician of the Soul," and Yao Shih Fō is worshiped as healer of physical as well as spiritual ills; while one of his manifestations, Binzuru, is very popular in Japan, where his image in wood sits outside the shrine, and is an undoubted source of disease through contagion, for the devotee touches Binzuru on the spot which is affected in himself until he becomes a veritable plague-spot. But the idea is good!

There are also dhyāni-bodhisattvas, such as Vajrapāni, who symbolizes power, and Titsang (Kshitigarbha),[2] who makes a strong appeal to human needs. He is vanquisher of hell, and protector of children—surely a noble conception of the divine. Buddhist art delights to paint him descending to the underworld, with children crowding round to welcome him; and one of the most

[1] Anesaki, *Buddhist Art*, p. 32. Less pleasing deities are Achāla (Jap., Fudō), the "immovable," type of wisdom and meditation—a form of Vairochana; and Aizen or Kongosatta—a god of love.

[2] "Earth Womb"—a reference, perhaps, to the widespread belief in a Limbo for the dead, situated in the womb of Earth.

touching sights in Japan is a Jizō shrine, where parents
are busy tying the tiny garments of some dead child
about the images of this strong and tender champion.
I have a little family shrine in which naked infants are
playing leap-frog as he comes, and offering their lilies to
him, and this whimsical note is very characteristic of
Buddhist art, one of the hallmarks of its genius and
inspiration.

Men, and especially women, cannot do without such
deities or such aspects of the Divine, and the new school
throve apace; for twelve centuries it has played a great
part in popularizing Buddhism, and though there is much
crude superstition in its dhārani, or charms, which the
priests do not pretend to understand, yet this has rather
added to its success; the people love to be mystified.
And the government itself in these early days seems to
have supported the new missionaries, sending Amogha
back to India to secure more Sanskrit texts and to study
its elaborate symbolism.   He came back after five years,
armed with new knowledge, and new stock-in-trade.
Among the rites in use today are masses for the dead, a
form of baptism based upon the consecration rite of Indian
kings, incantations against demons, fire-offerings, and
other bits of ancient Vedic ritual.   These met a felt need
in China, and local color was added in the form of charms
against mandarins and the brigands who have always
been a curse to his long-suffering land!   To all this was
added the charm of secrecy.   Men told one another in
whispers that the Day of Milei Fō, Maitri Buddha, was
at hand, and with it a new era.

The secrecy of the new movement, however, aroused
the suspicion of the government until it was proscribed;
but it flourished the more vigorously, and though today

it has been absorbed into the more orthodox Chan school, yet it has left its mark on both popular and monastic Buddhism, and is represented in the magic and mummery of Lama temples so common in Northern China, though these have been introduced from Mongolia and Tibet.

That the Tāntric school was strongly entrenched at Chang-ān in the ninth century is clear, for the Japanese scholar, Kūkai, after studying there for three years, took it back to his native land and there it flourishes, and may best be studied on the beautiful mountain Kōyasan. In these early centuries of its history in China it seems to have been free from the phallic symbolism and the priestly quackery of its later years, and its adherents led moral and even austere lives, and did much to make Buddhism a power among the common people.

Decadent as Chinese Buddhism undoubtedly is in many parts of the country, it has had an immense influence upon the civilization of this great people, beautifying it and helping to make it the pacific and democratic thing it is. Nor are there wanting here as elsewhere signs of a real awakening. In the early eighties a literary revival in China turned men's eyes to the Buddhist books, the beauty of whose language is still unsurpassed. In 1893 a lay-Buddhist from Ceylon, another Tamo for bluntness, did something to awake the monks of China from their torpor, and in the past two decades there has been a great activity in building at such places as Ningpo and Hangchow, and since the revolution many disillusioned men are seeking the quiet monastic retreats of Buddhism, as many as a thousand being ordained recently at one time in the city of Changchow. The training of these ordinands is improving, and there are among them some of real piety and devotion. Among laymen too there is an increasing interest in the philosophy of Buddhism; bookstores in the great cities stock from five hundred to a thousand different texts and commentaries; and magazines like *The New Buddhism* voice the interest of groups of the younger men who have reacted against the aggression of nominally Christian nations, and the impossible theology of some reactionaries in the devoted ranks of Christian missions.

Japanese influence is, moreover, at work, seeking to demonstrate the power of Buddhism to become once more an international bond between the peoples of Asia. In 1918 a Pan-Buddhist movement started in Tokyo, provoked a counter-move in the form of a Buddhist organization in Peking to combat Japanese influence, and the younger politicians look pensively at Buddhism as it offers itself as a basis for the new democracy.

Speaking more generally, there is an earnest endeavor being made to clothe Buddhism in modern garments, and to adapt it to modern needs, while philosophy clubs and popular lectures are making this "new thought" available to the masses. And on the practical side there are some efforts to do what Christian missions have so nobly demonstrated to be an essential part of true religion, in the relief of famine, in Red Cross work, in prison visitation and care for the infirm. Buddhism, in a word, is making one more effort to commend itself to the masses of China.

CHAPTER VII

KEUM KANGSAN, NĀRA, HIEISAN, KŌYASAN

Buddhism in Korea and Japan (ca. 400 A.D.)

"*Buddhism was the teacher under whose instruction the Japanese nation grew up.*"—CHAMBERLAIN.

"*It is only in Japan that the historic treasures of Asiatic culture can be studied in due order . . . . Japan is the museum of this civilization of Asia.*"—OKAKURA.

I

Buddhism entered Korea in the fourth and fifth centuries A.D. in several missions, of which at least three are famous. In 372 a Chinese monk, Sundo, came to Kokurai, the northern kingdom, in response to an invitation from its ruler to one of the Chinese kings; twelve years later came the "barbarian monk," Marānanda, an Indian, from China to the middle kingdom. In 424 the black or negro monk Mukocha established Buddhism in the southeastern kingdom of Silla. It seems clear that Korea welcomed Buddhism as a bond of union with China, and she certainly benefited greatly from the work of these missionaries. We know that by the middle of the sixth century all three kingdoms were strongly Buddhist, even sending a mission to Japan, where at Nagāno one may still see the Amitābha Triad, believed to have accompanied the missionaries; and for a thousand years the new religion prospered in Korea, helping to unite the three kingdoms into one, fostering education first by introducing the use of Chinese, and later by inventing an excellent and simple alphabet, and filling the

TWO HEAVENLY KINGS

(Sixth century, Korea)

land with temples which may still be studied very much in their original form in remote mountain fastnesses.

It is a delightful experience to follow the trail blazed by some of these early missionaries, and to visit the glorious mountain range of Keum Kangsan, known to Europeans as the Diamond Mountains and to the Japanese as Kongō San, where nearly fifty monasteries survive.

On the exquisite seashore near On Chung Ni may be seen to this day a rock in which the pious imagination sees the overturned junk which brought there fifty-three missionaries (now called "Buddhas"), and near by sits one of them himself turned to stone! Let us suppose that it was in the clear autumn weather after the typhoons were safely past that they landed somewhere on this rock-strewn shore. Around them sparkled a clear sea, and the peaceful valley stretched before them; but beyond towered the mountains, and their voice has always called louder to the Buddhist monk than that of the sea. Following the course of a rocky stream they began to climb and soon found themselves in one of the loveliest mountain ranges of the world. Their hearts must have leaped for joy as they passed now through glades where clear, deep pools reflect the autumn foliage of oak and chestnut; now through mountain gorges where the serrated battlements of gray peaks and the blaze of the maples stab the clear blue of the skies. And as they halted for their evening meditation their minds must have filled with wonder and awe and with a solemn peace, as the rocks flamed in the sunset and the great moon sailed into a cloudless sky. At last they stopped by babbling waters, and amid these spacious glades they built their first small hermitage, whose upturned gables and deep, sloping roof were to set the standard for all succeeding ages.   There were moments when these great waterfalls and deep pools seemed to them haunted, as Ruskin would have us believe, by demons and dragons, and many an ancient legend tells of how by the power of the Good Law they cast them out. Soon the towering rocks were crowned with little shrines to the merciful Kwanyin and other benign beings; it is not hard in these still places to believe that God is love, and to worship him under these kindly forms.   Moreover, monks who train themselves to meditate, and to find a unity in all life and the Buddha-nature in the exquisite things around them, cannot but develop a symbolic art, and soon the temples began to blaze with color within and without as they do to this day.

Here may be seen the old San Sin, or "Spirit of the Mountain," the gods of the Northern Bear, Chil Sun, and the Kitchen god, as they have been adopted into the Buddhist pantheon,[1] and side by side with them are the seven Buddhas, like flames of a seven-branched candlestick, or William Blake's "Sons of the Morning."   Before them, and before Titsang, pilgrim-worshipers bow in intercession for the souls of the departed, and make offerings of food.   Here too one may see upon the altars in the "Hall of the Great Hero" the trinities: Sākyamuni, Vairochana, and Lochana; or Sākyamuni, with Miroku and Kwanyin, surrounded by adoring Bodhisattvas (Posal) and Arhats (Lohan).   Here too are the other figures we have met in Chinese temples, and stereotyped as is the art of these temple frescoes and images, yet they breathe the spirit of devotion, and are, indeed,

[1] Another small shrine contains a figure of the old solitary Toksung, whom some identify with Chi-i, of T'ien t'ai, and some with the Arhat Pindola, the Binzuru of Japan who was a doctor, but is forbidden to enter the sacred precincts because of his abuse of miraculous power in ancient times.

A MOUNTAIN FASTNESS OF THE DHAMMA
(Diamond Mountains, Korea, with shrine of Kwanyin)

as the monks will tell you, aids to meditation rather than "idols," as they are often crudely called. In buildings known as Hannya (the equivalent of the Sanskrit prajñā) are found the libraries of the Chinese *Tripitaka;* and these too are little more than aids to meditation. For while it is the art of China, and especially of the pietistic and tantric schools which has prevailed, it is the spirit of the Indian or contemplative schools which survives in these Korean monasteries. Here the Hall of the Great Hero, Sākyamuni, and the Hall of Meditation are of central importance. Korean Buddhism is, in fact, a blending like that of China of these three schools, and one may find young acolytes studiously getting by heart the lists of the patriarchs through whom in an unbroken succession the teachings have descended. They will tell one how, when Buddhism was becoming too complex, a Korean monk, Taigo, went to China and brought back the simple and austere Dhyāna or Chan teachings, and Tamo is a greatly honored name.

At sunset I was invited to join the monks at their silent contemplation; after bowing to the Buddha images, they turned from them and sat in silence, meditating for two hours or more; after which we sat late into the night discussing the teachings of the school; and again long before dawn they were at this most difficult of arts. In some temples the praises of Amitābha are used as a help. In some the Vajra of tantric Buddhism is clasped between thumbs and fingers pressed tip to tip, and this too is an aid to meditation. For three or four years in the great monastic houses of Heian or Pomosā the novice is taught the preliminaries, and then follows a four-year course upon the great Mahāyāna books, the "Lotus," the "Awakening of Faith," the *Prajñā-Pāramitā Sūtras,* the Amitābha books,[1] and they maintain that these books have been since the sixth century their main scriptures. But many, in fact the majority, get their training in less formal ways; one kindly abbot, sixty-one years of age, told me that he had lived in the same monastery since, as a child of seven, he was adopted by the monks, and his calm, gentle bearing and sweetness of disposition are witness that the long years have not been spent in vain. These monks for the most part accept the T'ien t'ai classification of the Five Periods, and use some of the secret charms, or dhāranis, of Tāntra, such as the famous "Om mani padme hum" (om; the jewel in the Lotus: hum!). For into these monastic pools many streams have poured, although it is the still, deep waters of Dhyāna which have drunk them all in.

Such is Korean Buddhism in its mountain fastnesses, clearly a mixed Buddhism of the accommodated Mahāyāna with Sākyamuni as a central figure, with meditation as the chief exercise, with the philosophy of the Void and the T'ien t'ai classification tacitly assumed, and yet with some pietistic tendencies, as is evidenced by the place given to the Buddha of the Western Paradise. Ignorant the monks often are, and yet most of them will tell you that mind alone is real, that there is one universal mind; and these are living truths to them. "There is one moon in heaven," said a young monk to me as the great harvest-moon climbed over the shoulder of the mountain, "but men see it from many sides, and it is reflected in a myriad pools. There is one Buddha-nature," he went on, "in mountain, tree and bird"; "and in the mind of man," I added. This idealistic philosophy of the monks is akin to that of another moun-

[1] Korean Buddhists have printed scores of the chief Buddhist books.

tain lover, whose words remind us in the West how little we have developed our sense of the immanence of God. Wordsworth would be quite at home in these mountain monasteries, for here the Eternal Spirit is a living reality to many an earnest soul.

Of the Buddhism of the lay-people, though it was once a great and living faith, as is evidenced by the many stone Miryek, images of Maitri Buddha, and by the Buddhist names of many villages, it is more difficult to speak with enthusiasm. "It is no obstacle in our work," said the saintly bishop of the French mission; yet the bishop of the Anglican church in Korea is surely right when he finds:

In that indefinable charm and affectionateness of manner of the Korean a witness to the influence of that great Teacher who . . . . laid supreme stress on gentleness and kindness to others, and of whom we may say (with that stout old Christian traveller of the Middle Ages, Marco Polo): "*Si fuisset Christianus, fuisset apud Deum maxime sanctus.*"[1]

And it is easy to underestimate the hold which his religion has upon the Koreans.

Although the monasteries are in decay and the monks are despised, the laity are not lacking within the temple precincts, and they come to seek assistance at the Buddhist shrines in every kind of need. They bring offerings; they fill the brass dishes on the altar with rice, cake, nuts, apples, and pears; they light candles before the images and burn incense; they hire the monks to recite sacred passages to the sounds of drums, bells and cymbals; they fling themselves meanwhile repeatedly before the altar in prayer, with their foreheads in the dust, murmuring softly the words of supplication, of prayer, of sorrow.[2]

[1] Transactions: *R.A.S.*, Korea Branch, VIII, 40

[2] Hackmann, *Buddhism as a Religion*, pp. 264-65. The author notes that here as elsewhere Buddhists resort also to exorcists (Mudang) and soothsayers (Pansu) women and men, respectively, who from these spheres have ousted the Buddhist monk. And as in China so in Korea, behind all the Shamanism, Buddhism, and Confucianism of the people is a dim background of theism—the worship of the one great god, Hananim, whose name like that of Shang Ti has been adopted by the Protestant missionaries for God.

Today, though for complicity in a plot against the throne the monks were for centuries excluded from the capital and no temples were to be found within its walls, Buddhism has re-entered Seoul, and the Japanese are fostering it as a bond of union with the people of the land.

Yet Japanese Buddhism seems to make little protest against the high-handed methods of the military and police, and Korean Buddhists accept with languid interest the establishment of a Buddhist headquarters and training school, and a fostering of Buddhist propaganda. It is, in fact, doubtful whether these methods are not tending to drive the Koreans toward Christianity. And it is interesting that just across the border Buddhism is being preached as the most democratic of religions, while here it is relied upon to support a despotic government. No one can prophesy the future of religion in these eastern countries; but it needs no prophet to see that there is being developed a spiritual leadership in the Christian church in Korea which will mean much for the future of Christianity in the Far East. May it not be in the providence of God that a vital eastern Christianity is to be developed in Korea, and with it a renaissance of the old arts of which Korea is justly proud, and the discovery of a real democracy ? If so, then, Japan will owe Korea even more in the days to come than she did in the period we have now to consider. Meantime, a great white Buddha image of the eighth century gazes across the straits that separate the two lands, as who should say: "Much have my Korean disciples done for you. What return will you make ?" It is, indeed, a great debt which Japan owes to Sākyamuni and to Korea.

HŌRIŪJI
(Partly built in the seventh century A.D.)

II

The story of Buddhism in Japan is almost the story of her civilization; there is little in her rich treasury of art and religion which Buddhism has not inspired and molded. From this splendid background there stand out certain great and notable epochs and certain great names. First and most far-reaching in its achievements is the era of Shōtoku Taishi[1] (593–622), a contemporary of Muhammad and of Augustine of Canterbury, and like them a founder of a new civilization.

Amid the gentle slopes and stately trees of Nāra rise ancient shrines, visited by every tourist and honored by the Japanese as the cradle of their civilization. A few miles away stands a group more venerable still and far more interesting—the shrines of Hōriūji—perhaps the richest storehouse of Buddhist art and architecture in all the East. Here in 538 A.D., while Tamo and Chi-i were still at work in China, a Korean mission settled and laid the foundations of Japanese culture. Bringing a gilt image of one of the Buddhas, and copies of some of the scriptures, they carried also a personal message from the king of their country to the royal house of Japan, pointing out the excellences of the Dharma and its far-flung influence: was it not the religion of all the great nations? "These words," says Dr. Anesaki, "were a marvelous revelation to a people who knew only how to invoke spirits supposed to be little superior to men."[2]

The world has marveled at the meteoric progress of the Meiji era; that of the Nāra epoch was in some respects more remarkable, and a visit to Hōriūji will reveal some-

[1] For the earlier epoch of Buddhism in Japan see Appendix VI.

[2] *Encyclopaedia of Religion and Ethics*, VIII, 703.

thing of the incomparable debt which Japan owes to Korea, and still more to China, that mother of civilizations.

It not only marks the birth of Japan as a civilized power, but from it we can reconstruct the architecture of China now swept out of existence, and only a memory.   And its artistic value is no less; small as they are, these buildings are almost unequalled in Japan for absolute beauty, and they have remained the type from which all the architecture of the nation has developed. . . . . The general plan is noble and dignified and the grouping and composition consummately delicate.[1]

Japan was not slow in adapting and making her own these rich gifts, and within a century was to a great extent a civilized country.   Amid her glorious forests rose the stately roofs of Chinese and Korean temples, with curving gable and soaring pagoda; and within gleamed masterpieces of sculpture like the great Kwannon, which still speaks at Hōriūji of tenderness and spiritual repose, and haunts one with the mysterious other-worldly charm of the great things of religious art.

Prince Shōtoku, himself regarded as an incarnation of the Compassionate One, was, indeed, a remarkable figure whose authentic likeness, painted by a Korean artist, is treasured by the imperial family, and who is revered by the craftsmen of the land as their patron saint. Like Asoka and Kanishka he saw in Buddhism a wonderful bond of union for the divided and warring tribes of his people; and through its great doctrine of the oneness of all life political and racial barriers were overthrown, and a united people gathered about him.   Proclaiming it the state religion in 604, he based a constitution upon it, "for without Buddhism there is no way to turn men from wrong to right"; and at a port on the Inland Sea he established a great institution, the Shi-Tennōji, or "Shrine

[1] R. A. Cram, *Impressions of Japanese Architecture*, p. 32.

FROM SHŌTOKU TO NICHIREN

of the Four Heavenly Guardians," to demonstrate to his people the beneficent power of the new faith, and to prove to visitors from neighboring lands that Japan was now one with them in the religion of all civilized races! The first thing to greet the traveler on landing was this stately group of buildings with their schools of art and music, their hospitals and dispensaries clustering about the monastery and central shrine. What had the primitive cult to offer in comparison ?

Nor was the prince content with patronage of his adopted faith; he made an earnest and critical study of the scriptures, and selected from them three which were especially calculated to commend the new faith and to help him build up a united kingdom. These scriptures, upon which he himself wrote commentaries and gave lectures, were the "Lotus of the Good Law" (*Myōhō Renge Kyō* or *Hokke-kyō*),[1] the *Vimala-kirti-nidesa Sūtra* (*Yuima-gyō*),[2] and the *Srīmālā Sūtra* (*Shoman-gyō*).[3] In interpreting these scriptures he was a disciple of the Jojitsu school, whose chief book is the *Sātya-siddhi-śāstra*,[4] translated into Chinese by Kumārajiva in the fifth century. It contains, as we saw above, a philosophical treatment of the doctrine of "emptiness" and a practical application of this doctrine; let the disciple meditate upon the unreality of the "ego," and then apply the idea to the casting-out of self-will and the cultivation of unselfishness. All is unreal; most unreal of all is the illusion of "self."

But ruling princes are more concerned with applied than with theoretical teachings, and though Shōtoku was no mean thinker he knew that in the affairs of state a little philosophy goes a long way. His selection of books for the nation was a stroke of genius; and it would be

---

[1] *B.N.*, 134.　　[2] *Ibid.*, 146.　　[3] *Ibid.*, 59.　　[4] *Ibid.*, 1274.

hard for the modern scholar to beat it. The *Hokke-kyō*, which is still the most influential and popular of the Buddhist books in Japan, teaches a simple and picturesque religion, intelligible to the lay-mind; its optimistic note and democratic spirit in holding out the promise of salvation to all make it a book acceptable to ordinary folk, and its apocalyptic scenery has proved a great stimulus to art. But, above all, the splendid ideal of the Bodhisattva which it depicts is a useful reminder that loyalty is only attainable at a cost. To this challenge his people have made a generous response, and in the present period of transition Bodhisattvas are greatly in demand!

The other two books chosen by Shōtoku are sound lay-Buddhism, a proof to his subjects that the new religion is not merely monastic, but is capable of guiding men to good citizenship and even of swaying the throne, though "the King is to his subjects as Heaven to Earth." "Honesty," says the *Yuima-gyō*, "is the Paradise of the Bodhisattva." Vimalakirti was a burgess of Vaisālī and a stout lay-adherent of the Buddha; Srīmālā of Benares was a good wife, a model queen, and a staunch supporter of the Sangha. "The King is a father to his people," says the *Shoman-gyō*. A docile people and a grateful ward eagerly drank in these lessons, and for a time all went well. Yet we must not overlook the fact that in spite of the good example of the prince-regent the religion he was trying to secularize is at bottom a religion for monks and philosophers, and was being preached by missionaries from abroad, who took very different views of it, and were representatives of rival schools. "It furnished spiritual food for the intellectual and leisured classes; but it was not a gospel to the mass of the people."[1]

[1] Harada, *Faith of Japan*, p. 94.

Japanese Buddhism was in fact at the cross-roads; and as no nation is fortunate enough to be governed by a succession of Shōtokus, it was left to foreign monks and their converts in Japan to decide its fate. In the middle of the eighth century, under the great Buddhist Emperor Shōmu Tennō, a Chinese monk, Kanjin, was appointed head of the hierarchy, and an Indian ecclesiastic, Bodhisēna, exerted a great influence. Though they wisely encouraged social service, they made no attempt to put the scriptures into the vernacular, and tended more and more to keep in their own hands the arcana of the religion. With a hierarchy monastic in its teaching, exclusive and aristocratic in its practice, and still largely foreign in its personnel, Buddhism might well have remained an alien benefactor. But the genius of the Japanese began to assert itself, and Buddhism to make terms with the native Shintō. Gyogi, a monk descended from the royal house of Korea and a man of great ability, who was a social reformer as well as a religious leader, and who acted as adviser to the Emperor Shōmu, was the founder of this mixed or Ryōbu Shintō. He boldly proclaimed the identity of Vairochana with Amaterasu, the ancestress of the royal house (both being solar deities), and helped in the setting up of the Daibutsu at Nāra, a hideous colossus which represents Roshana,[1] an emanation of Vairochana, and thus published to the nation the new alliance. There is less to surprise us in this new move than at first may appear; the emperor, like Shōtoku and many another, was hailed as Avalokitesvara, and Gyogi himself as Mañjusrī, while the Indian Bodhisēna, who performed the ancient rite of "giving life" to the image by painting in its eyes,

[1] Other famous images of Roshana are the sixth-century rock carvings at Long-men near Loyāng, and elsewhere. It is only fair to the colossus of Nāra to note that it has twice been badly defaced by fire.

was regarded as Samantabhadra or Fugen. And in later days this Bodhisattva is even depicted as a geisha, who allures men to goodness by seeming to tempt them to merriment! Japanese Buddhism has pushed the principle of "accommodated truth" to extreme lengths, and these early exponents of this method were philosophers, followers of the difficult *Avatamsaka* of the Hosso and Kegon schools, and must needs give the people something more popular. Another great figure of this eighth-century Buddhism in Japan was Dosho, who at Chang-ān had been a pupil of the great Hiuen-Tsiang (known in Japan as Gensho), and who returned to Japan in 677. He and Gyogi are regarded as the founders of these *Avatamsaka* schools in Japan; and it would have gone ill with Japanese Buddhism, in spite of imperial patrons, but that the next century produced two great native leaders, who made Buddhism indigenous—even though they took it to the mountain tops and let it relapse to monasticism. Henceforward, for some centuries, the two mountains, Hieisan and Kōyasan, are the real centers of Buddhism in Japan. An eminent Buddhist scholar said to me:

These two mountains are the two lotuses of Japanese Buddhism: Kōyasan has been for eleven hundred years a lotus turned upward toward the sun and preserving its seeds intact; Hieisan has been for the same period a lotus turning itself downwards to the earth, and has scattered its seeds in many directions.

It is a true and picturesque image of these two great sacred mountains, and around them we may group our further study of Japanese Buddhism.

Born at a time when Buddhism was becoming too powerful in its influence in politics, and the hierarchy, divided among themselves, were intriguing also in affairs of state, Saichō, like many another earnest soul, had turned away in disgust, and had retired to a mountain side to meditate and find peace. In 794 when the government, suspicious of the power of the priests of Nāra, and for other reasons, removed to Miyako, Saichō was twenty-seven years old. Whether or not he had a share in the new move his hermitage of En-riaku on Mount Hiei began to attract attention, and was destined to become the center of a new and inclusive Buddhism. From the Chinese sect of T'ien t'ai, he had learned to find in the "Lotus" scripture the true Buddhism, and in opposition to the Nāra schools he began to teach the essential message of this book, that all are destined to Buddhahood, and that it is not necessary to pass through the stages Srāvaka and Pratyeka Buddha to become a Bodhisattva; an inference quite legitimately drawn from the ideas implicit in early Buddhism.[1]

In this democratic teaching was a solution, not only of his own spiritual struggles, but of the problem of uniting the nation. Buddhism had become aristocratic and exclusive, and the common people, no less than the court and the more earnest of the priests, were ready for the new teaching. Once more Buddhism was to do for a great people what it had done for the India of Asoka and of Kanishka, and for the China of Wu-ti and Fu-kien, and what it had already begun to do for Japan in the time of Shōtoku Taishi. Having worsted the Nāra monks in public debate, Saichō was sent in 804 to China "for a further search of truth." He spent a brief year studying at T'ien t'ai, and returned to make his beloved Hieisan the splendid home of a harmonized Buddhism. For eleven hundred years it has been the center of Japanese Tendai; and today, like the glorious cryptomerias guarding its

---

[1] See Prefatory Notes.

ancient shrines, it stands sentinel over a form of the faith which is dying if not dead; cemeteries, tombs, temples empty of worship are there in melancholy beauty as the memorial of a notable venture, which has spent itself. Here one may see towering among the trees the Sorintō a great bronze column set up by Saichō himself, and symbolizing, with its nine hoops encircling the central shaft, the multiplicity in unity of the new school; and possibly also the philosophy of Tendai, or pantheistic realism: behind and in the many is the One. In front of it stands a deserted but splendid shrine to Sākyamuni, for the "Lotus" leads back to the historic Founder too often forgotten in Japan; and here, half hidden among the trees, is an ancient stone image of Kwannon, as who should say: "Remember too Amida and his saving grace."

Beyond, united by a kind of "Bridge of Sighs," are preaching halls for the "Lotus" and the Amitābha scriptures, and here for many centuries these were expounded side by side. This ancient temple seems to utter a silent protest against the sectarian bitterness of today.

Here then in this group of buildings is epitomized the attempt of Saichō to establish an eclectic yet comprehensive Buddhism; and a little beyond them again is the central shrine, Kompōn Chudo, where a lamp lighted by him still burns in the dank and mildewed atmosphere, barely lighting up the gloom, and half revealing the altar with its eight volumes of the "Lotus," and images of the chief deities, Amida, Kwannon, Tai Seishi, Fudō, and "the Four Guardians,"[1] and without, hidden in the great archway which stands at the entrance of every Tendai

---

[1] Amida is Amitābha, Kwannon and Tai Seishi are Avolokitesvara and Mahāsthāmaprāpta.   Fudō is a Hindu deity, Acāla, adopted like Vairochana and Amaterasu, the sun-gods and Hachiman, god of war, into the pantheon of Buddhism, which like other pantheistic religions accommodates itself very easily.   The Four Guardians, Shintennō, are also Hindu guardians of the four quarters of the universe.

temple, is Monju (Mañjusrī), the Bodhisattva of wisdom, without whose help the elaborate system may not be mastered.

Here, though usually there are no worshipers, one may find services of praise to Amida; and more interesting, the venerable Homa sacrifice of Vedic India is still being performed. Burnt-offerings of cedar wood, oil, rice, and tea are made before the ferocious Fudō, and Buddhas and Bodhisattvas are summoned to be present, while strange mūdras, or gestures, accompany every invocation. The priest in his scarlet robes may dimly understand their hidden meaning, but no one else; and as one watches one begins to understand why in the days of its prosperity Tendai took from fifteen to twenty years to train its priests. It is as elaborate in its cult as in its tenets, and its eclecticism has not been critical. Today boys of fifteen are admitted to the novitiate by a service of ordination, the shamikai, taking the ten vows, and at the age of twenty are ordained bhikshu, or monk, taking the guzokukai, or two hundred and fifty vows. "Do they know much about the system?" I asked a learned Buddhist scholar.[1] "Not much," he replied, "but more than our famous scholars in the West."

But to return to Saichō; smiled on by the government, encouraged by what he had seen in China, inspired by the beauties of Hieisan, and by the vision of its slopes alive with worshiping multitudes, he moved steadily toward the goal. The first step was the planting of a school for monks. In this the "Lotus" was the foundation. The other chief books were also taught; and much was made of the books of the discipline and of ethical

---

[1] Mr. B. Petzold, who is at work upon an exhaustive treatise upon Tendai which will be eagerly awaited by scholars.

teaching, for to the twin pillars of Chinese Tendai Prajñā, wisdom, and Dhyāna, meditation, Saichō added Sīla, morality, as equally fundamental.

To all this sound Buddhism were added mystical contemplations, the use of magical gestures and charms, and an elaborate ritual containing such ancient rites as the Homa sacrifice and the abhisekha, or baptism, which we shall study in Shingon, or Japanese Mantra Buddhism.

The next step was the formation of a kind of third order of lay-people; and in spite of grave opposition, Saichō began to ordain monks at the central shrine. When he died in 822 he was the acknowledged head of a new school of Japanese Buddhism, and founder of a church soon to become too powerful, and to overawe the throne and the capital; and already his Buddhism contained at once the germs from which have developed the three great schools of Hōnen, Shinran, and Nichiren, and at the same time the seeds of its own disintegration. Before very long the innumerable temples of Hiei became veritable barracks, and the sound of its great bells the signal for a muster of armed monks, some houses putting as many as 3,000 into the field. Today, while animal life is sacred on Hiei, one cannot walk far along its splendid avenues without finding the graves of monks slain in the continual feuds between great and powerful rival monasteries.[1] Moreover, it became gradually clear that Saichō, or Dengyō, as he was now called, had attempted the impossible; like his master, Chi-i, he had mixed water and oil in a temporary emulsion, and they were bound to separate.

It is strange that ere this took place four hundred years went by, a time of great unrest and of intrigues both

[1] In the twelfth century Yoritomo had to forbid monks to carry arms.

political and ecclesiastical, and yet a time of steady devotion to the ideals of the monastic life, and of the arts of
which Japan is so justly proud. We may picture lonely
souls taking refuge from the hopeless corruption of the
hierarchy and the degeneracy of the court among the
quiet glades of Hiei. Such was the half-witted royal
monk, Kūya, who is said to have danced through the land
in the tenth century, reciting the praises of Amida, and
calling men to follow a simple, emotional faith. Such
was the learned artist, Genshin (942–1017), who wrote a
treatise on the vow of Amida and the communion of
saints in his Paradise, and Ryōnin (1072–1132), who
organized an Amida Society to work and pray—the
Yūdzū Nembutsu. Such pre-eminently was Genkū, or
Hōnen (1133–1212), the prophet of Amida, who in the
twelfth century broke away from Hiei, where he had spent
thirty years of meditation and study, and where at last
the truth of Amida's saving grace, as taught by Genshin
and Ryōnin, had seized and possessed him. With him
ends the Kyōto period, and begins that of Kamakura.
Satiated with rich food, "the honey of Shingon, the rich
butter of Tendai," he was hungry, he tells us, for the daily
rice. This all need, and even weak stomachs can digest!
We may imagine him in his exquisite hermitage of Kuro-
dani, where the glory of the maple blazes against a great
wall of cypress; here he would sit gazing at the setting sun,
meditating on Amida and his Pure Land, or repeating the
glowing passages of the *Sukhāvatī Vyūha*, until the vision
of the god flooded his being with joy and conviction.
Here at last was truth and reality. Like the vision of
our Lady Poverty to his contemporary, Francis, this
experience of a living Amida spurred Hōnen to the task
of awakening his people.

The present incumbent of the shrine will tell you the exact measurements of Amida, the color of his eyes, the marks on his body (identical with those of Sākyamuni), and may even carve for you a beautiful image of the gracious and compassionate Being whose praises Hōnen repeated in ecstasy innumerable times each day—praises which are heard today on every side in Japan.   In that dark age of decadence and corruption, how .restful to contemplate the ordered beauty of that Land of Bliss, where the Eternal King rules in righteousness.   Such is Amida Nyorai.   Great pictures of him descending on the clouds delight the eyes of the dying Buddhist.   Radiant light pours from him to all quarters of the universe, and about him, like stars around a central sun, stand the Bodhisattvas of whom Kwannon and Tai Seishi, embodiments of his love and might, stoop to welcome the passing soul into his paradise.   *"Namu Amida Butsu"*[1] is at once the prayer, the creed, and the hymn of the Pure Land sects, and it is expanded into a splendid hymnology; for the bulk of Japanese Buddhists are glad to escape from the "path of the sages" to "the path of bliss," from Jīriki to Tāriki, from self-reliance to self-surrender.   This doctrine we have already studied; here it must suffice to note that it was Hōnen, the Buddhist Francis or Wesley, who made it real and vital in Japan, and who in his "Selection," published in 1175, claims boldly that the only way open to all is the gateway to the Land of Bliss.   Though this book was publicly burned, yet his teaching fell on soil ploughed up, and ready to receive it, and the presence of Amida became a living and precious reality to many.[2]

[1] Sometimes shortened to Nembutsu.

[2] Famous disciples of Hōnen were Saigyo, poet, warrior, and knight-errant, and Kumagai, who having slain a young Samurai in battle put the sword from him forever and became a monk.

Its fruits are manifest not only in the art which it has inspired but in saintly lives like that of Hōnen, some of whose hymns have come down to us:

> The haze of morning veils the light of day,
> Or grudging filters some faint golden ray;
> But lo! behind the shrouding veil of mist
> The whole world by the Sun himself is kissed.[1]

This, of course, refers to the pervading love of Amida, which is there whether men respond to it or not. It was the nerve of his own belief; and when at the age of seventy-four he was sent into exile, he rejoiced that he might take the good news to far-off villagers. As he lay dying he comforted his followers with these words:

> What though these fragile bodies melt away
>   Like dew when Death has laid us low,
> Our souls abide and in a gladder day
>   Meet in the lotus-bed where now they grow . . . .
> On every side His beams the worlds pervade,
> His grace forsakes not one who calls for aid.

Here then, is a Buddhism which has entirely passed away from the rigid system of Karma and the vague allurements of Nirvāna, and which offers to men a religion of grace and a heaven of personal immortality of which the central joy is the beatific vision of a divine Buddha. Is he a personal God ? The Buddhist scholar replies:

No, yet truth accommodates itself; there is an absolute truth (Shintai) and an apparent truth (Zokutai) about the Buddha; and to the vulgar herd he is more real than a philosophical abstraction, more personal than the Dhamma, nearer and dearer than Sākyamuni. Let them worship a personal Amida.

---

[1] To Dr. M. Anesaki I am indebted not only for permission to versify some of his translations included in this chapter, but for much of the information contained in it. His *Quelques pages de l'histoire religieuse du Japan* he gave me in manuscript when I first visited Japan.

It is a religion for simple people, and yet, like other schools of Buddhism, it has its systematized philosophy, and teaches that there are four kinds of mind training, and three modes of thought. Yet all these are implicit in faith in Amida; the three kinds of thought are: profound reflection on the Buddha; sincere disgust with this present life, with earnest aspiration after the Land of Bliss; and the liberal resolve to dedicate all to the good cause. The four methods of training the mind are: instruction in and practice of faith; veneration for the three Jewels, and the exclusive utterance of the name of Amida. Hōnen ignored the "One Thought" doctrine of Tendai, that, as we are one with Buddha, we have only once to think of him and his grace to secure salvation; and even the teaching of the smaller *Sukhāvatī Vyūha,* that it is necessary to keep the name of Amida for seven days, or at least for one, in mind. He introduced, indeed, a "vain repetition" of the name of Amida, which was later to arouse the wrath of Nichiren; and this was in itself a remnant of the doctrine of merit which Buddhism, like Christianity, is tending more and more to reject.

It was left for Shinran (1173–1262) to take this final step, and to teach that no merit of ours is necessary, not even a parrot-cry, but only gratitude for the salvation which has already been accomplished. No wonder that the early Roman Catholic missionaries in Japan described Shin Shu as a kind of Lutheranism. Like Luther, Shinran cast away the last remnants of the "trashy doctrine" of merit, and like Wesley, he was an evangelist and a great hymn-writer, whose spirit may best be studied in the four hundred Wasan attributed to him; they are the equivalent of the Gāthās of India, and are best appreciated when placed in their proper setting. The great Hondo, or hall,

of a Buddhist temple in Japan is a thing of exquisite
beauty; the light falls through lattices and from old altar
lamps upon the faces of devout worshipers, wistful and
pathetic as their minds turn from present sorrow to future
joy.   Outside the children play in the sunny courtyard; for
youth, except in the modern Sunday schools of this sect,
is more concerned with the present than the future, and
has not yet learned the meaning of the other-worldly
joys that are within.   But for parents and grandparents
the influence of the chanting, the deep notes of gongs, the
dim lights, the burnished old gold of screen and altar,
colossal images, dimly seen through clouds of incense—
all this has an almost hypnotic influence, and those who
do not think too much are borne along on a tide of feeling
and æsthetic pleasure.

The central shrine is occupied throughout the temples
of the Shin sect by the figure of Shinran himself, and to the
left Amida, Hōnen, and Shōtoku, the great layman, who
typifies to the Shin Shu the fact that religion is for all,
and who is, indeed, the founder of Japanese Buddhism.
To the left of them are six other patriarchs: Nāgārjuna
and Vasubandhu, Indians; Donran, Dōshaku, and Shantao
(Zendō), Chinese;   and Genku, a Japanese.   Before the
central shrine is an altar with lights and incense, and a
priest is seated facing them.   Behind him are the heredi-
tary abbot in purple and scarlet, and next him his son,
a boy of seventeen, already proudly conscious of his
destiny as the next head of the great hierarchy.   Behind
them again are the choir in robes of old gold, and the
priests in black.   "*Namu Amida Butsu*,"[1] the praises of
Amida, alternate with Wasan, or hymns, the first line

---

[1] These and other meritorious words and deeds are like "good works after justifica-
tion"—effect not cause.

intoned by one voice, far away and solemn, and the three
remaining lines of each stanza taken up by choir, priest,
and people.   To a kind of Gregorian chant are sung such
words as these:

> Eternal Life, Eternal Light!
> Hail to Thee, Wisdom infinite,
> Hail to Thee, mercy shining clear,
> And limitless as is the air.
> Thou givest sight unto the blind,
> Thou sheddest mercy on mankind,
> Hail, gladdening Light,
> Hail, Generous Might,
> Whose peace is round us like the sea,
> And bathes us in infinity.[1]

Or it may be some patriarch who is being hymned, such
as Hōnen himself:

> What though great teachers led the way—
> Genshin and Zendō of Cathay—
> Did Hōnen not the truth declare
> How should we far-off sinners fare
> In this degenerate, evil day?

Occasionally a hymn, like the excellent preaching of some
of the priests, strikes a note of moral living whose motive
is gratitude to Amida:

> Eternal Father, on whose breast
> We sinful children find our rest,
> Thy mind in us is perfected
> When on all men Thy love we shed;
> So we in faith repeat Thy praise
> And gratefully live out our days.

---

[1] For permission to versify his prose renderings of some of these Wasan, I am much
indebted to the Reverend S. Yamabe, of Higachi Hongwanji. He has lately published
the entire collection ("Wisdom of the East," *Buddhist Psalms*). With this hymn we
may compare that of the Christian church beginning:
> "Thou Grace Divine, encircling all
> A soundless, shoreless sea. . . . ."

The Japanese, in whom gratitude is a very strong motive, find in the teachings of Shinran a Buddhism which is very Christian, and the words attributed to him, as he was nearing his journey's end, are a confession of sin which is worthy of a saint:

> What though in faith my way I wend
>   To that Pure Land of Thine,
> With all my flesh doth falsehood blend,
> And in my soul no spark of truth
>   No wholesome light doth shine.
> Too strong, too strong earth's clinging mesh,
>   My soul entangled lies;
> My very deeds of righteousness
>   Cry falsehood to the skies!
> And passion as a serpent's tooth
> Gnaws this poor heart of mine.
>
> What though my spirit steeped in shame,
>   Unmerciful and fickle be,
> Yet by the virtue of his Name
> And trusting in his Ark of love
>   I cross the waves of misery.
> All impotent as is my might,
>   My heart though cold and dead,
> Yet by his Grace, his saving light
>   Through me on darkened souls is shed,
> Enkindled from above.

It might be Luther or Wesley speaking; is it not the God of both speaking through this Buddhist saint?

The Shin Shu is a sect in which a great revival seems to be at work. Upward of 800 young priests are being trained in its two universities in Kyōto, and it claims 150,000 children in its Sunday schools, while it is teaching parents that religion is a matter of the home, and has broken away from the monasticism which for 1,700 years insisted upon celibacy as the higher life.

A modern disciple of Shinran thus sums up his creed:

1. Know thyself as thou art; it is worse than nothing.
2. Put absolute faith in the vows of Buddha Amida; it is every-thing and more.
3. Make joyous gratitude thy sole motive of conduct in life.
4. After being united with Buddha in the pure land, thou shalt be among us again to devote thy life to the work of Buddha to the end of the world.[1]

"It goes without saying," writes a modern handbook, "that this True Sect of the Pure Land is the doctrine preached by the world-honored Sākyamuni Buddha him-self," and heterodox as its doctrines undoubtedly are, the Shin Shu yet embodies much of the spirit of the Founder. He taught that the righteous are saved by their own merit, yet his mission was also to sinners, and a famous epigram of Shin Shu proclaims: "Even the righteous are saved by faith; how much more the sinning soul."[2]

The Western scholar may rub his eyes and protest that this is not Buddhism at all, but the Buddhist courteously replies that all living religion manifests itself through growth, and that the law of evolution is still at work. It is certainly true that the story of Buddhism must be read backward as well as forward if it is to be understood. If Hōnen and Shinran called themselves Buddhists we shall do well to leave it so. Yet critics of their systems as pernicious heresy are not wanting within the ranks of Buddhism, even of the Mahāyāna. One such we have to study now, a very different figure from the pietist Hōnen and the evangelist Shinran. Nichiren (1222–82) was a younger contemporary of the latter; trained like both on Hieisan, he also studied Shingon there, and his system

---

[1] *The Essence of Japanese Buddhism.*
[2] *Tannisho.*

is best understood as a development and a revolt from both Tendai and Shingon Buddhism. Born of fisher-folk among the virile peasants of Eastern Japan, he came like a strong sea breeze athwart the effeminate vaporings of thirteenth-century Japan, when Daimyo and priest alike were bathed in sickly sentiment, for the new pietism had quickly degenerated. While again the Pure Land teachers were turning men's eyes to a life beyond the present corruption and civil strife, Nichiren began to preach a religion directly concerned with the affairs of the nation, and with the everyday life of the people.[1] Like Amos, the shepherd of Tekoa, he saw with clear eyes through the prevailing religiosity, and insisted that repentance and righteousness alone could save the nation. This gospel he found embodied neither in the elaborate synthesis of Tendai nor in the mysteries of Shingon nor in the simple fervor of Jōdo Shu and Shin Shu; Shinran seemed to him to have wandered far from the teachings of Shaka, and to be leading men to hell, and Kōbō Daishi he branded as a "first-rate liar."   After long searching, he had convinced himself that the "Lotus" contained the true essence of religion, but that it needed reinterpreting to meet the needs of the new age. Today upon the Japanese stage one may see enacted the dramatic contest between this rugged prophet with his new formula: "Namu myōhōrenge-kyō, praise to the Lotus of the Truth," in his fierce struggle with the Pure Land sects. And today his disciples, vigorous and quarrelsome, carry on the tradition of pungency and aggressiveness, while the cynical layman looks on, and tells the story of the Jōdo priest who got so drunk that he repeated in his

---

[1] His earliest work is a semi-prophetic semi-political tract in which he announces impending invasion—1260 A.D.

cups the "Lotus" formula in place of that of the "Pure Land."

Arbitrary and exclusive in his demands, and critical of other heretics, Nichiren formulated his own quite fanciful interpretation of the scriptures. In the title of the book he claimed that the truth was fully embodied, and that as the worshiper repeated the mystic words he was identifying himself with the cosmic soul. Disgusted at finding the village children playing with the image of Sākyamuni, lately discarded in the new enthusiasm for Amida, he claimed to go back to the Founder himself— "No man can serve two masters"—yet he accepted the pantheistic realism of Tendai, and like Shingon found in union with the cosmic soul the true essence of Buddhism. At the same time he insisted that the Buddha is a personal Providence, and that natural catastrophes and threatened invasions are due to the withdrawal of his protection from faithless people and hypocritical priests. Like Isaiah, he announced impending doom: "Woe unto you who have forsaken the true teachings, and are fettered with false beliefs. Turn, ye men of little faith, and put your trust in the unique truth of the way of righteousness. Awake, awake. There is but one Sun in the sky." Mobbed, persecuted, exiled, and almost killed, delivered from the executioner's sword by a "miracle," he kept stoutly on, and, in spite of her degeneracy, saw in his beloved native land the destined Holy See of a universal church, and in himself the man of destiny. Was not the whole universe in its essential Buddha-nature behind him? And was not the whole long history of Buddhism about to find its fulfilment in a great day of the Lord Shaka? Had he, Nichiren, not himself, as Jogyo Bosatsu,[1] sat on the

[1] I.e., the Bodhisattva Visista Caritra.

Vulture Peak at the feet of the eternal Buddha? Yet
in all humility he confessed himself a common man and
a sinner, "not quite a messenger of the Tathāgata."

More than any other Buddhist teacher does he
approach to the authoritative "Thus saith the Lord" of
the Hebrew prophet, and at the end of his strenuous and
stormy life he set himself to watch and pray for the
consummation of the times, and for the establishment of
his church. Amid loneliness, exposure, and voluntary
poverty, the old prophet felt himself sustained by the
vision of a Buddhist universe, repentant and purified by
his teachings:

> Masses of fog and thickening cloud
> Close 'round about me like a shroud.
> Eternal from the Vulture Peak,
> Whence still eternal voices speak,
> Come, wind of Truth, drive error out
> As morning puts the night to rout.

Reformer, ecclesiastic, mystic, and poet, Nichiren was
also a schoolman and a philosopher. On a basis of
Tendai teaching he developed his "Three Esoteric Laws"
in which he gave a new interpretation to some of the
teachings of the "Lotus" and a new orientation to
Buddhism as a whole. The first law is the Daimoku, or
name of the "Lotus" Sūtra. It is by adoration of this
name that we attain to harmony and union with the Buddha, for in it is an embodiment of the cosmic soul, or of
the Buddha-nature. How this may be is incompre-
hensible, yet by faith it can be grasped and its virtues
appropriated. The second law is the Honzon, or object
of worship. Meditation on the mystical body of Buddha,
which is eternal and is yet named Sākyamuni, is the right
practice of Dhyāna, and the right medium of communica-

tion between each worshiper and the faithful; while the third law is the Kaidan, morality-platform, or ladder of moral instruction, representing the Sīla of the orthodox Buddhist Sangha. This too is summed up in the five words of the title, and the essence of it is faith in these words, by which we come to the Pure Land of Calm Light. In a word, "Our own body is the pre-existent Buddha (Honzon), our thought the good law (Daimoku), and our abode the Pure Land of Calm Light (Kaidan)."

To give one's heart and soul to meditation on the Honzon is superior thought; to repeat the title of the "Lotus" is superior knowledge; to believe and observe it is superior morality—such, in brief outline, is the system of Nichiren. Having worked it out stage by stage during the thirty years of an active life, in 1281 at the age of sixty-one he died, surrounded by his faithful followers and murmuring a verse from his beloved *Hokke-kyō*, serenely confident in the future. Had he not seen his own prophecy fulfilled and his authority vindicated?[1] His influence is by no means spent in Japan when brilliant scholars like Dr. Anesaki, trained in all the intricacies of Christianity and its theology, avow themselves his disciples; and when in recent years Takayama, an ardent disciple of Nietzsche and of Tolstoi, died in calm confidence in the teachings of Nichiren, and did not hesitate to compare him with Jesus of Nazareth. Did they not both put first the unseen and the eternal? Did not both suffer for the truth?

Nichiren Shu is one more proof of the vitality of this ancient religion, which after twenty-five centuries is seeking to renew its youth and adapt itself to a changing world. It is also, alas! one more evidence that religion

[1] From his little hermitage at Minobu at the foot of Fujiyama Nichiren saw his prophecy of a Mongol invasion fulfilled and the Armada scattered by a typhoon, and mocked the boasts of Jōdo and Shingon priests that their prayers had prevailed.

KOBO DAISHI AMONG THE TOMBS OF KŌYASAN

in Japan as in other lands is apt to play the chauvinist. In his imperialistic teachings Nichiren was something of a megalomaniac.

Such are the schools which have originated on Hieisan; numbering among them more than three-fourths of the Buddhists of Japan, and showing considerable vitality at the present day, they are worthy of careful and sympathetic study much more detailed than is possible here. All are pantheistic in their underlying philosophy, polytheistic in common practice, and orthodox as to the final goal, Nirvāna. But they differ as to method, and, as we have seen, they differ profoundly as to their main emphasis in appealing to the popular mind.

If Hieisan is the solemn memorial of a dead past, it is because it has shed its life-giving seeds; Kōyasan is by contrast a center of life and energy. Here Kūkai, or Kōbō, to give him his posthumous name, a younger contemporary of Saichō, founded a new Japanese Buddhist church, introducing and making indigenous as Shingon (True Word) the esoteric or Mantra Buddhism. Like Saichō he had studied in China, and at Chang-ān had met a disciple of Amoghavajra of the Mantra school of Buddhism, lately introduced.

Kūkai was a man of enormous energy and inquiring spirit, and had begun his career with a careful comparative study of the three religions of China. The politico-social ethic of Confucius, the mysticism of Lao-tze, the philosophy of Buddhism—in all he found food for his spiritual hunger. During his stay of nearly three years at Chang-ān we may be sure that he studied the conflict of religions, learned something of the electicism of the Chinese, and watched the growing complexity of Buddhism itself; nor is it unreasonable to suppose that he made acquaintance with

Christianity, which was somewhat widely established at this time in China and summarized on such monuments as the Nestorian stone, in which a very limited Christian theology is set forth in Taoist guise. But it was Tāntric Buddhism which fired his imagination and captured his allegiance, and one book in particular, the *Mahāvairochana Sambōdhi Sūtra*, known in Japan as *Dainichi-kyō*, riveted his attention. In later years he made a masterly adaptation of its generalizations, classifying for the purpose of propaganda the existing Buddhist schools. This "lengthwise classification" is a useful commentary on the evolution of Buddhist doctrine, and if one remembers that it is propaganda and does not take it too seriously, it is well worthy of study as a remarkably acute essay in the comparative study of religion.

The Buddhist and other schools are divided into ten stages:

1. At the bottom are beings of brute passions, human and demoniac, ignorant of the law of cause and effect and of the difference between good and evil. They are like the "Ram," stupid and passionate.

2. There is an enlightened as well as a brute stupidity! The second stage is known as that of the "Stupid boy who practises fasting." It includes those who, like the layman of Hīnayāna and the Confucianists, practice "mere morality" with a view to worldly success, and are not spiritually minded. Shingon disciples, who practice the "Three Mysteries of Body, Word, and Thought," belong to this class.

3. Wiser than the stupid boy is "the fearless infant"! Folk like Brahmins and the monks who follow the ten precepts of Hīnayāna belong to this stage; ignorant and weak, they yet have some thought of the Unseen. The

Shingon disciple reaches this stage when he makes progress in the practice of the "Three Mysteries."

4. Next comes the stage of the Srāvakas, known as the "Skandhas without self"; these have begun to think philosophically, and are typified by the Kusha sect.

5. Fifth is the stage of the Pratyeka Buddhas, the thought which gets rid of the seeds and cause of action and of rebirth, reaching enlightenment through meditating on the twelve Nidānas. Such are the followers of Jojitsu; and the Shingon disciple reaches this stage when he realizes the unreality of the phenomenal world, and knows that it is like an image of the moon in water.

6. Now begins the Mahāyāna, the "altruistic great vehicle"! Realizing that thought alone is real, idealists such as the Hosso sect stir up compassion for those who are deluded by the unreal phenomenal world, and convey others to Nirvāna. Right in their idealism, they are wrong in their nihilism concerning phenomena.

7. Those who belong to the Middle Path, and accept Nāgārjuna's "Eight Noes," such as the Sanron school, belong to a further stage, and, with those of the foregoing class, to a stage of freedom of thought reached in the Yoga practices of Shingon. Though the teaching of unreality may not be sound philosophy yet when practically applied it leads on to the realization of transcendental truth.

8. Those of the "One Thought Way," who like the Tendai school believe in an ultimate reality, and find it expressed in phenomena—pantheistic realists—are one stage nearer truth. The phenomenal is real because it is identified with the noumenal.

9. Higher still are those who, like the Kegon school, believe in the absolute cosmic soul immanent in all phenomena, and find the Buddha-nature in both.

10. Last and highest are those who hold to the esoteric "Thought Adorned with Mystery," and work out the full practical consequences for religion of this idealistic philosophy. Such is Shingon:

The exoteric doctrine having cleansed away the dust of evil,
Lo! the treasury of mystic truth is opened in the True Word,
Made real now are all virtues and potencies.

The first nine stages, in a word, representing all the other schools of Buddhism, are only means of suppressing passion and of annihilating false beliefs; it is only as he reaches the tenth stage that the climber gets beyond the mists into the radiant light of day, and finds the real meaning of his own thought and the secret of Buddhahood in this present life. Then the cosmic soul is embodied for him in every act, but most intensely and truly in the performance of mystic ritual, and in the utterances of mantras. The divine is most real when it is most realized; and in this ritual, philosophy comes down from the clouds to earth; the ideal is realized, and the cosmic soul becomes truly incarnate.

Such is the triumphant apologetic of Shingon, and Kūkai stands revealed as a systematic thinker of real genius. He was also a great artist, and the true books of his school are pictures. In addition to his "lengthwise system" he introduced to Japan the "side-by-side" teaching in graphic form of the Mantra school. This can only be understood by close and careful study of two elaborate Mandaras, in which every detail is the expression of a fanciful, yet closely seasoned system. The first Mandara represents the Vajra Dhātu (Kongōkai), or "diamond element" at once unbreakable, and able to cut through the obstacles of passion. The second represents the matrix, or Garbha Dhātu (Taizōkai), which is

like a womb producing and containing the seeds of all
being. The former is wisdom, the latter reason; the
former can destroy passion in one's self; the latter, insep-
arable from it, is essential to the salvation of others.
The former is the ideal, or potential, aspect of the universal life revealed as Vairochana or Dainichi, the great
Sun; the latter is the dynamic aspect of the universal
life; and both are represented pictorially, for art is
philosophy made concrete. In the Vajra Dhātu Mandara
Dainichi is seated as a central sun in contemplation, which
is typified by a white disk. In the Garbha Dhātu Mandara he is enthroned in the heart of an eight-leaved lotus,
and his double halo of red typifies activity. In the
former he is surrounded by various "emanations," all
in white disks; in the latter by various "powers" or
activities personified as deities with red haloes. Both
aspects, potential and dynamic, reveal the life of this
cosmic being, whose "emanations" and powers embody
his inexhaustible goodness. Transcendent, he is also
immanent in the phenomenal world. By mystic rite, by
mūdra and mantra, the worshiper identifies himself with
this source of his being, and makes dynamic what before
has been potential.

The great Sun is thus the principle of life identified
with the Tathatā, whose energy dwells in and sustains the
smallest grain of sand, or drop of water. It is his purpose
to bring men back to a knowledge of their kinship with
him and to restore them to union with the cosmic lord.
By a stroke of genius, Kūkai, having accepted Vairochana
as the Dharmakāya, followed Gyogi in now identifying
him with the sun-goddess, Amaterasu, from whom the
Mikado traces his descent. The pantheism of Buddhist
philosophy made this an easy step:

The Buddhas in innumerable Buddha-lands
Are but the cosmic Buddha in us all;
The golden Lotus, countless as the sands,
Are our own mortal selves corporeal.
Each mystic word a universe conceals,
Each work of art the cosmic life reveals:
So in this fragile body may we find
The glorious potencies of life combined.

Kūkai was poet as well as artist and philosopher, and the graphic pantheism of Shingon has been a great stimulus to art and letters. In more material ways too it has appealed to the imagination of the Japanese, by laying hold of certain secrets of bodily and spiritual health. Long before one comes upon the art-treasures of Kōya-san one meets, climbing the long, gentle slopes, a steady stream of white-clad pilgrims; and among them is many a palanquin bearing some sick person in search of health. Do they find it on the sacred mountain ? It is claimed that many do. One such pilgrim, a picturesque figure in his peaked hat with rosary and conch, with vajra, wheel, and other symbols of his faith, told me that he had been sick in body as well as in soul until a Shingon priest had healed him, and now his whole life was given to pilgrimage and to the mystic arts of healing. Some of his mūdras he showed me, and to my question as to whether faith were needed in the patient: "No," he replied, "my own faith suffices." But when I would have questiond him further my interpreter rebuked me gently as one might chide a botanizer on his mother's grave! Was I not intruding upon holy things, and what had science to do with faith ?

It is clear that Japan is eager for a religion which affects bodily health, and some of the new sects of Shintō, such as Tenri-kyō, and Omōto-kyō, which in a few years have gathered millions of adherents, embody a kind of Chris-

JIZO AT THE GATES OF KŌYASAN

tian science as one of their chief "planks." Many are the
miracles of healing attributed to Kūkai, and so great an impression did he create that when in 835 he passed away he
was believed merely to have retired into a shrine, there to
await the coming of Miroku.[1] Around him beneath glorious trees and hideous tombstones[2] lie the faithful in their
thousands, and among the tombs is many an indication that
in this strange esoteric development the religion of Sākyamuni has not forgotten its central message of loving-
kindness. Possibly unique among the monuments of war
is one erected here by the warlike prince of Satsuma in
the sixteenth century in honor alike of friend and foe and
dedicated to their spiritual welfare. Here too one may
study the mysterious Abhisekha, or baptism-ceremony,
which would seem to be based on the coronation rite of
Indian kings, and possibly to be colored by Nestorian
practices. Handed down from Mahāvairōchana himself
this rite reached Kūkai through an august succession of
patriarchs, and today among the Shingon sect "baptism
for the dead" is a regular part of the funeral ceremonies,
the gift being transmitted through the living to the
departed.

But mysticism too often degenerates into magic, and
Shingon has not been free from the corruptions of *Tantra*,
which we shall study in the following chapter.

[1] His work was carried on by his disciples, Jitte, Jikaku, and Chisha, all of whom
studied in China.

[2] Many containing mystic words probably traceable to the Manichees.

CHAPTER VIII

SVĀYAMBHŪ-NATH AND LHĀSA

Buddhism in Nepal and Tibet (ca. 800 A.D.)

" This beautiful statue is the sum and climax of Tibet. It would be difficult to surpass its exquisite workmanship."—PERCIVAL LANDON.

" A repellent image . . . . with goggle eyes and a coarse, sensual face, and of very rude workmanship."—WADDELL.

I

Amid the green ricefields and the wooded valleys of Nepal, and in sight of the great snow rampart of Himālaya, Gotama was born, and here today one may see the Asokan pillar which marks the spot in the pleasaunce of Lumbini, and trace the course of the Rapti by whose banks he meditated. Hence too flowed the little stream of Buddhism which we have watched as it grew to a mighty river; and hither by circuitous ways it returned after a thousand years, polluted and hardly to be recognized.

It is in the land of Sākyamuni that Buddhist theology has perhaps reached its greatest elaboration, and that Buddhist toleration has worked itself out in the most amazing hotch-potch of polytheism, tantrism, and demonism, accepting alliance not only with the early animism but with Saivite Hinduism, naked and unashamed. Climbing the five hundred steps to the shrine of Svāyambhū-nath, pilgrims from Sikkim, from Bhutan, and even from Tibet and distant parts of India jostle one another as they go to worship the giant Dor-ji, or thunderbolt of Indra, with which he transfixes the demon of drought and releases the longed-for rains, and here Buddhist stūpas and Hindu lingams compete for their worship. The hideous Kālī with her skull-necklace, trampling upon her prostrate lord, stands side by side with the pure and lofty Sākyamuni; or worse still Buddhas, of whom he is prototype, embrace their *saktis* in corybantic ecstasy, and Hanuman the ape sits cheek by jowl with the gentle Avalokitesvara. Here among the *Nine Dharmas*—the great Mahāyāna scriptures which Nepal has so long preserved and now worships—the apocalyptic "Lotus" and the philosophical *Prajñā-pāramitā* find themselves side by side with the sex-orgies of the *Tathāgata-guhyaka,* which "has all the characteristics of the worst specimens of Sakta works," says Rajendralal Mitra.[1] Here incest and other bestiality is made the path to illumination and release. In Nepal Hodgson discovered and gave to the world priceless manuscripts of these and other works preserved for a thousand years in the dry air of this inaccessible land, and, as he said, in the streets of its old towns "it is often requisite to walk heedfully . . . . lest perchance you break your shins against an image of a Buddha."

Here above all we may study the cult and doctrine of the Adi-Buddha and his emanations, which is the key to much that is puzzling in the iconography of later Mahāyāna. Though we are not yet in a position to state without qualification the origin and nature of this doctrine, it seems a final stage of the trikāya theology and of the ālaya of the Yogācāra. Some selection from the mass of material accumulated by Hodgson, De la Vallée Poussin, and other scholars may be of value to the student who is not a specialist.

[1] *Nepalese Buddhist Literature,* p. 261.

It is clear that in Nepal we have a Buddhism of a
distinct theistic type, which Burnouf considers must be
distinguished from the Hīnayāna and the Mahāyāna
alike. Poussin admirably contrasts it with the former
by setting over against the old formula, "Of all that
proceeds from causes the Tathāgata has explained the
cause," a new one, "Of all that proceeds from causes the
Tathāgata *is* the cause." The historic Buddha is now,
in a word, the representative of a First Cause, unorigi-
nated, self-existing Svāyambhū; and this is the deity
worshiped at the capital of Nepal, Kathmandu, and at the
shrine of Svāyambhū-nath. "He has never been seen;
he is in Nirvāna. Nevertheless he is pure light, he issues
from the 'void' (suñyatā) and his names are innumerable."[1] By his contemplative power (dhyāna) he pro-
duces five Jinas, or Dhyāni-Buddhas: Vairochana, the
Brilliant; Akshobya, the Imperturbable; Ratnasamb-
hava, the Jewel-born; Amoghasiddhi, Sure Success; and
Amitābha, Endless Light; they are creators of corporeal
forms, to whom is sometimes added Vajrasattva, who from
being an early attendant-spirit of Sākyamuni is promoted
to be creator of immaterial things. From these Dhyāni-
Buddhas are born Dhyāni-Bodhisattvas, Samantabhadra,
Vajrapāni, Avalokitesvara (or Padmapāni), Ratnapāni,
and Visvapāni, and their reflexes, the historic Buddhas.
Thus Sākyamuni is the reflex of Avalokitesvara, who is the
Dhyāni-Bodhisattva of Amitābha, in whom the invisible
Adi-Buddha is revealed; the historic Kanakamuni is
the reflex of Akshobya, while the coming Buddha, Maitreya, will represent Amogha-siddhi.

In the *Avalokitesvara-guna-Karandavyūha* in its metrical form this hierarchy of Buddhas is set forth. Here

[1] "Adibuddha," *E.R.E.*, Vol. I.

Avalokitesvara is derived from the meditation of Adi-Buddha, and co-operates in the creation of the world by giving his eyes to form sun and moon, his teeth to form Saraswatī, goddess of eloquence, and so on.   Here too we read of the descent of this great spirit into hell, which forthwith becomes a paradise.

How did this elaborate system arise ? We cannot be certain, but some points to be taken into account are—(a) the appearance in such early sculptures as those of Gandhāra of two Bodhisattvas, one Maitreya with long hair and with a flask in his hand, and another, almost certainly Avalokitesvara, in whose tiara sits a Buddha who is in teaching mūdra, but may be Amitābha; (b) very early in the developed Mahāyāna we meet with the grouping of Avalokitesvara and Mahāsthāmaprāpta as the attendants and spiritual sons of Amitābha; in the *Amitāyur-dhyāna Sūtra*, for example, they play an important part; (c) there is considerable confusion of idea, the Bodhisattva being sometimes the spiritual son and pupil of the Buddhas, sometimes a potential Buddha, who out of compassion to the world refrains from entering Nirvāna, and is more effective than the Buddhas, who, though they are majestic beings, are not of much practical help to their devotees; (d) the pantheistic background from which all these figures emerge is, as we have seen, a development of earlier Buddhology and of the idealistic philosophy of the Vijñānavāda.

These ideas are all to be seen blending in the cult of Adi-Buddha; it is theistic, not in virtue of worship paid to him as supreme but rather because one of his emanations is often promoted to what Poussin calls the "presidency"; and we find in Japanese Buddhism, for example, a similar process at work, Vairochana at times being supreme, with Amitābha as his reflex, as in Shingon Shu, and Amitābha himself wresting the "presidency" from him in Jōdo Shu, much as in Hinduism the shadowy Brahman retires behind some Avatar, now Vishnu, now Krishna, now Siva. Indeed, in the whole Buddhist theory of emanations and of the substantial identity of Jina and Jinaputra, or Buddha and Bodhisattva, we see the Hindu mind at work.

This elaborate theology is clearly an attempt to work out the Trikāya doctrine for popular presentation; how readily the idea of a Tathāgata-garbha, or "Womb of the Buddhas," leads to the identification of the Dharmakāya with an original cause, the Adi-Buddha; the Nirmāna-kāya, as the adaptation of the Eternal to temporal needs, expresses itself naturally in the phraseology of generation or spiritual sonship, while the Sambhogakāya, invisible yet real and effective, is at once a glorified being, and the Eternal and Absolute in action. He has been compared, indeed, both to the glorified Christ, and to the Holy Spirit of Christian theology.

In such ways the Adi-Buddha doctrine was worked out. It is a remarkable attempt to bring order out of the growing chaos, and to provide a hierarchy for the faithful. We may summarize it in some such form as this:

In the beginning, when all was void was the Om, and from it the self-existent Svāyambhū,[1] the Adi-Buddha, by his own will was manifest, who was before all. As a flame he issued from the Lotus, and from him, who is without form, all things proceed; from him proceed the Dhyāni-Buddhas, and from them the Dhyāni-Bodhisattvas, through whom the worlds are made.

In eternal calm of contemplation dwell Adi-Buddha and Dhyāni Buddhas; to whom shall prayer be made? To the creative and sus-

[1] This title occurs first in Buddhist literature in *Milinda Pañhā*, p. 214, where it meant "self-enlightened."

taining powers, the Dhyāni-Bodhisattvas, who are to them as his hand is to man. Compassionate are they to the world, and obedient to his behest.

If that were all, the study of the pantheon would be a simple matter, but as we have seen there is much confusion; often in Nepal, for instance, the Bodhisattva Mañjusrī is honored as Adi-Buddha, and Vairochana, Vajrasattva, and Vajrapāni are all used as names of the Svāyambhū. The Aisvarikas of Nepal, moreover, have another trinity, a strange development of the "Three Jewels"—the Buddha symbolizing generative power, the Dharma productivity, and the Sangha their son, who is the active creator and ruler! Nor has the Self-existent escaped this tantric enthusiasm for matrimony: his consort is Adi-prajñā or Adi-dharma, and in their esoteric form they appear together in close embrace as Yogambara and Jñānasvari. In Tibet they appear as Vajradhāra and his Sakti, who holds a skull-cap and a vajra, and are the chief deities, in theory at least, of Red and Yellow Cap alike. Let us glance at this turbid inland lake in which the stream of Buddhism lies befouled and stagnant. We may find some lotus blossoms even there, for streams from India and from China as well as from Nepal have poured their waters into it.

II

On a plateau, "the Plain of Milk," 1,200 feet above the sea and girdled with vast snowy peaks, rises the forbidden city of Lhāsa, and on a rocky spur above it towers the great Potala, the palace of a "living Buddha," the Dalai Lama, in whom is incarnate Avalokitesvara. Many times in the history of China and Japan some good emperor or some holy monk has been acclaimed as the Compassionate One come down to earth, but here in this ancient city he has his abiding place. Apart from this, Tibetan Buddhism is not essentially different from much in China and Japan, and is very much like that of Nepal. It is Mahāyāna in tantric guise, and it has made terms with a darker animistic cult than in any other land.

As we have seen, the Yogācāra school of Asanga, founded in the fourth century, is idealistic in its philosophy, maintaining that only thought exists, and in its practice makes meditation, long-continued, the only way to the goal. In order to attain to Bodhi, the universal and only Reality, the seeker must become a Bodhisattva and practice Yogācāra continually. To help him in this arduous task, dhāranis, charms or spells, are provided, and he is encouraged to look for miracles, for there is only one Reality, and we must expect that as the veil of illusion wears thin it will break through. We can best understand the developments of this school if we remind ourselves that Buddhism in India is a Hindu reform movement, promoted for a brief period to be the religion of Asokan India, but subject to reabsorption in the amazingly plastic system of Hinduism. When, therefore, between 500 and 900 A.D. the Sakta systems with their goddesses, their occult practices, their hypnotic meditation, their medico-religious quackeries, appeared, Buddhism did not escape the infection, and it was this contaminated type which entered Tibet in the seventh century. According to the stone edicts of Lhāsa this was before the time of the great Srong Btsan Gampo (630–98 A.D.), but we may accept his reign as the epoch which saw at once the introduction of Buddhism and of the script of the Indian alphabet current in Northern India. The first booklet translated into Tibetan in the new letters was a hymn to Avalokitesvara, using the "Om mani padme hum" formula now so familiar. One of the first temples to be built for the new religion was the Jokkhang,[1] or "Lord's House," which formed a nucleus and a Holy of Holies, unholiest of all, for the great cathedral of today, whose golden roof flashes amid dark trees in the center of the town.

But Buddhism had to face a strong and ignorant opposition from priests and people, in whom the Bön animism was strong, and, as in other lands, it needed the patronage of the throne to set it upon its feet. SriSrong De-Btsan, the son of a Chinese princess, was the Tibetan Asoka who summoned the great scholar, Padmasmabhava, from Nālandā, where he had learned the idealist philosophy and also the magic and occultism of the Yogācāra school. In 747 he settled in Tibet with a company of other Indian monks and some Tibetan novices, of whom one Dpal-bangs became the first Lama, or abbot, some thirteen years later, and a great translator of the Sanskrit texts. These pioneers were great and notable scholars, and it is a wonderful fact that their translations, wherever they have been tested, "display such scrupulous literary accuracy, even down to the smallest etymological detail, as to excite the admiration of all modern scholars who have examined them.[2] The *Canon*, or *Ka-gyur*, in one hundred and eight volumes, is divided into seven sections, for in addition to the *Vinaya* and *Sūtras* it contains *Tāntras;* and some of the *Sūtras* have been subdivided. "It is the word of the Buddha," says S. Lévi.[3] "The commentary,

[1] Jo means "lord." "By a curious perversion of the Mahāyānist doctrine of the Kāyatraya (i.e., Trikāya), they say that the Lhasa Jo is the Dharmakāya, the Peking Jo is the Sambhogakāya, and the Kumbum Jo is the Nirmānakāya."—Rockhill, *The Land of the Lamas*, p. 105.

The quotations at the head of this chapter describe the treasure of the Jokkhang—a statue of the youthful Sākyamuni.

[2] Waddell, "Lamaism," *E.R.E.*

[3] Among its contents he notes *Prajñāpāramitā* in twenty-eight volumes; the *Vinaya* in thirteen volumes; *Avatamsaka* in six volumes; and *Tāntra* in twenty-two volumes.

Tan-gyur, in two hundred and fifty volumes, contains the Fathers of the Church"; it is a great encyclopedic library of ancient Indian lore or metaphysics, logic, composition, arts, alchemy, etc., including the commentaries of ancient Indian Buddhist writers, Nāgārjuna, and others, also some texts by Tsong Ka-pa and other Tibetan saints. Its contents have not yet been fully examined. The translation of the *Canon* and of most of the commentary was completed by the latter half of the ninth century, and the patron under whom this great work was accomplished, Ral-pa-chan, endowed monasteries and did so much at the expense of the state as to lead to his assassination by his own brother, who put himself at the head of a Bön conspiracy, and began a savage persecution of the invading cult. His reward came swiftly, and the popular "miracle-plays" of Tibet have no more popular scene than that of his murder by a Buddhist monk disguised as a Bön devil-exorcist. Alas that the disguise has become a habit! With its genius for compromise Buddhism in Tibet has made terms with the primitive cult, though it is difficult to say how much of the superstition and quackery that goes on in the name of Buddhism belongs to Saivite Hinduism and is an importation from India, and how much is distinctively Bön. In any case, it is there because Buddhism made terms with it, and it has done the people of Tibet untold harm and the religion of Sākyamuni great and lasting disgrace.

Yet we may do now what Buddhist leaders should have done long since, and cutting away the rank tropic growth of magic, of obscurantism, and of cruel exploitation of the people, may lay bare the genuine Buddhism that lies like an august and aged trunk hidden and rotting underneath. The majority of the monks belong to the

Ge-lug, or Yellow Hats, and are celibate, keeping the two hundred and fifty-three rules of Mahāyāna monasticism, and claiming to derive their authority from Maitreya Buddha, as revealed in the succession from Asanga down to Tsong Ka-pa. But they have also a Yi-dam, or tutelary deity, Vajrabhairava, a manifestation of Yamantaka, most fearsome of all Mahāyāna deities. He is the ferocious emanation of Mañjusrī with a bulgy head, scowling brows, and three eyes, and sometimes he has the head of a bull, and a chaplet of skulls. With him is usually depicted his Sakti, or female counterpart, embracing him, while underfoot he tramples animals and birds. Their Dharmapāla, or guardian, is no less atrocious, the "six-armed lord," Hayagriva, horse-headed and often crowned with skulls, while under his feet are demons, and about him clings his Sakti.

Here are clearly Indian tantric deities, and one clasps the mystic Vajra, or thunderbolt, a phallus symbolizing Mystic Truth, indestructible and potent in exorcism, a weapon introduced to Tibet by Padmasambhava, and known as the Dor-je, and now familiar in all Mahāyāna temples. These deities represent two ranks in the hierarchy of gods who surround Avalokitesvara, the Yi-dam being of the Buddha rank and the Dharmapāla being of the rank of Bodhisattva; and their images are to be seen painted on the limestone rocks of Lhāsa and on innumerable temple banners. To them worship of an elaborate and ritualistic kind is paid, an honor they share with the nine sacred books, or *Dharmaparyayas*, and the Living Buddhas.

It was this strange doctrine introduced by Tsong ka-pa which really distinguished the Buddhism of Tibet from that of India, and which has given so disatrous a power to the Lamas, culminating in 1640 in the creation of the Dalai Lama as sole head, temporal and spiritual, of all Tibet.

Side by side with the Ge-lug-pa monks are the Kar-gyu, or white Lamas, more ascetic and given to solitary meditation and at times to great austerity. On their hats is a St. Andrew's cross, typifying the cross-kneed posture of meditation, and their Yi-dam also is Vajradhāra; but their guardian is Bar-nag, "the lord of the black cloak," and their practice of mystical insight is different.

Several subsects have arisen out of this austere and unpopular Kar-gyu, but it is still next to Ge-lug the most powerful of the sects; and next to it Waddell places the Sas-kya, founded in 1073, and setting up a hierarchy of great power. Its great Bodhisattva is Mañjusrī, regarded as supreme, and it traces its authority to Nāgārjuna. Its tutelary god is Vajraphurpa, and it belongs to the orthodox Red Caps. Its monks are not celibate and yet it is to some extent reformed, having been stimulated to activity by the reformation of Atisa, and it has given birth to two reforming subsects.

Such are the great schools of Tibetan Buddhism, and it is to the Indian monk, Atisa, that we must look if we are to understand their significance. By the early eleventh century Tibetan monks were legion, had made terms with the old Bön-pa, and had departed from the Middle Path, not only marrying but living openly with mistresses, as many do today. In 1038 Atisa arrived from India and started to clean the Augean stables, and the Yellow Hat sect is the Ge-lug, or "Virtuous Order," which has developed from his Ka-dam, or "Men under Discipline." The other two great sects, Kar-gyu and Sas-kya, are also to some extent reformation movements, and though they are all three tantric, and tainted with Bön superstitions, they are nevertheless schools of the Mahāyāna, and their gods and Bodhisattvas are for the most part Buddhist.

But in addition to these there are those who have refused to reform—the Nying-ma—and they have had to defend their old Bön practices by inventing "revelations," or hidden gospels, and attributing them to Padmasambhava. These are known as Ter-ma, and their authors claimed that they had been in former births disciples of the great teacher, and had learned from him that the rites they defended were really good Buddhist practices. To him almost more honor is paid than to Sākyamuni, or to the Ādi-Buddha.

Thus the religion of Tibet, whatever Western scholars may feel, claims to be good Buddhism, more or less orthodox as it has submitted to reforms and expurgations. Strangely enough the Yellow Hats, who are most orthodox in doctrine, are most unlike their co-religionists elsewhere in being organized as a regular hierarchy, with a Grand Lama exercising a priest-kingship over all Tibet, and appointing other great Lamas at Tashi-lhumpo, at Urga, and at Peking.[1]

This was a gradual process, the fifth Grand Lama inventing the doctrine of his divine origin, and claiming that he and the first incumbent were both incarnations of the great Srong Btsan Gampo, and that he was the great and merciful "Spirit of the Mountains," identical with Avalokitesvara, Chan-ra-zi, the "god who is clad with eyes," and whose favor is won by uttering the mystic spell, "Om mani padme hum." Strangely enough too

---

[1] Here, in striking contrast to the dignity and simplicity of the Confucian shrines, the Lama temples may be conveniently studied.

he invented, with unexpected modesty, a higher destiny for his colleague at Tashi-lhumpo, proclaiming that he was Amitābha. The Grand Lamas at Urga and Peking are of less august descent, and their jurisdiction, spiritual and temporal, is more limited, as is their asceticism, his holiness of Urga having a harem, and both having to keep the favor of the Dalai Lama. None of these "Living Buddhas" is respected by the Red Hats, whom they in turn despise for their laxity.

Below these great ones are the four grades of monks so numerous as to be a curse to the country (more than one-third of the entire population of Tibet and more than half in Mongolia being enrolled in them). In Lhāsa itself two-thirds of the population are said to be monks dwelling in three vast monasteries and some smaller ones. They are: (1) lay-adherents, upāsikas, or ge-snen, usually children under instruction, but sometimes adults also; (2) neophytes, ordained as probationers and taking part in the services, having bound themselves to keep the thirty-six vows; these correspond to the samanēras of Ceylon, and are the majority of the order; (3) the Bhikkhus, or Ge-long, are the Elders, or Thera, who have taken the full vows of the order, and (4) the abbots, or K'an-po, who rule over monastic houses and need to be strong disciplinarians. They alone are really Lamas, or teachers (Guru). There are also nuns much less numerous, and even less literate, than the majority of the monks; of them we have little knowledge, but it may be that there are pious women among them.

In Tibet, monastic Buddhism has had free course and provides a *reductio ad absurdum* of the system; the easy tolerance of Buddhism has allowed the Dharma to be prostituted to the base uses of an unscrupulous priesthood, and the noble figures of the Buddhist deities have given place to corybantic and erotic demons. *Facilis descensus Averno!*

Yet even here the religion has shown powers of recuperation, as in the reforms of Atisa, and there is mingled with the magic and quackery some genuine mysticism. Each great sect has its own Yoga, and there are devotees and adepts who, we may believe, arrive at mystic states of mental clarity. Nor can we fail to respect the stoic endurance of the solitaries of the ascetic school; here as one passes by steep and gloomy ways through some mountain pass a thin and feeble hand may be seen to flicker from a crevice in the gray rock, and peering into the gloom one may dimly see the hermit, who with wistful, sunken eyes looks out upon a world he has forever left. Or it may be he has immured himself completely and only a hand is to be seen, while within he is lying in filth and misery unspeakable, self-immolated in a death-in-life, seeking to find in some paradise beyond a solace and joy as poignant as his pain in this fleeting world. No one who has read it can forget Colonel Waddell's description of such a colony of solitary hermits in their "cave of happy musing upon misery"; "poor ghostly tenants of a subterranean world . . . . sinking miserably into a lethargy of driveling imbecility."[1]

Such was Milaraspa, an Indian hermit-saint of the eleventh century, whose hymns are still popular, to whom magic powers are attributed and who had his chief cell on Mount Everest.

Of the strange power of these men over the people it is difficult for Western minds to conceive, for the East venerates austerity, and believes that it brings an exceed-

[1] *Lhāsa and Its Mysteries*, pp. 236–44.

ingly great reward.   And even the ordinary monk, lazy
and corrupt though he be, is accepted as the intermediary
between the suppliant and his gods, Tāra or Dölma alone
being at all times directly accessible to human prayer.
So from the mud of corruption flowers this lotus bloom
upon the ancient stem, and it is good to pause and contemplate the goodness and power of God, and the yearn-
ing of the heart of man, as even here it vindicates itself.

The goddess Tāra seems to have found a place in
the Buddhist pantheon in the sixth century, and Hiuen-
Tsiang found her cult strongly established in Northern
India, until, as the centuries went by, every house had
its image of this deliveress.   That seems to be the meaning
of her name, and beautiful stories are told of her begetting;
one that she sprang from a blue ray that streamed from
Amitābha's eye, another that a tear from the compassionate Avalokitesvara grew into a lake, from out of which
arose a lotus bloom, and in its fragrant heart lay the pure
and lovely Tāra.   She is incarnate in all good women,
and was first revealed to Tibet in the queens of Srong-
tsan-gampo.   So grew the belief in her twofold manifestation as the white and the green Tāra, one a full-blown,
open lotus, the other closed.   The white Tāra, like the
open lotus, symbolizes day;   and the green, a closed
bloom, symbolizes night, for the compassion of the good
Avalokitesvara is ever vigilant.   In support of this
interpretation are many pictures in which she holds a
full-blown lotus, and above her are Sun and Moon.   Yet
even this lovely figure was not allowed to go unsullied,
and to her were added the ferocious manifestations, red,
yellow, and blue, which, with her two kindly forms, were
all regarded as the Sakti, or female energies, of the five
Dhyāni-Bodhisattvas.

As Sakti of Avalokitesvara the white Tāra symbolizes Transcendent Wisdom, and has often the third eye of fore-knowledge, and the green Tāra often has four arms, symbolizing her gifts to mankind, while among their titles are such noble names as these—"dispeller of grief," "subduer of evil passion," "giver of happiness," "assuaging strife," and "potent in all nature."

The symbolism of these various forms is in itself an elaborate study, and indeed Tibetan Buddhism has carried symbolism to a wonderful perfection, and its art is unique in its blending of microscopic detail and bold, decorative schemes. Upon its altars with their rich trappings are the "eight glorious emblems"—the parasol of royal rank, the two fishes of joy and luck, the conch of right conduct whose whorls turn to the right, the lotus of salvation, the bowl of treasure, the diagram of transmigration, the standard of victory, and the wheel of the Dharma. With them are the seven Jewels of a Cakravarti, or universal emperor; and before them are set out seven bowls with the offerings of ancient Indian hospitality—water for feet and hands, flowers and perfumes, a lamp, food, and drink.

Here too on special occasions are incense, the "eight glorious offerings," and sometimes the symbols of the five senses dedicated to the gods—a mirror for sight, a shell for hearing, nutmegs for smell, sugar or fruit for taste, and silk for touch. There are also bells, vajras, skulls, at times filled with blood, at others used as drums; all this under a baldachino of silk and gold almost hiding the images of the gods, of whom there are said to be at least five hundred. For a study of some of these the student will find Miss Getty's fine work, *The Gods of Northern Buddhism*, most useful. It is too intricate a subject, however, for all except specialists; and even they work at it with some of the faith of the pathologist, that from his close study of the abnormal and the morbid light may be cast upon the normal and healthy. So from Tibetan Buddhism we may find light yet breaking out and illuminating some of the many obscure places in the vast field of the development of religion. Even in its iconography there is displayed an ingenuity and an art which may, to many of us, seem misapplied, and yet which have kept alight the torch of faith in dark days, and have, as we saw in the case of Tāra, held it high at times for all to see.

In the libraries of the great temples there are rich treasures for the scholar; and to these books the priests pay a superstitious veneration which does not, however, often go to the length of study! Bound in wooden covers and weighing several pounds, each volume is placed reverently on the head of any who handle it; and they are taken at times in solemn procession to drive away evil spirits from beds of sickness, or from newly planted fields, when the services of the monks are duly bought. No one who has attended a service of this kind will forget the childlike faith of the peasantry, wholly in bondage to the priests, nor the deep, guttural chanting of these custodians of all knowledge and of divine powers.

A High Mass resembles that in a Japanese or Chinese temple, that is to say, it is like a service of the Catholic church:

The deep, organ-like bass of the singers, the swell and fall, the intoning, the silvery-toned bells, accentuated at times by the muffled roll of the drums, gave altogether a majestic and sacred character to the service, whilst the flickering lights and the figures of the priests, looming out of the darkness and through the thin clouds of incense fumes, like shadows vivid yet veiled, made up a most impressive spectacle.

So writes Waddell, and reminds us of the belief of the Abbé Huc that the devil had taught the Lamas to perform this ritual, that they might be forearmed against his mission.

There are, indeed, many things in Tibetan Buddhism which might without bias be ascribed to the subtlety of the Evil One; but I should not select the ritual, which apart from its blood-offerings, may well be derived from early missions of the Christian church. Today that church has greater gifts for Tibet, and is even now helping to awake her out of lethargy and dull despair. Yet the services in such great shrines as the Potala need not become dull and colorless because they become respectable. And there is surely a place for a Tibetan Christianity, for a hermit order of Christian Tibetans, less austere and more human, and for a Trinitarian theology not different in essentials from the doctrine of Adi-Buddha. Nor need the Western church refuse to learn from the artist-monks, for instance, who understood their beliefs clearly enough to put them into such admirable charts as the well-known "Wheel of Life." Artists the Buddhism of Nepal and Tibet has produced, especially in bronze, who surely have rich gifts for the church of Christ. And it is good to contemplate the work of emancipation which His Spirit will do among these sturdy mountain-folk, freeing them from fear and slavery, from poverty and dirt, and setting free the blind devotion which now spends itself so lavishly on "Living Buddhas," on prayers which are mechanical yet often voice the cry of the human heart, on the support of a vast army of drones and tyrants, and on the cult of degenerate gods.

That the peoples of these northern lands are naturally religious is clear; no nation on earth supports its church at greater cost or with more cheerful sacrifice. No food is taken without offerings being made to the gods of the four quarters; prayer-cylinders and flags are everywhere, the use of such formulas as "Om mani padme hum" is universal, and indeed the land is filled with evidences that religion means much to its people. Yet Rockhill can say, "It is surprising how small a place the performance of religious ceremonies occupies in their daily life," only to go on and describe a daily even-song such as can be found in few Western lands:

As night falls lamps are lit on the altars of every Buddhist temple, and a short service is chanted, while lamas seated on the porch play a rather mournful hymn on long copper horns and clarinets. This is the signal for the housewife to light bundles of aromatic juniper boughs in the ovens made for the purpose on the roofs of their homes, and as the fragrant smoke ascends to heaven they sing a hymn or litany in which the men of the house often join, the deep voices of the latter and the clear high notes of the former blending most agreeably with the distant music in the lamaseries.[1]

In the morning offerings are placed before the household gods; and the veneration paid to "Living Buddhas" amounts too to a ceremonial observance. I shall never forget the prostrations made before the young Mahārāja of Sikkim, an Oxford man somewhat restive under this excessive adulation. But, as he said to me, "My land is not lacking in the spirit of religion," and wherever the eye rested it found ample proof of this.

But of Mahātmas, or of the great spiritual and mental achievements described by the theosophists, there is no trace. Their medical science is quackery, their religion a raw material terribly perverted too often by blind leaders. Here, as in other Buddhist lands, the gospel of Christ awaits great and signal triumphs. It will replace countless capricious deities and demons by a loving Father-God, and will bring to fruition the devotion of these spiritually hungry peoples, filling with new meaning whatever is lovely and of good repute.

[1] The Land of the Lamas, p. 248.

APPENDIX I

FĀ-HIAN IN LANKĀ[1]

(*Ca. 400 A.D.*)

The sun has gone, and velvet night apace
Begins to hang her lanterns in the sky.
Fragrance of champak and of jessamine,
Breathing their sweetness to the silver moon,
Bewitches all my senses.   Far below
The pipes and tomtoms call the worshippers,
And points of light creep upward to the shrine,
Inviting me to worship with the rest.
Yet I sit on alone and meditate,
Heartsick for mine own countrymen and home.
To-day at worship, as I knelt before
The jasper image (which I told thee of,
Rare miracle of art), a fan of taffeta
Painted with hills and clustering temple roofs,
And circling mists about their gable-ends,
Moved me to childish weeping. . . . .
So do I yearn towards my dear, dear land,
And longing fills my breast to sit once more
Encircled by the faces that I love,
And see Chang-ān and mine own monastery.
. . . .

Ah me! "From love springs sorrow; very sorrowful
Is separation from the thing we love."
So spake the Master.   True his word, yet harsh
To us who know not yet detachment's calm,
Which, craving none, has sympathy with all.
The way is long and very steep the slope
And stern the struggle to attain the goal;
And I am very weary and alone! . . . .
Enough!   Grant me to ease my heart's desire

[1] From the *International Review of Missions.*

By telling of my sojourn in this land.
Thou knowest already of our journeyings
Across the deserts of Yarkand, and thence,
Scaling the mountains, how we came at last
To places trodden by those holy feet.
Of which the crown and flower is this
Lovely Tamrāvati, the Holy Isle;
Whose beauties would that I might chronicle,
And tell thee of the triumph of the Law,
Whose Wheel yet runneth its triumphant course.
Gayā is derelict; the grove of Lumbini,
The Master's birthplace, sore neglected lies;
Vultures alone frequent the Vulture Peak,
Where Arahats once communed with their Lord.
But here the puissant Sangha doth proclaim
On monuments of stone how great its power
To make a nation prosperous and strong.
Fragrant as champak is the Noble Law
Pervading and enriching all the Earth!
Here in Tamrāvati Asoka's son
Six centuries ago established it.
Heir to his father's throne, he rather chose
To be the herald of the Dhamma's realm,
Embracing exile, that its influence
Might make this lovely isle a land of bliss.
Heroic prince! His courage shameth me.
But yesterday I pondered in the cave
Where once Mahinda, rapt in holy thought,
Would gaze o'er Lankā's forests league on league.
His home he left, his kindred and his throne;
And how shall I, poor weakling, thus repine?
For I have found the books I sought, and soon
Do purpose to return (if Heaven grant,
And Karma) and will bring with me their lore.
Know then I had them from the learned sage
Great Buddhaghosa's self; he doth translate
Back to the ancient tongue of Magadha
The treasured writings of the islanders,

Guarded with reverence down the centuries—
A very learned man. We held converse
Seated beneath a rocky canopy,
Where palm leaves rustled in the evening breeze
And plashing waters soothed and charmed the ear.
To whom with bitter shame I fain must tell
How poor and ignorant our monks, contrasting them
With the great abbots, who in Lankā here
Puissant and learned, overawe the King,
And bend him to the purpose of the Law.
Of other things we spoke, and most of how
The Dhamma doth develop in the North.
Austere, I argued, in its origin,
Beauteous as moonlight, and as coldly clear;
Yet something lacking grace, which mortals need
Who long to pray, to feel an answering touch,
When to the heavens they lift the hands of faith.
To which the sage made answer, "Saving grace
We find in sacrificial lives of Bodhisat.
More than the Ocean is the blood he shed,
More than the stars of Heaven the eyes he gave.
Which merit, running over, doth avail
For all the pain and sorrow of the world.
So potent is the Master's saving love!"
"Such is the germ," I answered, "growing whence
By ordered steps our doctrine doth unfold.
This saving love in Amitābha see,
Whose grace abounds when our poor merit fails;
Who brings us to his Western Paradise,
More winsome to the heart of mortal man
Than cold Nirvāna's solitary bliss."
Of our Compassionate Lady, too, we spoke
Kwanyin, who hearkens to the cries of men.
And here in Lankā is another Name
Which links our doctrine with the Master's Norm,
Arguing the oneness of the Holy Law
The Greater and the Lesser Vehicles.
For here they reverence Metteyya, King

Of Love, the Coming Buddha whom our Lord
Foretold.   Far off, they say, his coming;
Yet he comes, to nerve the struggling efforts of the world;
So in his Name they pray, and find new strength.
And in his Name do fathers bless their sons,
"May ye be born to see the Lord of Love."
For so is man; not made for solitude
And lonely striving, but for love and prayer;
So only can he steel his wavering will
To drive out Tanhā from its citadel. . . . .
Last must I tell thee of another Lord,
Whose story moved me strangely.   At the shrine
A merchant-sailor, out of Jaffa come,
Who spoke the language of the islanders,
Held converse with the Bhikkhu, and with joy
—Ecstatic joy as of a man in love—
Told him of one, the Anointed King of Peace,
Who for the mighty love He bore the world
Became a servant, and endured to die.
In short his story seemed like Bodhisat's,
Save that this Syrian Lord was done to death
By men whose eyes were blinded by the dust
Of pride and anger to his righteousness . . . .
Our people do not slay their prophets thus!
And then the merchant told of stranger things;
Of how this Lord of Love did conquer death
And liveth yet to judge and rule the world:
Whose Kingdom is a reign of righteousness,
Goodwill on earth and hearts atoned to God.
A winsome doctrine, making visible
The Unseen Love, and bringing Him to dwell
Homely and courteous with sinful men,
Until in triumph He doth take his power and reign.
Strange doctrine, which our hearts acclaim,
And yet repugnant to the calmer intellect.
Physicians say it cannot be believed
That spirit should reanimate the flesh,
And turn the processes of nature back.

Yet righteousness hath wondrous power to change
The course of things.   Thou knowest how the saint
Can rise in air, as spirit doth prevail
O'er flesh, and can escape the bonds of space
And time, beholding things of the dead past,
The unborn future yet in Karma's womb.
Sainthood hath wondrous power, and ye know
The "Lotus of the Holy Law" doth teach
Our Master liveth yet upon the Vulture Peak,
For he too conquered death. . . . .
Indeed I see the Christ, this Syrian Lord,
Because I first have seen the Bodhisat!
This thing demandeth converse, and deep thought:
And the man's joy itself were surely proof
Of some strange secret which his soul hath found,
Which works within him like a potent wine.
And now farewell: the sky flames with the dawn
And the pale moon fades at the rising sun.
E'en so, if this strange Syrian tale be true,
Shall the Anointed brighten all the East
And our clear moonlight yield to radiant Dawn.
Hath not the moon herself a borrowed glow,
Nor grudgeth yielding to the Source of Light?

APPENDIX II

SOME BUDDHIST PRAYERS AND VOWS

A. FROM MODERN BURMA

A MONK'S PRAYER[1]

Awgatha, Awgatha, I worship with the body, with the mouth, and with the mind, with these three "kans." The first, the second, the third; once, twice, until three times. The Lord, the precious one; the Law, the precious one; the Assembly, the precious one—these three precious things. I, the worshiper, most humbly, with fervid zeal, with clasped hands, pay reverence, give offerings, and with pious gaze bow me down. Thus by this worshiping I gain merit and increase in earnestness and purity of heart, and am freed from the Four States of Punishment; from the Three Evil Things, starvation, plague, and warfare; from the Eight Chambers of Hell; and from the Five Enemies. And at the end, when the last existence has come for me, may I pass into Nirvāna.

B. FROM INDIA

THE KING OF VOWS[2]

When I attain to be Buddha—I will not accept Buddhahood if all who believe in integrity of heart and long to be born into my Kingdom are not born therein. Nay, if even they who think on me ten times be not born therein will I not enter; nay, more, if all save they who are guilty of the deadly sins enter not in, neither will I enter upon Buddhahood.

C. FROM CHINA

A LAYMAN'S PRAYER TO KWANYIN[3]

Mother of Pity, hear my prayer,
That in the endless round of birth
No more may break my heart on earth,

[1] From Shway Yoe (J. G. Scott), *The Burman: His Life and Notions*, I, 223. London: Macmillan & Co., 1882.

[2] The eighteenth vow of Dharmākara Bhikkhu, later to become Amitābha Buddha. See *S.B.E.*, Vol. XLIX, Part II, pp. 15, 73.

[3] Translated by L. Cranmer Byng in *A Feast of Lanterns* from a tomb on Fu Kin Mountain in the Kiang Su province.

Nor by the windless waters of the Blest
Weary of rest;
That drifting, drifting, I abide not anywhere.
Yet if by Karma's law I must
Resume this mantle of the dust,
Grant me, I pray
One dew-drop from thy willow spray
And in the double lotus keep
My hidden heart asleep.

D. FROM CHINA

A Monk's Prayer to Kwanyin[1]

I am indeed filled with thankfulness that it has been granted me to know the Buddha's way of salvation; but although I am a monk and have abandoned the world, I am bitterly conscious that my heart is not yet penetrated with the truth. I am sorely lacking in true knowledge, and have many vain thoughts and wrong opinions. I am deficient in the moral force necessary for spiritual advancement. I study the scriptures with diligence and yet I am incapable of fully understanding and assimilating their holy wisdom. I fear that few blessings are in store for me, that my life is destined to be cut short, and that I have devoted myself all in vain to the religious life. I have wasted my days, and dare hope for nothing but a spendthrift's death. Behold, in my longing to purify this heart of mine, I am shedding tears of anguish. In reverence and humiliation I kneel before Thee; day and night my thoughts dwell on Thy holy countenance. I hold fast to Thy holy name, and prostrate myself before Thy sacred image. Incline Thy heavenly ear, O Pusa, to hearken unto me; of Thy divine love save me from misery; grant me Thy pity and Thy protection; let Thy spiritual light shine upon my body and illumine my heart. Baptize me with Thy sweet dew, so that it may wash away all stains of hatred and ill-will, cleanse me from all sin and foulness, and make me pure in thought and deed. Guard me both day and night from all evil. Be ever with me, O Pusa, when I wake and when I sleep. Grant that my understanding may awaken under the rays of Thy glory. Grant that I may increase in spiritual intelligence and discernment. Grant that when I read the scriptures the words may remain stored in my

[1] From R. F. Johnston, *Buddhist China*, pp. 309-11.

memory, and that when the sacred truths are expounded I may have wisdom to understand them.   May I be endowed with good judgment and insight; may my days be long; may I attain happiness and peace; may I ever be absorbed in the contemplation of Thy truth; may evil spirits keep far from me; may I awaken to a clear perception of the futility of living through generation after generation without spiritual progress; may I walk in the way of the pusas; may I show gratitude for all mercies; may I put my trust in the Buddha, the Law, and the company of the saints; and wherever the Law holds sway, may all living beings attain union in the perfect wisdom that leads to the peace of Buddhahood.

E. FROM CHINA

THE VOW OF A MAHĀYĀNA MONK

I shall never cherish any thought of breaking the precepts which I have now accepted.   From today up to the attainment of Buddhahood I shall never cherish any idea of pride toward the elders. . . . . I shall never arouse any angry thought toward any fellow-being. . . . . I shall never envy any others their bodily excellence or beauty. . . . . I shall never arouse arrogant thought concerning all things, whether subjective or objective. . . . . I shall never accumulate wealth for my own sake but give out all that I shall receive to help poor and suffering people. . . . . I shall practise the four embracing methods (sangraha) not only for myself but for the sake of all beings, and thus, being free from attachment, never being weary (of my work), and being without any entanglement in the mind, shall embrace all fellow-beings into the same communion. . . . . Whenever I shall meet any unfortunate people, orphans, deserted, imprisoned, or suffering from various mishaps and tribulations I shall never leave them unhelped nor stop until they be saved and freed from sufferings, through righteous means. . . . . Whenever I shall see any people offending rules of decency or committing crimes, I shall never pass them by without trying to correct them, but try to persuade or coerce them, according to the degree and nature of the offences.   For persuasion and coercion are the methods of perpetuating righteousness; and when righteousness is perpetuated, the beings in the heavenly resorts grow in number while those in the woeful resorts diminish, and thus the wheel of truth will perpetually be turned, to the benefit of all beings. . . . . I shall never cease to embrace the perfect truths, since thus, and thus alone, we can remain mindful of the Buddha, the Communion and the Pāramitās.

Now let me take the vow to save innumerable fellow-beings and to attain the perfectly right view of truth throughout all my coming lives. Let me take the vow to preach the truth to all without ceasing, on having realized the perfect truth. Let me take the vow, for the sake of embracing the perfect truth, to dedicate my body, my life and my wealth to guarding the truth.

F. FROM JAPAN
Two Prayers for the Dead[1]

I

Praised be the Buddha Amitābha (Namu Amida Butsu)!

This monument is erected in memory of the men and animals, whether friends or foes, who fell in the campaigns of the 23rd and 24th year of Oei (commencing on the 6th of the 10th month). Do you, priests and lay believers, offer your sincere prayers to the Buddha Amitābha in behalf of the dead.

II

On the 15th of the 8th month in the 2nd year of Keicho, at Nangen in the Zenra Do, several thousands of soldiers of the Ming Army laid down their lives, among whom 420 were killed by the Japanese troops under my direct command.

On the 1st of the 10th month more than eighty thousand men of the same hostile army were killed at Shisen in the Keisho Do.

May the Buddhas bestow protection upon each soul, who took part on either side and found his last resting place in Korea, being loyal to the end to his own fatherland!

In those different engagements the slain on both sides numbered over three thousand, and those who died of disease or lost their lives by some accident either on land or sea were too numerous to count.

G. FROM CHINA
Confession of Shantao (Zendo)

Be merciful unto me, nor count my iniquities which are as the grass for multitude. Receive my confession and accept me. Past sin— may it be blotted out; sins of the future may they never be sinned.

---

[1] 1416 A.D. and 1599 A.D., respectively.

Past good—may it increase; good yet undone—may it come to the birth. Saith the Buddha, "I am manifested to destroy sin; declare ye, therefore, your sins of unbelief in former births, make confession to the Elder Brethren, prostrate yourselves and your eyes will be opened to behold the shining form of the Buddha in glory."

H. FROM INDIA

A CONFESSION[1]

The disciple shall enumerate his sins in former lives from eternity until now—sins in deed, thought, and word, whether he has himself committed them or caused others to do so or rejoiced at their commission; such sins are cursing, envy, lying, cheating, and unbelief. Let him say, "I confess before the Buddhas of the ten regions. I will not commit such offenses either in this world or in worlds to come. I dare not deceive him, the all-seeing; I dare not cover my iniquities: nay, henceforth forever I dare not commit these sins."

[1] Translated into Chinese by Anshikao (148–70 A.D.).

APPENDIX III

SYNONYMS OF NIBBĀNA AND NIRVĀNA IN THE THERAVĀDA AND THE MAHĀYĀNA

I. IN THE PĀLI BOOKS

Negative	Positive
Extinction of lust (Tanhākkhayo)	Ambrosia (Amatam) (lit.: "not dead")
Destruction of passion (Virāgo)	
Extinction of becoming (Bhavani-rodho)	Bliss (Sivam)
	Freedom (Vimutti)
Extinction of rebirth (Jatikkhayo)	Purity (Suddhi)
Destruction of sorrow (Dukkhāk-khayo)	Refuge (Lenam) (Saranam)
	Simple state (Dhuvam)
Endless state (Anantam)	Calm (Santi)
Uncompounded state (Asam-khatam)	Island (Dīpam)
	Coolness (Sītibhūtam)
Uncreated (Akhatam)	Truth (Saccam)
Sorrowless (Asokham)	Supreme (Param)
Ineffable (Anakkhatam)	Everlasting (Accutam)
Abstract (Nipunam)	Security (Yogakkhema)
Formless (Arupam)	

II. IN THE SANSKRIT AND CHINESE BOOKS

Negative	Positive
Non-duality	Reality
Incomprehensibleness	Truth
Unchangeableness	Absolute
Absolute void (Sūnyatā)	Supreme good
Inaction	Enjoyment
Not falling back	Fulness
Formlessness	Home
Undefiled state	Sameness
Immovableness	Honorable state
Without sign or token	Ease
The invisible	Unique

The unthinkable
The unparalleled
The unfettered
The indestructible
The unworried
The infallible
Being without remnant
Neither going nor coming
Escape from Mara, sorrow, rebirth, etc.
Neither single nor double
Without beginning or end

Purity
The far shore
Nectar
Excellent
City of peace
Suchness (Tathatā)
Ideal world
Wisdom (Prajñā)
Buddhahood
The womb of Buddhahood
Deliverance

"No measure is there for the being freed,
    By which to speak and think upon his state,
    For wholly done away are ways of thought,
    Blocked are the channels of our daily speech."
                                    —*Sutta Nipāta.*

"Trackless as birds upon the viewless air,
    In Emptiness the Saints find Liberty."
                                    —*Theragāthā.*

"Nirvāna is neither death nor destruction, but Bliss,
    Freedom and Purity."—*Lankāvatāra.*

APPENDICES IV–VI

CHARTS OF THE BUDDHIST SCHOOLS OF INDIA, CHINA, AND JAPAN

APPENDIX IV

THREE GREAT SCHOOLS OF THE HĪNAYĀNA

TABLE I*

	Theravāda or Sthavira	Sarvāstivāda (A Subsect of the First)	Mahāsānghika
Chief beliefs	Semi-realists: The world and consciousness are real, but are an ever changing flux — "unreal" from the standpoint of eternity. The Arhat cannot lapse. Gotama, a real historic person	Realists both as to the phenomenal and the noumenal, but in the Sautrāntika subsect an idealistic tendency. The Arhat can lapse. Gotama a real historic person	Idealistic: developed Bodhisattva doctrine; docetic view of Gotama
Chief books expounding differentia	Kathāvatthu	1. *Jñāna-prasthāna* 2. *Mahā Vibhāsa* (early third cent. A.D.) 3. *Abhidharmakośa* 4. *Divyāvadāna*	Portions of *Mahāvastu*
Chief exponents	Tissa or Upagupta; Buddhaghosa, etc.	Katyāyaniputra Vasubandhu Sanghabhadra Hiuen-Tsiang (in part) Fu Kuang and Fa Pao (Chinese commentators on *Abhidharmakosa*)	
Subsects	Sautrāntika, Sarvāstivādino, and others	A. Gandhāra Abhidharmikas Kasmīra Abhidharmikas (Using Textbook 1) B. Vaibhāsika Sāstrins (Using Textbook 2) C. Neo-Vaibhāsika Sāstrins (Using Textbook 3) 1. Sautrāntikas 2. Orthodox Abhidharmikas	Lokottaravāda and seven others

* After Takakusu and others.

APPENDIX V

BUDDHIST SECTS OF CHINA

TABLE II*

Name	Founder or Introducer	Chief Scriptures	Chief Characteristics, etc.
I. Ch'an	Tamo, 526 A.D.	*Vajrācchedika* and *Prajñā pāramitā Sūtras*	Meditation. This sect "has practically absorbed all the rest" (*Encycl. Sinica*). (Cf. *Zenshu* in Japanese sects.) It teaches that the Buddha or Dharmakāya is in the heart
II. Chiao-men (so called by I) Book sects	Tao Hsuan, 595–667 A.D.	*Vinaya*	Monastic discipline and asceticism. (Cf. *Ris-shu* in Japanese sects)
a) Lü			
b) T'ient'ai	Chi-i, d. 597 A.D.	*Prajñā pāramitā Saddharma Pundarīka Nirvāna Sūtra*	Harmony of teachings, pantheistic realism. (See *Tendai* in Japanese sects)
c) Hsien-Shou or Hua Yen	Buddha-bhadra, fourth cent.	*Hua Yēn Ching* (*Avatamsaka Sūtra*)	(Cf. *Kegon* in Japanese sects)
d) Tz'u-En or Fa Hsiang	Hsüan Chuang	*Wei Shih Lun*	Scholastic philosophy, idealism
e) Ching T'u	Hui Yuan, 333–416 A.D.	Three *Amitābha* scriptures	Pietistic devotion to Omitofō; salvation by faith. (Cf. *Jōdo* in Japanese sects)
III. Absorbed or defunct	Paramartha, 563 A.D.; Hiuen-Tsiang, 564 A.D.	*O-phi-Tamo Ku-sho-Lun* (*Abhidharmakośa*)	Philosophical; semi-materialistic. (See *Kusha* in Japanese sects)
a) Chu She			
b) Cheng Shih	Kumārajiva, 402 A.D.	*Chan-shih-lun*	Philosophical; "nihilistic." (See *Jōjitsu* in Japanese sects)
c) San Lun	Kumārajiva, 402 A.D.	Nāgārjuna's three chief works	Philosophical nihilism. (See *Sanron* in Japanese sects)
d) Mi or Chen Yen	Vajrabodhi, eighth cent.	*Ta-Jih-Cheng* (*Mahā Vairochana Sambodhi sāstra*) and *Mandaras*	Symbolic pantheism, esoteric and mystical; magic. (See *Shingon* in Japanese sects)

*After Hackmann and *Encyclopedia Sinica*.

INDEX

INDEX

Abbots, 204; *see* K'an-po

Abhidhamma, 12 n., 34, 39, 44, 107, 111, 115, 118

Abhidhamma Sangaha, 111

Abhidharmakośa, 43

Abhiñña, 20, 109, 117; *see* Meditation

Abhisekha (baptism), 78, 172, 191

Absolute, 72, 83, 98, 100, 146, 149, 196; transcendence of, 102; Truth (Dharmakāya), 72, 79, 84 (Shintai), 175; Void, 81; within, 80; *see* Tathatā

Acchuta, 17, 221

Accommodated truth, 168

Acolytes, 159

Ādāna, 95; *see* Ālaya

Ādi-Buddha, First Cause, xv, xix, 193, 194, 196, 197, 203

Ādi-dharma, 197

Ādi-prajñā, 197

Aditthāna (persistency), 91

Āgama period, 147

Agavamsa, 111 n.

Agra (original essence), 62

Aisvarikas, 197

Aizen, god of love, 152 n.; *see* Kong-osatta

Ajātasattu, 29, 85

Akazome Emon, 80

Akhatam, 221

Akshobya, 194

Akuto-bhāya, 17

Ālaya, 94, 95, 193

Ālayavijñāna, xv, 94, 96, 98

Alexander, 47

Alexandria, 107

Alphabet, 156; Indian script, 198

Altruism, 19, 22

Amatam, 17, 221

Amaterasu, 167, 170 n., 189

Amida, 170, 177; Nyorai, 174; Society, 173

Amitābha, 58, 59, 60, 78, 126, 159, 194; books, 159; Buddha, Paradise

of, xviii, xix, 59, 100, 126; cult, 83, 84; Pure Land of Bliss, 85; schools, 140; scriptures, 170; sects, 125, 131; Triad, 156

Amitāyu, 59

Amitāyur-dyhāna Sūtra, xix, 85, 87, 93, 125, 195

Amitāyus-Sutropadesa, 127

Amogha, 151

Amoghasiddhi, 194

Amoghavajra, 151 n., 185

Anakkhatam (ineffable), 221

Analects, 123

Ānanda, 25, 35, 58, 78, 87; second patriarch, 137

Anantam, 221

Anattā, xiv, 6, 10, 12, 53, 72, 110, 111, 136

Anawrata, 110, 111, 113

Ancestor cults, 38

Anesaki, Dr. M., ix, x n., 19 n., 59 n., 61, 91, 97 n., 139, 163, 175 n., 184; *Buddhist Art*, 152 n.; *Nichiren*, 2 n., 60, 146 n.

Anguttara Nikāya, 33, 38

Aniccā, xiv, 72, 80, 110, 111, 136

Animism, 111, 120, 128, 192

Annihilation, 14, 15 n., 16 n., 110

Annihilists, 16, 18

Anshikao, 58, 125, 126

Antoninus Pius, 125 n.

Anurādhapura, 89 n., 105, 106

Anuruddha, 111

Anussati (ten recollections), 116

Apocalypse, 62

Arahatta, 14

Architecture, Buddhist, 163; of China, 164

Arhat, 14, 21, 25, 31, 37, 43, 53, 54, 112, 117; ideal, xvi, 124, 147; in Nibbāna, xvii

Arhats (Lohan), 158

Arhatship, xiv, xviii, 9, 35, 43; candidates for, 64; four stages of, 44, 123; ideal of, 54

227